Wounded Healers

Wounded Healers

*Mental Health Workers' Experiences
of Depression*

Edited by
VICKY RIPPERE

and

RUTH WILLIAMS
Institute of Psychiatry, London

With a Foreword by
DR JOSEPH CONNOLLY

JOHN WILEY & SONS
Chichester · New York · Brisbane · Toronto · Singapore

Library of Congress Cataloging in Publication Data
Main entry under title:

Wounded healers.

  Bibliography: p.
  Includes index.
  1. Depression, Mental—Addresses, essays, lectures.
2. Affective disorders—Addresses, essays, lectures.
3. Mental health personnel—Biography.   4. Mental health
personnel—Mental health—Addresses, essays, lectures.
I. Rippere, Vicky.   II. Williams, Ruth.   [DNLM: 1. Depressive
Disorder.   2. Mental Health Services—manpower.
WM 171 W938]
RC537.W67   1985   616.85'27   84–29118
ISBN 0 471 90592 5 (paper)
ISBN 0 471 90746 4 (cloth)

British Library Cataloguing in Publication Data

Wounded healers: mental health workers' experiences
  of depression.
  1. Depression, Mental
  I. Rippere, Vicky   II. Williams, Ruth
  616.85'27   RC537

  ISBN 0 471 90592 5 (paper)
  ISBN 0 471 90746 4 (cloth)

Printed and bound in Great Britain

'At the philosophical level, a disease, though considered to be a disgraceful episode, may be beneficial, since it gives an awareness of psychological and corporeal zones that normally work silently. This knowledge of one's self enriches personal experience. Therefore, we become more accepting and understanding creatures.'

Yaryura-Tobias and Neziroglu (1983)

For Monte Shapiro,
who taught us both a lot

Contents

Foreword

Everyone knows what 'depression' means, so it's a fair bet that few know what it means at all. The very term is a metaphor – something to do with low mood. But 'low' and 'high' as descriptions for mood states are themselves images. Do they describe them better than the 'black' (melancholic) or 'red' (sanguine) – derived from now discredited physiological ideas? The notion of mood as low may have semantically spilled over from the below-normal functioning of the depressed person. This is described (largely for the convenience of those who describe) in the languages of psychology, physiology, and sociology. Functions are imaged as 'pressed down'. But what is pressing on what? The weather men, by contrast, know exactly what they mean by depression – greater weight of the Earth's atmosphere at a particular time and place.

'Depression' has become poetic shorthand for the myriad states – unwanted, unpleasant, unsought, unenviable and a whole Thesaurus-load of uns – of worse-than-normal functioning of the most complex creatures we know, ourselves.

The reasons why this book was written are to be found in the second and third paragraphs of the editors' Introduction. Wondering whether to borrow or buy it, you could do no better than read them – now?

This book, then, brings together personal accounts of severely depressed states by those who have survived them. The authors, moreover, are 'in the trade'. Their job was, is, or became that of caring for others who are depressed. They have reflected on what they have seen in others and in themselves.

This, then, is a travel guide written by several who have been there – to the desolate landscape (mindscape?) inadequately called 'depression' on the map of human experience.

Many who care for the depressed will not have made that trip themselves, though no one can be sure it won't be made before life ends. They will try to use their own experience of loss, bereavement, and rejection to feel into, and with, the depressed person. How do the depressed view this striving? Do they feel even dimly understood? Patronized, perhaps pitied but poorly comprehended?

The experiences recounted in this book have been seen by several of their authors as 'creative maladies', informing and shaping their personal development and their professional lives. Some will read these travellers' tales and know that they have been there too, and perhaps find solace in just that. Others will be briskly glad that some of the mapping has been done and is on file.

Those, however, who find themselves caring for a depressed relative, friend, or patient, and are puzzled by what they see, will discover some of their bearings with this guidebook. And those they care for will then, too, feel less lost.

Everyone knows what 'depression' means. Few know all that it means. Wherever we have reached in this understanding, these accounts can take us only further.

JOSEPH CONNOLLY

Acknowledgements

In compiling *Wounded Healers* we have been grateful to many people for their help. The Editors of the *British Journal of Occupational Therapy*, *Social Work Today*, *Nursing Times*, *Nursing Mirror*, *Bulletin of the Royal College of Psychiatrists* and *Journal of the Royal College of General Practitioners* helped us to contact prospective contributors by including notices about our project in their respective journals. Gordon Smith of Tavistock Publications suggested adding general practitioners. Dr Dorothy Rowe provided encouragement at an early stage of the project and also put us in touch with one contributor. Dr Frances Clegg and Professor Cheryl Richey drew our attention to some useful references. Drs John Crammer and Robin Murray offered helpful comments on an early draft of the introduction. Jean Morgan, Kathy Coomes, and especially Eileen Markham helped with the typing. Finally, our authors provided the material on which the book is based. However, the assembly and interpretations are our responsibility.

VICKY RIPPERE
RUTH WILLIAMS

Notes on the Contributors

Annie Altschul, SRN, RMN, RNT, BA (Hons), MSc (Soc. Sci.), is currently a Professor of Nursing Studies. She was formerly Senior Lecturer in Nursing Studies in Edinburgh and Principal Tutor, Bethlem Royal Hospital and Maudsley Hospital.

Rudi Arnold, BA, MA, is a training officer in a social services department.

George Bellis, SRN, RMN, Obst. Cert., HV Cert., N. Admin (Hosp.) Cert., RCN, MRIPHH, is a Nursing Officer (Health Visiting) in Islington.

Brian Daines, MA, is a psychotherapist at Shore in Sheffield and a marital therapist at Whiteley Wood Clinic in Sheffield.

'A Doctor Patient', MRCS, LRCP, MRCGP.

'GP', MB, BS, DCH, is a general practitioner in the East of England.

Elizabeth Jardine, BA (Hons), PhD, is a psychologist in the State Public Service, South Australia.

Katy, MB, ChB, DRCOG, MRGCP, is an inner city GP with special interest in the health of women. She has been involved in groups, courses, and campaigns concerned with womens' health for over eight years.

Margaret, MB, ChB, was a general practitioner in Central Scotland. She took her own life in July 1982 after 17 years of illness.

Frewen Moor, MD, FRCGP, was a retired general practitioner who practised at Westgate-on-Sea and at Norwich. He died in October 1983 at the age of 90.

'Phoenix', MB, BS, FRCPsych, DPM, is a retired consultant psychiatrist.

Vicky Rippere, BA, MA, PhD, BSc (Hons), MPhil, is a lecturer in psychology at the Institute of Psychiatry in London and Honorary Principal Psychologist at the Bethlem Royal Hospital and Maudsley Hospital.

David Roberts, SRN, ONC, RMN, RN, is a charge nurse in a large teaching hospital.

Lydia Scotting, MBAOT, is head of the Department of Occupational Therapy at an auxiliary hospital in Edmonton, Alberta, Canada.

Catherine Series, MBAOT, SROT, is a senior occupational therapist in a psychiatric day hospital in Malvern.

Georgette Smith, BSc (Hons), MPhil, was a clinical psychologist at a London teaching hospital. She is now looking after a young baby.

Celia Talbot, BA, CQSW, is unemployed.

Patrick Wakeling, MB, ChB, BAO, DPM, MRCPsych, is a consultant child and family psychiatrist in North Lincolnshire.

Ruth Williams, MA (Oxon), DipPsych, is a lecturer in psychology at the Institute of Psychiatry in London and Honorary Principal Psychologist at the Bethlem Royal Hospital and Maudsley Hospital.

Introduction

This collection of essays is about the experience of depression in mental health workers. All three terms of reference require commentary. Each of the 19 chapters is a personal account of what it was like to be depressed; the focus is intended to fall on the phenomenology of depression, though our authors have also addressed themselves to other aspects of their respective journeys through the Slough of Despond. By 'depression' we mean primarily affective disorders that would be so classified by the average British psychiatrist following the Registrar General's classification (HMSO, 1968): bipolar and unipolar, neurotic and psychotic, agitated and retarded depressed states are included. However, not all of our contributors sought psychiatric treatment, so not all of their depressions were officially diagnosed. Finally, under the heading of mental health workers we include individuals belonging to the main professions involved in the care of psychiatrically distressed people at all levels of the health care delivery system from primary care on up. Thus we include general practitioners, psychiatrists, psychiatric nurses, a psychotherapist, clinical psychologists, psychiatric social workers, and occupational therapists. Not all the authors whose work is represented were mental health workers at the time of the depressive episode described, but in these cases the experience was a crucial determinant of their subsequent choice of a mental health career. In other cases the author was a mental health worker at the relevant time but has subsequently either retired early or moved to a non-clinical field of work or a non-psychiatric field of clinical work. But some have remained in the same mental health field they were in when their depression occurred. While it might have made for a more homogeneous book to have restricted participation only to mental health workers who had their depressions while 'in harness', such a restriction would not only have precluded us from considering a number of important issues which these other cases raise but might also have given a misleading impression of the ways in which people's experiences of depression may interact with their mental health careers.

Having said briefly what the collection is, we must now say a bit about what it is in aid of. The aims of the book are multiple. The most basic purpose is to make available a more comprehensive collection of phenomenological accounts of depressive experience than appears to exist in English at the present time. Although recent years have seen a steady trickle of articles, book chapters, and full-length books about depressive experience written by professionals in and around the fields of medicine and mental health (i.e. A Practising Psychiatrist, 1965; Sutherland, 1976; Burns, 1981; A Doctor Patient, 1981; Endler, 1982; Lehmann, 1982), experiential reports on depression are still scanty in comparison with the wealth of available phenomenological accounts of schizophrenia, which have been a fruitful source of hypothesis-building (i.e. McGhie and Chapman, 1961). (Readers who are not interested in the 'mental health worker' aspects of the collection may read it at this level.)

Over and above this sheer descriptive aspect, the collection has a number of what might be called philosophical dimensions. One of these is the editors' view that there is a tremendous gap between the complex and changing mental states that are conventionally lumped together under the general rubric of affective disorders and the fixed and skeletal schemas conventionally used thus to describe them. Of course we recognize that it may not be the proper job of classificatory systems to reflect the breadth and diversity of human experience, but we are nonetheless impressed by the contrast between the richness of depressive experience and the poverty of official labels used to allocate these states to approved addresses in semantic space. We suspect that perhaps one reason why depressed patients feel misunderstood is that the complexity of their experience isn't adequately represented in contemporary explanatory and descriptive schemas. If so, then wider appreciation of the complexity might lead to better understanding of how depressed people feel. While better understanding of feelings might not automatically lead to better treatment, it might at least reduce some of the subjective costs of available treatment, one of which may be having to bear the isolating feeling that 'nobody understands'.

A related philosophical concern is the question of how experiences of depression are to be conceptualized. When we speak of depression, are we speaking of an illness (a kind of measles of the mind), a weakness to be dealt with by the hoisting of socks, an interpersonal psychosocial problem, a result of distorted thinking, a product of Western social aspirations or of the oppression of women, or the result of an inherited tendency to biochemical derangement? This list is, of course, not exhaustive. The experiences described in the collection cover most of these possibilities and add several dimensions to our appreciation of the quandry which these alternative formulations pose. We do not propose to adjudicate between these contending schemas, since we reckon that different explanations are required for different depressions and these are not all mutually exclusive in any case: having an inherited tendency to a particular form of biochemical derangement is not known to make people exempt from interpersonal problems, for example. But how the experience of depression is conceptualized may have vital significance. If a young doctor's depression is conceived as a sign of immaturity or inadequacy, he/she may be unlikely to be promoted into positions of responsibility; if it means a temporary biochemical dysfunction, promotion may be more easily considered, if cautiously; if it means the possession of perfectionistic standards of behaviour he might, with reason, be welcomed with open arms. One of our main aims is to call attention to an alternative conceptualization which we expect will seem paradoxical to many readers who habitually construe depression in one of the commonplace ways.

This alternative possibility, adumbrated by several of our authors, is that a depressive episode may be a critical point on one's trajectory through life, an object lesson in understanding the frailty and conditionality of human purposiveness (including one's own). If used constructively, it can be a growth point, a springboard for personal development: that is, if the message conveyed by the depression to the self is heard and heeded. In short, a depressive episode can be a source of information that all is not well in the way one's life is going and, because it is so exquisitely unpleasant a state to be in, provide the often considerable impetus needed to reset one's course. Not all depressive episodes necessarily lead to such a potentially beneficial outcome, but since it is almost never acknowledged that *some* depressions can be positively useful, we feel the need to emphasize this point.

At the other extreme, some depressions lead inexorably to despair, personal disaster, and death. In proposing that some episodes of affective disorder may, like acute pain, be adaptive in drawing the sufferer's attention to the existence of threat to the self, we remain poignantly aware that some depressions, like chronic pain, may cease to convey adaptive information and simply overwhelm the sufferer with meaningless suffering which it seems impossible to alleviate by rational – or any – means. One of our authors took her own life shortly after completing her chapter describing her 16 year history of recurrent depression. She had evidently had enough.

Between these two extremes of personal regeneration and suicide are, as we implied earlier on, a variety of possible outcomes. Another of our philosophical purposes is to emphasize this diversity, particularly the more benign possibilities. Our choice of emphasis is consistent with the trend of our authors' reported experiences and also with previous, if rare, observations in the voluminous literature on mental illness in doctors, that a history of even very serious mental illness need not spell the end of a worker's effective career (Small, Small, Assue, and Moore, 1969; Crammer, 1978). Uncommon as such observations are, we feel that they need to be given more notice, especially in view of the overwhelming emphasis in this literature on suicide as the most noteworthy outcome of depression in doctors (i.e. Blachly, Osterud and Josslin, 1963; *British Medical Journal*, 1964; Freeman, 1967; Blachly, Dishner and Roduner, 1968; Craig and Pitts, 1968; Simon and Lumry, 1968; De Sole, Singer and Aronson, 1969; Rose and Rosow, 1973; Steppacher and Mausner, 1974; Rich and Pitts, 1979; Pitts, Schuller, Rich and Pitts, 1979). Even if the rate of suicide in male doctors in England and Wales has been recorded as being two and a quarter times higher than in all males and one and a half times that of males in social class I (BMJ, 1964), suicides are still only a minority among the depressed. We believe there is a need to pay more attention to the survivors who recover from a depression, pick themselves up, and uneventfully return to normal life. It is only by studying survivors that anyone is likely to find out what factors enable them to survive. We suspect that these may prove to be potentially more amenable to modification than the demographic characteristics, such as age and sex, which have been found to be associated with increasing the risk of suicide.

In this context it is of special interest to consider how our contributors report having been treated by their professions in consequence of their histories of depression. Some appear to have had considerable help and support from bosses and colleagues, some to have met with virtually no discernible reaction at all, others to have met with considerable hostility and harrassment, and others still to have encountered wildly different receptions from different representatives of their respective professions. The perceived reception – as opposed to whatever official or statutory arrangements may exist for dealing with formerly depressed employees – of employers is a topic which, to our knowledge, has not yet been systematically studied. Our data, such as they are, could hardly be called systematic, but they do suggest the potential of the area for study. We strongly suspect that some employers would not wish their response to particular individuals to be on record. Several authors suggest that a curious double standard may operate, such that it is considered acceptable for clients to have depressions ('Anyone can become depressed, dear') but not considered acceptable for staff to do likewise ('Except mental health workers, that is!'). Is there a sociologist in the house?

Another topic which we found to be conspicuous by its absence from the literature is the question of whether surviving an episode of depression might contribute to improving a therapist's performance through enhancing empathy with patients. Even the voluminous second edition of the *Handbook of Psychotherapy and Behaviour Change* (Garfield and Bergin, 1978), which reviews many studies of therapist variables thought to be relevant to therapy outcomes, says nothing about this matter. It was because of this large apparent gap in the literature that we decided to enquire specifically into our contributors' views on this question when we came to elicit material for the book.

Now we come to the question of why and how the book came about. The impetus came from the experience of the two editors, who for some time shared, with several dozen plants, a small office on the third floor of the Institute of Psychiatry. After a period of sizing each other up, we felt safe enough to share our mutual 'skeleton' of having a 'history of depression'. We found that we shared both a gnawing secret worry about the implications of this stigmatizing state of affairs for our future careers and at the same time a sneaking suspicion that the 'skeleton' was not an entirely Bad Thing to be bringing with us. We realized that our experiences of suffering and survival had taught us things that we were finding useful in our professional work and wondered whether we were the only formerly depressed mental health workers who felt this way about their histories.

Eventually we decided to find out. A phenomenological data base seemed to us to be an essential first step in identifying and exposing the issues that might be involved in our quandry, so we set about asking fellow mental health workers to write about their experiences of depression, addressing themselves to five straightforward questions:

1. What sort of experience of depression had they had?
2. Under what circumstances had they become depressed?
3. What did they do about it themselves and what did others, whether lay or professional, do about it?
4. What of all this did they personally find helpful and what did they find unhelpful?
5. Having survived to tell the tale, what did they feel they learnt from the experience, both personally and in their susbsequent work as therapists?

We deliberately refrained from posing an explicit question about the reaction of their employers, actual or prospective, to learning of their affliction, in order to ensure that any comments our authors made about the matter were spontaneous and not just a case of telling us what they thought we wanted to hear.

Once our plan was drawn up, we faced the problem of contacting prospective authors. We began by inviting several psychologist colleagues whom we knew to have suffered from depression to contribute to the book. In order to contact members of other professional groups, we wrote to the Editors of relevant journals – the *Bulletin of the Royal College of Psychiatrists*, *Social Work Today*, *Nursing Times*, *Nursing Mirror* and the *British Journal of Occupational Therapy* – describing our project and inviting interested parties to get in touch with us. Later, at the suggestion of Gordon Smith of Tavistock Press, we also wrote to the Editor of the *Journal of the Royal College of General Practitioners*. We are grateful to all of these kind people, because we were soon in correspondence with depressed or formerly depressed mental health workers from all over the country as well as a few from abroad. All expressed keen interest – of the 'It's about time someone looked into this' variety – in the project. Some sent articles they had already either had accepted for publication or had drafted at the time of their difficulties with a view to eventual publication. Others produced new material for the occasion. Several correspondents, all of them nurses, sent anonymous short essays without return addresses and with short covering notes to say they didn't dare identify themselves, lest dire things happen to their future employability. By the early summer of 1980, we had the names of enough people to hold two informal meetings with prospective contributors to discuss the proposed book. By midsummer, the first drafts had begun to arrive in the post. Over the next two years, we accepted some 19 essays for the book.

In order to ensure that the different accounts were all written independently of each other, we established the 'ground rule' that authors could only read others' chapters after having drafted their own. Thus each essay represents the individual writer's own personal approach to describing his or her depression, with varying degrees of reference to the guidelines we had suggested for them to follow. While part of the thematic overlap which the reader will readily

discern results from these shared guidelines, another, and probably considerably larger, part reflects broad similarities in the depressive experience of
mental health workers which transcend individual differences in profession,
circumstances, temperament, and personal style. But despite the considerable
degree of thematic overlap, the 19 accounts remain uniquely individual and
remind us forcibly that while outsiders may conceptualize it under a generic
category heading, suffering remains an essentially personal affair.

Our conviction that personal experience of at least some of the kinds of
suffering as one's clients experience may be useful preparation for work in the
helping professions is reflected in the title we have chosen for the collection.
The notion of the 'wounded healer' is the topic of a provocative chapter by
Bennet (1979) on doctor–patient relations. Bennet notes that patients respond
positively to the elusive quality of empathy which they perceive in some
professional helpers with whom they come into contact. One of the circumstances which favour the development of this quality is, he argues, 'the idea of
the wound' (Bennet, 1979, p. 184). By this he means that while most professional people wear a protective mask to keep clients at a distance, some rare
ones do not:

> 'A few people seem to go through life without the need for such armour, but what is
> common to all people who have either shed, or have never had, a protective mask is
> the idea of vulnerability. By laying down their armour they are declaring that they are
> not perfect and inviolable. Although perhaps not actually indicating their weakness,
> they are accepting the possibility of personal weakness and it is that potential which
> other people can discern and relate to' (Bennet, 1979, p. 185).

Bennet goes on to observe that in Greek mythology, in Christian symbolism
of the crucifixion, and in primitive shamanistic societies, healers have been
associated with a weakness or wound to which valuable properties are
attributed:

> 'In many cultures it has been expected that the healer will also be a sufferer, and this is
> most vividly demonstrated in those societies where there are Shamans. These are
> people regarded as having a mixture of priestly and healing powers, but a requirement
> for the role is that they should possess some defect such as in Western society would be
> recognized as an illness or disability often of a spectacular kind such as epilepsy,
> although it would be expected that they had mastered the condition or else somehow
> come to terms with it. In their own culture what might seem to Westerners as a
> weakness was seen as evidence of the ability to communicate with the spirit world, and
> thus was conceptualized in positive terms' (Bennet, 1979, pp. 185–86).

These observations about traditional evaluations of the 'wounded healer' are
relevant to our efforts to transmute the stigma of a 'history of depression' into a
potentially positive asset. In view of these ample historical precedents, we
reckon that our efforts to rehabilitate these 'histories' cannot be dismissed as
idiosyncratic special pleading; it is, rather, a belated rediscovery of something
which has been known for millennia but which has been lost sight of amongst
contemporary mythologies of 'professionalism'.

Having said what the book is, what it is meant to be in aid of, and how it came about, we must briefly say what it is *not*. First, it is not a book about so-called 'burnout', which has been described as a syndrome of 'emotional exhaustion, depersonalization, and reduced personal accomplishment that can occur among individuals who do "people work" of some kind' (Maslach, 1982, p. 3). While we certainly recognize that mental health workers can become depressed in the context of extreme 'people pressure', none of our authors has described his or her experience in these terms, so that the topic has excluded itself from our scope. For the same reason, it is also not a book about the pressures, such as they may be, of working in a mental health career; it is not about 'job stress' (i.e. Marshall, 1980; Hammen and de Mayo, 1982; McCue, 1982), because our authors do not for the most part conceptualize their difficulties in these terms either. Thirdly, it is not a book about the psychology and psychiatry of depression, though we expect that workers in these fields might learn things from reading our contributors' observations. Finally, we would like to emphasize that the book is not intended to be a *roman à clef*. The authors' professional positions appear on the opening page of each chapter and their names or pseudonyms in the list of contributors. But except where authors have specifically requested that their name or pseudonym be explicitly associated with their chapters, they are not attributed to individual authors. The decision to present the material in this oblique manner was reached only after much editorial deliberation. There are two main reasons for the veil of mystery. The first is to protect the authors' (and their families') privacy and their relationships with friends, colleagues, clients, and employers. And the second is to make it easier for the reader to read the accounts without distraction. Though each chapter is highly individual and personal, the identity of the author is, in a paradoxical sense, basically irrelevant. The accounts describe generic experiences — becoming depressed after bereavement, or out of the blue, or whatever – which could happen to almost anyone. It is better that each should be read for its own sake rather than as a whodunnit.

Section I   Trouble at work

The three chapters comprising this first section share the common theme of an experience of depression precipitated by trouble in the writer's work. The three authors belong to different professions – psychiatry, social work, and clinical psychology, respectively – and their work and life circumstances are all different. But differences in circumstances and profession do not obscure the common ground between their reports and indeed between their reports and others which appear later in the collection.

These authors describe their encounters with difficult occupational situations: a traditional 'bin' where slipshod psychiatry is endemic and which an idealistic senior registrar can do nothing to reform; a bureaucratic junta aimed at obstructing a senior social worker's promised promotion; and an academic trap in which a young PhD student is caught between conflicting pressures from her boss-cum-supervisor.

Although all three writers became depressed in inimical work circumstances, none of their accounts corresponds closely to the notion of 'professional burnout' as formulated in the American literature. Rather than suddenly or gradually grinding to a complete professional halt, each one made efforts to remain 'on course', though with varying degrees of opposition and success. One has remained in his previous line of work, the second was forcibly retired early on medical grounds, and the third changed to her present career. Neither the cause nor the course of their depressions is stereotyped.

These accounts raise the important question of the role of work in the depressions of mental health workers. In the past decade, several investigators have examined the role of work in the depression of patients who are not mental health workers and the effects of depression upon their occupational performance. The main findings are worth considering. Weissman and Paykel (1974) reported that a sample of middle-aged depressed women of social classes 3, 4, and 5 showed less maladjustment in their work roles in jobs outside the home than comparable depressed women who were full-time housewives. The authors suggested that there might be 'something protective in the work situation which enables function in this context to be preserved' (Weissman and Paykel, 1974, p. 72). In a similar vein, Mostow and Newberry (1975) compared depressed housewives from New Haven and Boston with a matched sample of depressed women who were employed outside the home. Although the depressed workers were more depressed at the outset, they tended both to recover faster and to make a more marked overall improvement than the housewives. The authors suggested that their jobs provided the depressed workers with both distraction and protection. The findings of Brown and Harris (1978) in Britain lend support to these suggestions. In a sample of women from working-class Camberwell, they found that not having a job outside the home contributed to vulnerability to becoming depressed in the face of provoking events. Having an outside job afforded some protection.

These findings suggest that, in working-class women at least, outside employment may confer protection against becoming depressed, protection of social role performance in depression, and stimulus to recovery, through mechanisms which at present remain conjectural but which are likely to involve such factors as social support and enhancement of self-esteem. What they do not tell us, however, is what happens to professionals, who are presumably liable to the same basic human needs for support and feelings of self-worth, when they encounter trouble at work.

The recent findings of Fredén (1982) from a survey conducted in Sweden appear relevant to this question. He found that people in specialized professions appeared to be better equipped than manual workers to cope with a depression *not* concerned with their work, but they were at greater risk of becoming depressed as a result of their work situation. Like the previous authors, Fredén proposed an explanation based on self-esteem. In this context, he discussed the reluctance of professionals to seek help when they become depressed. If the experience of our authors is anything to go by, his suggestions apply *a fortiori* to mental health professionals:

> 'Perhaps . . . the cultural convention that emphasizes the importance of personal strength in high-powered, high-status jobs discourages any idea of seeking professional help. "I will (should) manage to cope with this depression myself; I don't need to bother a psychiatrist". The specialist is pressed for time, his job calls for personal continuity; it is difficult to be away for sickness or for undergoing treatment. Furthermore, the specialist occupies a particular cultural role in our society; he has a "career". It is hardly likely to help him in the promotion stakes if he becomes known as a man with mental troubles. Or at any rate, this is what he may believe; he must put a good face on things and go on fighting' (Fredén, 1982, p. 104).

The general strictures applying to professionals would seem to be particularly acute in the case of mental health professionals who become depressed in the context of a work problem.

'Awakenings' (Chapter 1) concerns the plight of a depressed psychiatrist. 'There is no lonelier man', observes the author. Like several writers in the collection, he notes the lack of a recognized way for a depressed mental health worker to seek professional help for his or her depression. The psychiatrist author's reluctance to confess his infirmity to colleagues derives, as Fredén suggests, from shame at not fulfilling the expectation that he should be a tower of strength, as well as from his concern for the possible effects of his illness upon his promotion prospects at a critical point in his career.

Similar concerns are voiced in 'Hitting rock bottom' (Chapter 2) and 'Surviving depression' (Chapter 3). The social worker author of the former notes that 'I felt desperately ashamed of myself for not coping'. She, too, holds the expectation of herself that she *should* cope and the effects of her illness upon her career suggest that her employers held the same expectation. And for the author of the latter chapter, though not a mental health professional at the time of the events described, the question of references for future jobs looms large, as does the prospect of social invalidation resulting from her anticipated inability to live up to others' expectations: 'Being a failed PhD on grounds of assumed stupidity was bad enough, but on grounds of mental instability it was pretty unthinkable'.

This passage raises the question of taboos within the professional ethos. The close similarity of theme between these three chapters and others appearing later in the collection suggests the possibility that one of the covert norms internalized during professional socialization – whether or not within the mental health professions specifically but probably more troublemaking within them – is the expectation of psychiatric invulnerability. The shame expressed by our psychiatrist and social worker at finding themselves unable to live up to this expectation and implicit in the future psychologist's view of failure to conform to it as 'unthinkable' foreshadow the possibility that the unspoken taboo may be a very strong one, more of the order of sibling incest than, say, of using the wrong fork to eat the gateau. We shall have more to say of hidden taboos affecting mental health workers at a later point.

Meanwhile, to end this brief introduction on a less gloomy note, we may consider another theme which emerges from these accounts, namely the importance of self-help in depression. All three writers received treatment from others in the mental health system, whether GPs, psychiatrists, or psychotherapists. All had pharmacotherapy and one underwent ECT. But alongside, and in some cases despite, these externally administered treatments, all engaged in active self-help. Their accounts emphasize the necessity of working out one's own solutions in one's own way and in one's own time. Again, this is a recurring theme in later chapters.

This section has been chosen to lead off the collection because the theme of trouble at work seems to be such a salient one for depressed mental health workers and because they adumbrate so many of the themes presented in other essays in the book.

1 Awakenings

By a Consultant Psychiatrist

Where does one start? When does depression begin? It is easier to trace the source of a river. Looking back on my first depression – like the shock of unrequited love it was the hardest to bear – I recollect awakenings; moments of transition of the greatest importance to my life. There were four. Three were part of the depression; the fourth occurred three years later. When we wake each day we have put distance between us and all the events before we slept. We get as near as we can to making a fresh beginning; and just for a little while, in that short interval preceding the preparations for another day into which we have been drilled over the years, we are detached, uninvolved as we stare at the ceiling, or look out at the trees, growing whether we notice them or not; at the other houses whose blank sameness mocks the striving of their occupants. But the awakenings I shall describe were quite different from all the rest – dramatically so. There were moments when it seemed my past had overtaken me on the road; seized me roughly and demanded to know what the hell I thought I was doing walking off like that, with so much unsaid and undone. 'Not another step will you take', said the past, 'unless you settle your account with me. If you refuse I'll dog you to the end of your days. I'll wait for you behind every corner.'

I was in my middle thirties: a senior registrar in adult psychiatry. My wife then worked at home, in our hospital house, looking after our five children, three of whom attended the primary school. The area provided good post-graduate training, but the hospital could not, by any stretch of loyalty, be regarded as 'progressive'. Its lifeblood had long since congealed; its purpose dissipated by the almost ceaseless warring of personalities; its old ideals degraded; its original humanity blunted by excessive chemotherapy and ECT. It was, in a word – as I found to my cost – a 'bin'. What resources of my own did I bring to this discouraging place? Let me say just this. There was a gulf between my aspirations (often unrealistic) and the opportunities for their fulfilment. I do not profer this as the sole cause of the depression, but rather as a contributing factor. My daily routine occasioned more self-reproach than one of robuster personality would have tolerated. I considered that I was in the midst of unimaginative, slipshod psychiatry and tortured myself because I could not put it right. I am surprised that I lasted as long as I did. But my facility for self-deception sustained an impassive facade not only to the world but to my inner self. Kept it up, that is, until one fine summer's evening I felt the first tremors of the force about to engulf me. During the afternoon I had been puzzled by an anxiety possessing neither object nor explanation. It became worse, so I went to the pub and drank three or four pints of beer. I might as well have drunk water. Retreating from the place in some alarm I returned home and went to bed quite early. Sleep followed easily enough, but the following morning at precisely five o'clock I awoke into a world that had changed, and to a state of mind of which I had no previous experience. There was no doubt at all. I was depressed. I lay there filled by the horror of my condition, like a man who has been told he has cancer. I lay on past the time of rising, bursting in tears like a child when my wife asked me what was the matter.

Ordinary objects were altered. Tables and chairs, or whatever it might be, now appeared as sinister, devoid of familiarity, drained of the feeling formerly invested in them. I felt the cold acutely. That, and the steady pressure on the top of my head, made me feel ill. I would grip anything within reach as though trying to derive warmth and comfort; or reassuring myself that something, at any rate, was real. I sat motionless for hours, not bothering to turn on the light. Everything invoked and reflected my depression. I was drawn to whatever seemed in sympathy with my mood. One evening I picked up a book of Rembrandt etchings – reading was beyond my concentration – and stared, fascinated, at a crucifixion scene whose Christ appeared as an extension of my own sufferings. To this day Rembrandt stirs uneasy feelings within me. There was copious weeping. Going to bed was dreaded. Two hours sleep at the most, troubled by violent, repugnant dreams. I cannot recall their content in any detail, except that in one my mouth was crammed with stinking butcher's refuse. I marvelled that my wife and children were able to accomplish so much. I lived in a world geared exclusively to the interests and capabilities of a race of people from whom I was set apart. The children's irrepressible play, their laughter, their excited comings and goings and, above all, their sound sleep, filled me with envy. They seemed as angels viewed from the depths of hell: their gaiety did nothing to lighten my misery. In fact I was extremely irritable, and totally unable to tolerate the least demands put upon me. At the same time I was fearful of being left alone. Time passed but I was hardly aware of it. So retarded in mind and body had I become as to be incapable of any act of self-destruction. I don't recall – in the first few days, at least – thinking about suicide. In a sense I was dead already: my mind a black mass – celebrating despair; mocking hope – from which I could obtain neither grace nor comfort. I had no appetite for good, no sexual needs. I didn't even bother to get myself a glass of water. I just didn't bother about anything.

I brooded – it could hardly be called thinking – upon my plight as a depressed psychiatrist. There is no lonelier man. After a day or two at home I struggled back to work, which I succeeded in reducing to the barest minimum. I avoided as many of my colleagues as possible. It was like being made of glass: a walking transparent cabinet filled with a shapeless jumble of bruised, bleeding nervous tissue. This wretched showcase bore a label informing anyone I chanced to meet: 'This psychiatrist is depressed because he is inadequate'. I was bitterly ashamed at not being a tower of strength and I feared detection more than anything. After three or four weeks, desperation overcame pathetic pride and I decided to approach a colleague – a man of medical assistant grade whose warmth and kindness exceeded a knowledge of psychiatry (I wished to be helped, not understood, you realize). The irony is intended. As a hospital psychiatrist trying to inspire confidence from senior colleagues for the purposes of good references, one has, indeed, to feel desperate before confessing one's infirmity. God, how I longed then that my depression be magically changed into a decent, straightforward physical ailment! The psychiatric hospital is intolerant of weakness in its staff. Compassion is for patients; for 'them' not 'us'. When the dreaded plague strikes a doctor's house, the rest put up their shutters and circulate the comforting notion that the victim's illness is the direct consequence of the sterling qualities possessed by every member of the caring professions: an excess of virtue, if you like, turning upon its owner like a two-edged sword. But in their secret thoughts the survivors are saying to themselves, 'Always knew there was something rum about him. Not surprised really'. I knew there was no recognized way of getting help. Perhaps some could have braved it out, but disclosures do not always make for 'good' professional relationships, and there are very few junior doctors who would risk endangering their prospects by coming clean to those consultants whose work is built upon the ever-pressing need to defend themselves against precisely the same fate.

So, summoning such courage and initiative as remained to me, I invited my nice colleague to the hospital social club for a drink. After a pint or two I said as casually as I could, 'You know I've been feeling very depressed lately'. To which he replied, just as casually, that he was surprised because I certainly didn't look that way. Although this was immensely reassuring I persisted and rather in the manner of one humouring the whim of an over-scrupulous colleague who, presumably, knew more about these things, he wrote out a prescription for antidepressant drugs. This medication brought me no relief. One day I had a row with one of the consultants: an overbearing man for whom I had no respect whatsoever. I was stung by his insensitivity and I gave back as good as I got. But I felt terribly hurt; misunderstood and unappreciated. He revelled in quarrels. I did not. I stormed out of his room and went home immediately, trembling with anger. It was early evening. I told my wife that I felt unusually tired and that I was going to bed. Once in the bedroom I took out the drug bottle and swallowed its contents. My hand shook as I gulped down a fistful or more of capsules. It must have taken a couple of minutes to finish them, but I persevered sustained by the mounting excitement of a unique occasion. What I was doing was unambiguous. No obscurity of purpose this time. I lay on the bed wrapped in a blanket of peace and deep satisfaction. Certain of having done the right thing at last, and undisturbed by any thoughts of my family, I slid comfortably into oblivion.

A white wall and a dazzling light from which there was no relief. Total silence. No memories, except that I knew who I was. Pain and stiffness in my back suggested that I was lying supine. Some force prevented movement. At length I discovered I could move my head. This brought no comfort as I scanned the glaring, featureless monotony of a white hell. For without any effort of mind I knew I was in hell. Now it was clear. I had died, and this was my punishment. I could recall no crime, no 'judgement'. I must lie here for eternity – 'for ever, and ever, and ever, and ever . . . '. The horror of endlessness. If only someone would turn down that accursed light. Suddenly my right arm moved as though independent of my will. My left arm was tied. The fingers fumbled for a knot, but in vain. Then a childhood memory. Trying to find the doorknob in the bedroom. Wandering round and round suffocated by the darkness, wishing, praying that someone would come. My free hand continued like a frightened child blindly to explore. It found my penis. Horribly long, it seemed to extend downward out of reach as though tethered somewhere. Frantic tugging caused intense pain. What shameful deformity was this? The air was unbearably hot. As far as I could tell I was naked, drenched in sweat, but, strangely, suffering no thirst. One misery the less. The futile gropings and stirrings continued. I tried again to retrieve some memory, some slender clue as to what had led to this unhappy state.

'He's awake.' There was no doubt – a human voice. Then a white figure just to my left. It commanded, 'Leave that alone. You've given us enough trouble as it is'. Another voice joined the first. A face bent over me. 'Please turn the light down', I pleaded. No reply. Then, 'You can take the drip down now, but leave the catheter in'. Finally, to me, 'We're taking you to the ward now. We had to keep you here in casualty because we need the beds for the people who are really ill. You've taken up a lot of our time'.

Clearly, I had been put in my place in the medical scheme of things, but this troubled me less than the disappointment of not discovering a life after death. That, at least, would have been something. As it was I had to accommodate the banal reality of being a damned nuisance; of keeping the doctors and nurses from their proper task of attending the legitimately ill.

In a surprisingly short time something of my old rationality returned. It had deserted me when the going really got tough, calmly slipping back when the danger was over. But it had forfeited much of my respect and I felt less inclined to listen to its advice. In contrast, the beliefs, the certitudes of childhood had been touchingly loyal, despite my neglect of them. Guilt and the inevitability of punishment had been lying low waiting for their moment. Coming round in the casualty department was an awakening with a vengeance. I was trundled to the ward along an intricate route indicated by the changing patterns of the ceiling. The drugs were not yet completely washed out of me, and I felt a little euphoric for some hours. It seemed merely amusing that one of my consultant colleagues stood by my bed declaring that the massive overdose had to be seen as a serious attempt at suicide; and that if I did not agree to become an 'informal' patient then there would be nothing for it but to put me on a 'section'. Good-humouredly and with condescension I agreed to his terms. I was admitted on the following day to a psychiatric hospital some 20 miles or so away from my own.

The third awakening occurred many times – 12 at least, it is hard now to remember. Always it was like coming round before the brain was ready. I saw people and things but could not recognize them or know their purpose. A foretaste of dementia. I lay there struggling to piece together what was surely the fragment of a dream. Nothing made sense until, in an instant, full awareness supervened and it didn't matter anymore. I would regain normal consciousness with all the relief of a child rushing out into the sunshine, released from the lesson it couldn't understand. I was left with a sense of confusion, with the recollection of the faint residue of a frightening perception. All I can say is that things as they are are frightening simply because they have no meaning. We must exude meaning so that life may become digestible and the world made nourishing. The worst moment of all was that of fighting to remember my identity. I always felt I would never succeed until, just in the nick of time, the nightmare was dispelled. Quite often there was headache. Also, the feel of the temples made damp by saline solution. Then I would be very thirsty and hungry, consuming my tea and biscuits greedily. This was remarked on by the gentle nurse – not one of your brisk, jolly kind, thank goodness — who sat beside me like a mother. I am talking, of course, of electroconvulsive treatment, suggested to me by the consultant, into whose hands I had been received, as the best treatment to have. Poetic justice in this. I, who had passed enough electricity through the brains of my patients to illuminate a city, now submitted to the same nostrum. I, who wearied of pressing the button, and who would have gladly burnt Volta in effigy, was at last brought to the same extremity. My consultant had said, 'Well, old chap, what would you do with someone as depressed as you? You'd give him ECT wouldn't you?'

Apart from the quiet attentions of that particular nurse, the only other satisfaction afforded by the treatment was the intravenous anaesthetic, Pentothal. Almost immediately, it imparted an extraordinarily intense sensation of pleasurable relaxation. Then 10 seconds or so later, one's brain crumbling like a sandcastle before the tide, one fell asleep with a deep sigh. A fellow patient reckoned it beat an orgasm any day.

So far, then, I had received medication which had not succeeded, and ECT which rid me of my symptoms, no doubt for all manner of incidental, unacknowledged but important reasons. Something must now be said of my experience as an in-patient, and something too of the doctors whose kindnesses could not be faulted, but whose relationship with me was characterized by a collusion into which, it has to be admitted, I readily entered. First the doctors.

I developed a positive talent for divining the 'needs' of my interlocutors. My intuitively composed history succeeded in relieving their anxieties by enabling them to allocate my symptoms to a category with which they felt most at home, and of which they clearly 'approved'. In this essentially defensive game my doctor was allowed to display superior skill. I had a sharp eye for necessary fiction. I knew from sheer experience that consultants of the usual calibre are reluctant to be led into the dark places of what is tritely called depression. I felt that to tell the whole story would not have been a worthwhile investment of time and effort. My editing of the truth was prompted by a deep need for sympathy, for 'understanding'.

My dread of being readily explicable within the terms that apply to others was concealed by claims to be as others are. I was thus allowed to pass through customs with relatively little to declare, travelling on to that friendly land (which half of me yearned to inhabit) of jolly good, salt-of-the-earth chaps who are all (bless them) likely to get depressed from time to time. So I went along with the cliché, which my doctors seemed never tired of reaffirming, of the conscientious doctor who works too hard and who succumbs to an illness, 'which really, you know, is just like any other'.

On admission I was given a side room to myself. At first the privacy was welcome, but I soon longed for the mateyness of the open ward. I was, accordingly, moved, and introduced to psychiatry in action as experienced by the punters. I was now one of 'them'. The whole business was about being a helpless 'patient' – a passive, inert lump of problems, some intractable. The days were endless. We waited around, sitting and lounging for drugs, meals, ECT, and doctors' visits. I was fitted neither by training nor inclination to man a lathe in the industrial rehabilitation unit to which a chosen few disappeared each day. The rest suffered a kind of stimulus deprivation in that all normal events had been removed from our lives. Consequently our attention became riveted, once the worst of the symptoms were past, upon any and every trivial occurrence. Otherwise unexceptional people became, as soon as they had stepped into our domain, veritable Falstaffs in the fullness and variety of their idiosyncrasies. There was a hugely obese Irish cleaning woman with a tongue as foul as the NCOs of my national service days. A bloated send-up of a Sean O'Casey character, she waddled about emitting an unbroken stream of obscenities larded with Dublin slang. Then there was the nursing assistant, a dreamy, impractical girl who seemed merely to be tolerating her job because she could think of nothing else to do. She was attractive enough to interest men whose sex lives had been interrupted, and, conscious of her central position on our sad little stage, she played it for all it was worth. A fragment of dialogue:

Patient: 'Be careful love, if you do that again we'll all see your drawers.'

Nurse: 'Never wear 'em, dear. Not 'igeenick.'

My presence excited all manner of fantasies in my fellow sufferers, once they knew my profession:
  'What's your job then, mate?'
  'I'm a doctor.'
  'What kind, like?'
  'I'm a psychiatrist.'
  'Christ, if you're in here what chance have we buggers got?'

We all became very anxious about the doctors' visits, hanging about waiting for our particular consultant to show up. One noticed that the doctors always made a beeline for the office and would spend as much time with the nurses as with us. I realized later that I must have displayed all the child-like dependence of the others. The nurses tried their hand at discovering why a psychiatrist who knew about mental illness should, even so, land up in hospital. One staff nurse was particularly anxious on the point, and after having me in the office (always a privileged place to be) for a few amateurish interviews, which in my hunger for attention I was pleased to grant, reached the conclusion that worrying about promotion had brought on my illness. Even the doctors fell into the same trap of confusing their own anxieties and preoccupations with mine. One who couldn't stand children ascribed my depression to having five of my own. Another – a devout Catholic doctor – decided that sexual frustration was what we should be talking about.

The ward was a worthwhile experience. It seemed to me that patients did more for one another than did the staff. When I began to feel better I tried to be helpful in my turn. I loved their humour and admired their courage. Shared suffering is a great cohesive force. I remember them with affection and gratitude.

And what of the fourth wakening? It occurred three years or so after discharge from hospital, and was part of another depression, but this time of only moderate severity. It was a metaphorical awakening, in which thought and feeling became better acquainted. My wife played a large part. She was midwife, counsellor, and much else besides. Never, during my three weeks absence from work, was time so well spent. Together we began to make sense of what we both knew of my life and personality. This fruitful process has continued, though it has been very difficult at times.

What else have I learnt? It seems to me that from depression itself one learns nothing. Rather it is from what one makes of depression that benefit derives. Depression is depression. It lays waste and may prove, too, a total waste of time unless one uses the experience, and all its consequences, to build anew. In that sense, it is an experience like any other; yet simultaneously unique in the opportunities it affords.

To begin with I have gained an insight into the predicament of those in the hands of doctors and nurses, which I could not possibly have obtained in any other way. Again, I have been enriched in more personal ways: self-awareness and enhanced creativity amongst them. These bonuses have accrued, as I have implied, despite the treatment prescribed by the doctors, who were, as I can now see, attempting to fulfil their own personal and/or professional needs. Admittedly, I colluded in this, but I think my instinct was right. Progress has to be on my terms and in my own good time.

Perhaps the most precious outcome of this personal development – of which depression was a vital part – has been the certain knowledge that, for me, depression is a sign of not dealing honestly with my problems. That when I am overwhelmed with difficulties, and wonder how I can possibly find a way through, and experience at the same time a feeling of really struggling with it all, then I know that I am, after all, coping. The paradox consists in using the feeling of not coping to know that I am. Being depressed – severely so, I mean, is to have avoided the challenge; to have thrown in the towel without even having faced up to the contest. It's like saying, 'You take over, I can't do anything. I'm a patient. I'm depressed'. I am sure, too, that for many others, depression may be related to what is called 'growth' (for which, as I have said, it provided unrivalled opportunities) and that better arrangements should be made to give psychiatrists the right kind of help. The psychiatrist's family, too, needs special consideration. I have witnessed enormous suffering – compounded of anguish, insecurity, embarrassment, and downright humili- ation, in a colleague's family subjected to the brutally insensitive attentions, and arrangements, of attendant consultants who were, in truth, acting out their own neuroses. On the whole, I consider that I've been relatively fortunate compared to some I've know or heard about. Perhaps the most salutary lesson has been that one must not take one's professional status for granted. What matters most to the patient is what mattered most to me: namely, the personal 'accessibility' of the psychiatrist – those subtle qualities of personality render- ing him non-judgemental and a fully paid-up member of the human race. Someone who listens to more than the mere words one falteringly utters. Above all, he must be able to distinguish his problems from those of his client. To be a good psychiatrist requires the same honesty and courage expected of the good patient.

Patrick Wakeling

Wounded Healers
Edited by V. Rippere and R. Williams
© 1985 John Wiley & Sons Ltd.

2   *Hitting rock bottom*

By a Senior Social Worker

I had always known that the traumatic events of my childhood had left me vulnerable to depression. I had clocked up most of the items on the list produced by psychiatrists as events predisposing to depression, e.g. loss of parents (and siblings) in childhood, instability of ties to a locality, and being 'different' from peers. (I'd had over 60 addresses by my late twenties.) I'd also survived a lot of stress and trauma unsought which is not on the standard lists and life was made more difficult by having intelligence and ability above the level to which I'd been educated, so that I was always being cramped rather than stretched, which is a much less healthy situation for the human psyche.

There were, however, many positives as well. I knew how to obtain knowledge and to overcome social and practical obstacles, and I had lots of experiences in adapting to different people and cultures. Necessity having been my only mother from the age of 12, I also possessed a whole host of practical coping skills self-taught for the initiatives needed to survive. I had, however, thought that the only thing to do with my kind of childhood was to forget it, so I had buried it pretty deep and formed for myself another new personality as a capable wife and mother, freelance writer, secretary, senior social worker, and politically active citizen, gaining most of my education for these functions in my spare time. I still feel that I had earned this self-image, that I had a right to keep it, and was entitled to my repressions, or at least to deal with them in my own way and at my own pace through my writing, fantasy life, etc., and that *no one* had the right to make me relive my intolerable past, for any reason whatever. However, that is what happened and I went through it like a lamb to the slaughter, believing that hard work, ability, and efficiency must sooner or later be recognized and appreciated. How wrong my experience proved that delusion to be.

I first trained as a social worker with the Church and, therefore, hold very strong ethical values about the rights of individuals and I have always been prepared to fight for the rights of others whenever these were infringed.

After a decade of acting as a kind of camp follower to my husband's job, I finally insisted on a settled home so that my children could be educated and my husband used this home as his London base. I had considered myself fortunate when my children were aged three and five respectively to obtain a social work post with a 'term-time only' contract of employment, which made it possible for me to have some sort of a career whilst running a professional home and bringing up my children, for I abhorred the idea, forced on many of my husband's colleagues, of sending my children off to boarding school and seeing them scarcely once a year. I believed that both education and a settled home were of paramount importance for them – the more so because I had myself suffered such tremendous lacks on both scores and because my husband – of necessity – spent a good deal of his time in transit.

I had held this post for a decade, reached a fairly senior stage in my career and my children were growing up when my boss (on account of Seebohm) asked me to undertake a CQSW course on secondment as a prerequisite to promotion, since new policies now made this an imperative. Although I already held better social work qualifications than anyone in my department, I saw this as a way of quenching my unsatisfied thirst for knowledge and enjoying the student life I had been denied as an adolescent (like many of my generation). I was made more conscious of this earlier deprivation by my son starting his 'A' levels and gaining a place at Cambridge. When I made application for the CQSW course, however, I was very worried at having to submit a social history, for (a) I felt people would say I'd been reading too much Dickens; (b) there was too big a discrepancy between my middle-class image and my early social history and only a small amount of adverse social reaction had taught me never to make revelations; and (c) I felt I had long ago left behind the deprived child I had been and I wished only to develop the woman I had become with the fulfilment and further enrichment of the education I felt lacking. I doubt if I shall ever get over the anger about the course, which viewed education as a process of breaking down students rather than nourishing them and building them up, which is what I believe the purpose of education to be.

However, on this and other occasions I placed my faith in the officially published literature which stated that the social history was only for interview purposes. What a lie! Thus, in this manner, I was made to provide the ammunition which wrought my own destruction, because I was foolish or gullible enough to read what was officially published as policy.

Trouble started right at the beginning of this course. I went for my first tutorial to a tiny, cupboard-like room where I heard from the mouth of the well-educated, refined, middle-class spinster tutor the words, 'We're going to change you, we'll alter you, make you over afresh – you'll forget everything you've ever learned and learn it all afresh – so your life will be completely changed'. I sank into myself, frozen, my voice sounding as if it came from somewhere else. Only the cultured tones, lack of physical violence, swear words, threatening countenance and the wielding of a dolly stick round my squirming buttocks, thighs, back, and person, differentiated the situation from many I had endured in my early teens, prior to being locked up in a cupboard by an irate mother-substitute. The cupboard-like room regressed me, but still my defences refused memory of the events; only the fear, coldness, and numbness were present. I made some remark about having spent 30-odd years getting my life into the orderly state in which it was found and that since it suited myself and my family, I denied anyone else the right to change it, but I had come like a lamb to the slaughter. I took one look at the image in which I was to be remade and the earlier hate for the substitute mother's cruelty fused. I got up. I said, 'I am, after all, my own unaided work'. I deliberately twisted my engagement ring so that flashes from the diamonds nearly blinded her and then I escaped. This was the first time I'd been conscious of a really mean side to my personality emerging, for, after all, perhaps she chose her spinster state. I had to make haste to the 'ladies' though, for I had commenced to menstruate heavily and was annoyed at the near ruin of an expensive dress. At that moment, however, I realized that the monthly beatings I had received as an adolescent had had more to do with the older woman's menopause than with my puberty – nothing at all in fact to do with my puberty.

The shame I felt about my early sufferings began to be converted to anger and I realized I should have great difficulty in controlling myself towards this wretched tutor. When locked up as an adolescent I had always had the conviction that I was the one who was sane, but this time the sheer weight of the educational establishment I was in made me much less sure about this. The situation depressed me. My doctor knew a little of my history and each time I went to him for antidepressants (a fairly mild variety) he tried to persuade me not to subject myself to this further misery. I insisted that I must have the piece of paper and that one can endure anything for two years. I had proved that to myself more than once; when one has no past the future is all the more precious. Against his better judgement he gave me the tablets to keep me going through this two years of hell. Despite these and all my will-power, however, the tutor affected my work and my whole life and I could not react normally to her, do justice to myself, or concentrate fully throughout the whole two years. On one occasion I even actually vomited during her tutorial.

At the end of the year she commented on the difference in my work for her and for other tutors and I agreed that she affected me adversely 'Why didn't you ask for another tutor?' she queried, having given me a bad report. 'And have you say I couldn't cope with you', I spat – the only moment of triumph I recall. She signified her willingness to change the report if I would explain myself fully to her. 'No thank you', I said, almost snatching the report and signing it. She was almost in tears when I handed it back to her. In *my* final report I mentioned that during the first year I carried around Rudyard Kipling's 'If' and in the second year the official police warning about 'the evidence you shall give'.

Finally the two years of inquisition were over, a brown envelope with some extra letters after my name arrived on my doorstep with a card of congratulation which I threw straight into the rubbish bin. For some brief months I thought I was back to normal, I had the piece of paper and I did not need any more Tryptizol or to see my GP. Alas, however, that had only been the preamble to much worse that was to come.

A few months before the course had ended, my former boss retired through ill-health to cause me further sadness. I then received a letter from another older spinster (who'd always been jealous of something – either my children, popularity, ability, social status or the sum of all) in which I was told that my employers were unilaterally altering my contract of employment. As I have already said, the term-time only contract was the main reason that had kept me in the same job while my children were at school, and my son was still in the sixth form then. My husband had just earned a good promotion himself and the sum total of the alteration to my contract would have meant that I got more responsibility, more difficulty at home, etc., and would have to pay high costs to employ help for all the household responsibilities I normally left for the school holidays, so that his net financial gain would accrue to the Inland Revenue and not to us.

I tried for months at all levels to obtain an interview to discuss this but without success. I was then deliberately interviewed on three occasions for the anticipated promotion (I had been bound in a legal agreement to obtain the CQSW for this purpose) and each time I saw an unqualified, male applicant with less experience, shorter service, less education – but conspicuous political affiliation – appointed. I was then called for the interview refused for 14 months and told, 'You'll always be at the bottom of the pile as long as you have this contract'. The Establishment Officer of the Authority also told me that he 'recognized no moral obligation towards any employee', that he 'would have sacked my former boss for urging on me the Authority's own published rules as an incentive to promotion', and that he 'had only seen me so I would not feel brushed off'. I flounced out angrily at the most ill-mannered brush-off I could ever have imagined.

There followed 18 more months of misery when I felt like a criminal, with poisoned arrows being shot at me from dozens of different sections of the bureaucracy, till I had breast-pangs every time I saw a buff envelope. The legal wrangling went on, I amassed a dossier four inches thick, and this finally culminated in an Industrial Tribunal at which an official apology was made and an interview to redress matters promised. The interview proved very difficult to obtain. During this 18 months I had had to go back to my GP again and was taking the mild antidepressants and also heavy doses of sleeping pills. I started to wake with severe chest pains, but an X-ray showed nothing abnormal and no amount of sleeping pills suppressed the pain. The GP I had known for 16 years suddenly retired unexpectedly and I felt bereft, utterly unable to trust another doctor with such a complex situation and without even the will to talk about it any more. I finally knew I could no longer go on, however.

Fortunately, my knowledge of the 'scene' enabled me to obtain a self-referral to a psychiatrist who was 'right' for me, given all one's notions about Freud, Jung, Klein, Laing, et al. He made a house call at once, which was the equivalent of being thrown a lifebelt when drowning. At once this made me feel that I was now being diagnosed by someone with real expertise. He cared.

After two or three weeks of improvement with the effective antidepressants he prescribed for me, my anger was again simmering over the injustice and I was girding my loins to get back to the fight when *the* crisis occurred.

I had been completely frank with my psychiatrst, who agreed that my ability to analyse myself and do my own 'mind work' were very positive factors for me. After this improvement, when he expressed pleasure at my progress. I had a very bad, restless night. I finally dozed fitfully and woke late from a very vivid dream. In my dream I had been watching myself lying inside a coffin lined with rich purple, which was the source of a beautiful incandescent light surrounding it. I knew that the coffin was the womb, all warm, soft, velvety, safe, and free of trouble and noise and I was closing the lid down on myself. I woke from this dream all trembling and shivering in my head, but still absolutely mesmerized by the attraction and overwhelming desire that coffin had exercised over me. It was so vivid that two years later I recall it as clearly as I do the births of my two children (which were also pretty fraught and eventful).

After several minutes of shivering I realized that I still felt as cold, stiff, and numb as a corpse, though I had been lying in bed with an electric blanket on high for some hours. A number of realizations crowded in on me simultaneously. They were that (1) my husband had told me not to use the blanket as it was faulty; (2) I had for some weeks been sleeping on my back in the stiff, posed position of a corpse; (3) I had had over the previous few months a number of falls, accidents, etc. I realized that my subconscious was trying to kill me and – because of my children – make it look like an accident.

I turned off the electric blanket and with the slow movements of the depressed patient swallowed three times my prescribed dose of antidepressant in much the kind of way that primitive man must have chanted incantations or pulled up mandrake roots. I waited for some time for them to work, made a hot drink, wrapped myself in a blanket, and sat in a chair in front of a fire trying to thaw. I don't know how many hours I sat there, petrified, wondering whether my subconscious or conscious mind would be in control. Finally I wrote it all down in a letter to the psychiatrist to ask him, as I knew I would never have the courage to tell it to him at consultation.

Then I made myself do something else. Having had much trauma in my life, I have a very strong will and a trained concentration to switch to other channels. I therefore tried to get on with some work for an Open University course I was doing. Unfortunately, it was *Oedipus* and the inevitability in Greek drama set my mind on tramlines – I could only parallel my own situation with that of Oedipus, seeing how for years I had kept on taking what I thought was completely constructive action and all I was doing was working towards my own destruction. I put it away as I felt terrified of murdering my child or blinding myself. I knew that a lot of this feeling stemmed from air-raid experiences, the death of my mother, and other childhood miseries and griefs which had all followed so rapidly on one another that there had been no time to resolve them.

I obtained by devious means a list of films and books dealing with related themes. After this I spent many days reading, going to films when my anti-depressants held me in an '*up*' state and sobbing heart-rendingly and for many hours over the fictional events. Thus very slowly and cautiously I was able to approach my own loss and grief and – for the first time in my life – admit that I was actually worth crying over and the child in me worth nurturing. I was able to accept all my husband's anger and impatience with me for not coping and functioning as I had been accustomed to, because – on the physical level – when he was at home he was a very good and capable father to an infuriating, helpless, and exasperating child-figure whom he could no longer understand on any level. When my son was home from Cambridge he demonstrated anger that I no longer functioned as the mother he knew. We had some angry quarrels on account of my jealousy of his good fortune compared to my early disadvantage and on account of his youthful rebellion and thoughtlessness. Fortunately my superego or overself nearly always had the last word so these were the means of a better understanding emerging and the altering of the balance of relationship between us. He now wears the MCP tie which I gave him with wry humour and a certain panache.

For years I had been able to reach out to distressed people and make contact with them, but my *cri de coeur* seemed summed up in the title of Olwen Wymark's play, *Find Me*, which no one can hear, for I have always been a person on whom others leaned, so no one could guess that I was lost. Although I am normally an outgoing, gregarious person, in my depressed state I could inflict myself on no one, so I gradually lost all social contacts. There were, at the best of times, very few people with whom I could communicate intimately. When I did try to verbalize and unburden myself to someone, the reaction was one of defending themselves from my misery. Usually there was a natural human wish to help, but it generally found an outlet in a pep talk, in lecturing me about all the material blessings I possess (as a result of years of hard work) and attempts to make me feel guilty about my neglect of home and family (guaranteed to increase my depression, so causing me to shrink further from the contact) or other versions of the 'pull yourself together' theme. If I had been able to do that, nothing on Earth would have made me lay myself open to this kind of reaction, but I was desperately lonely as well as low, not being allowed to go to work.

I felt desperately ashamed of myself for not coping, too, although it was like having lead weights tied to my arms and legs and body so that superhuman effort and an hour of bracing my will was sometimes needed just to crawl out of bed. My GP was helpful, but since my case was complicated by hypertension and stress-induced menopause, there was some conflict over treatment and some element of blaming me for being ill. No doubt if I had driven myself less hard I might have been spared some of this illness, but I know now that I have a personality which could only admit defeat when the physical batteries were utterly drained and on a negative charge, which removed any further charges of energy and libido or normal adaptive functioning.

Each blow from bureaucracy (and these would fill a three volume book) sent me back to the pit, until my pen spat fire. I was sneered at as 'Joan of Arc', experienced every twist of the 'sociology of blaming the victim' that a complicated system could maliciously, vindictively, thoughtlessly, or just by the gaps in between, promote. I walked on eggshells, having to remain blameless and fight for principles, though there were so many guilty consciences at work against me that I really learned just how that poor Old Testament scapegoat felt when he was being tarred, tied, beaten, and drummed out into the wilderness. Although the vileness I felt got into my soul and made it harder to fight back – almost like trying to keep oneself clean in a cesspit – somehow I had to convince myself I was worth fighting for and I guess the antidepressants provided the physical energy base which fired the anger afresh each time. Also, although I was in contact with many people who were clearly doing tasks which were distasteful to them, such as the Authority's doctor, who had never seen me before but conveyed to me remarks which he agreed were actionable as defamation of character, the non-verbal sympathy and admiration which was expressed in conjunction with the distasteful messages allowed me to retain my basic faith in human nature on the personal level.

The loneliness and isolation were – are still – the hardest part for me to bear, denied the contact with interesting work and a busy life to which I had been accustomed. In retrospect I feel that if one consistent helper had been able to 'phone me for 10 minutes each morning to ask how I was, I would have recovered more quickly – but I could not have brought myself to ask anyone; after all, my social circle is full of busy, professional people with many responsibilities, whose time could be better spent than on me in that worthless state of being. There were days on end when I spoke to no one, couldn't drag myself out of the house, wondered if anyone was alive out there, or if I was really dead or in limbo. I would dial a wrong number just to hear a human voice or switch on the radio, though I couldn't bear the noise, just to reassure myself that the world had not stopped. I did 'phone my psychiatrist once or twice when I felt suicidal, but then I felt guilty even about doing that.

At the very worst times, when I lost all physical sensation and my body felt like a block of ice, the warmth of a fur blanket both comforted me and made me fear it was my shroud. Like characters in a Beckett play I suppose we all have this association between birth and death, but I could not feel that there was very much in between at those times. With the help of the psychiatrist I graded my medication. I also allowed myself many childish regressions, which my strong superego would formerly have been very shocked by – like guzzling a half-pound box of chocolates instead of having lunch. I rationalized it by thinking that I didn't feel well enough to cook anything and that chocolate is nutritious. It would take me hours to get up enough energy to have a bath, though I knew this helped – for I did as much friction rubbing as physical energy could be mustered for. I had problems with my husband over this, for his mother died of hypertension after a hot bath and as I saw so little of him, I might have begun to need a strong disinfectant.

Also at the time I could not appreciate any of the positive aspects of my situation. I had some near-miraculous answers to prayer. One of these came through a misdirected letter from America, which made me a new friend with whom I had so much in common we started where normally 20 years of association might not have reached. She came to me twice, though a very busy person, and comforted my terrifying need when I was on the verge of suicide.

Expert help was also available within my own resources of knowledge. When I was worried that I seemed to be getting worse instead of better I was able to study my son's pharmacology textbooks and go and ask the relevant questions of various consultants, which achieved much improvement. Also – whilst my professional identity was disgusted with me for having become a dependent personality and I was so angry with my body for not allowing me to drive it even further – the professional knowledge helped me to know what was happening in my mind and body and play the patient game – patient both as noun and adjective – thus being as constructive as was possible even amongst the ruins of my identity, drive having always been my main characteristic, rather than patience.

I cannot honestly say that I have gained anything from this breakdown, by which I mean I would rather not have learned most of what I have experienced. I'd rather still believe that tutors think education is to encourage, stimulate, and share enthusiasms with students than to wield power to break them. I'd rather not have known that one of the largest education authorities in the UK could publish policy documents which could bind me to these years of misery and were no more binding on them than toffee wrappers. I'd rather not have met senior professionals paying lip-service to what I believe in and criticizing me for 'over-reaction' when I defended British principles of the rule of law. The Chairman of the Education Committee 'has no executive power', so who is responsible for seeing that local authorities do their job with integrity? Millions of pounds change hands daily on the Stock Exchange on the basis of trust between entrepreneurs and is my experience the norm for the so-called 'caring' profession? Is a moral sense really superfluous in our society? At the root of my depression is the discovery that in our so-called democracy might is the only right, money the only morality, and principles something only the aristocracy can afford.

I wonder how many times I have heard an exasperated social worker say in a pejorative tone, 'what a manipulative client'. I guess I'll be the manipulative client *par excellence* if I'm ever admitted to an alocholic unit or home for destitute aged social workers (come to think of it, I'd better write an auto-biography before then or the social history-taking will never get finished). Each night I used to add a postscript to my prayers, 'Oh, God, let me never be a social worker's interesting case' and I really feared contact with other social workers whilst I was depressed. Consciously or unconsciously, individuals know their needs. In my book, manipulation is the way each person uses the world in trying to satisfy those needs and to use his talents. Like many others in society, I am now denied the opportunity of giving service which many of the recipients assured me had been of real worth to them.

Now I am faced with the problem of finding a way to go on living when the future seems utterly bleak. I am not the kind of person who can find meaning in life without a sense of purpose and a feeling of being useful, and my work is now denied to me. I have always admired the sheer guts of the average person, who keeps going in the face of incredible adversity; now I wonder if they are the fools and perhaps the wise ones are those who let Nanny State carry their responsibilities if they can get away with it. How can I ever trust anyone again when very highly paid officials can write official letters to me and then reinterpret them to make black mean white a month or so later?

I keep reminding myself of all the goodwill, kindness, initiative, generosity, and human compassion of ordinary people, but I cannot find it enough if all public standards are the sham I have found them to be.

The life problems produced by my experience of the last six years are greater than ever. I feel enough anger to want to fight all the grievances of all who ever had their faces ground by Bureaucracy but know that my body cannot carry this anger to constructive action. I still have to hold to my principles, however, even more strongly though more warily, because they have been crushed to dust and welded together again piece by piece. No one will forgive me for having been the victim of their negligence, lies, or inefficiency, but I do not find it difficult to forgive except in instances where viciousness and deliberate malice were the motivating factors.

In view of the fact that I can be compelled to accept a medical retirement at a very early age, thus having my livelihood effectively removed, perhaps I shall have to concede that, after all, money is the only thing which is of any importance. I am back at a subsistence level which more than 25 years of hard, grinding work fighting against obstacles and overcoming adversity had made me forget, for no employer had ever been able to find fault with my work on any score. How do I fill in the blank of 15 years of stable work record, references, seniority, the need to find fresh work after a long illness and recover the self-confidence which all these bitter experiences have so completely destroyed? I don't know the answers to these questions yet. I only know that I am trying to use memory of all that was commended and many appreciative associates as the assurance I need and as grounds for hope, but it is difficult. I feel no hope, no confidence, but as during the depression I took an intellectual decision, put it into effect, and the feeling eventually followed in its wake, so now I attempt the long, slow crawl upwards and back in just that way if there is to be any future at all.

The experience has made me more selfish, less ready to be used by everyone towards whom I have duties and responsibilities – perhaps after all I was the fool in not pressing my own needs and personal values at an earlier stage. I am also more suspicious, less likely to take anything on trust, to make the smallest assumption, and altogether more cautious, less enthusiastic, and slower to react or respond. I can spend so much time thinking things over that the need for action is completely eliminated. I am more hedonistic, yet still feel extremely empty without the satisfaction of work which I know I did well. I feel for the thousands of unemployed who perhaps feel they are on the rubbish heap, the wrong equation felt by all unemployed between money and leisure.

I try to tell myself that from the bottom of the pit one can go no lower and so, with all my heart, I try to make myself believe that from here on the only way is up. I wish I could feel real conviction about that.

3 Surviving depression

By a Clinical Psychologist

Between the ages of 23 and 33 I experienced major environmental harrass-ment that took many forms but was never absent in some form. During this time I also experienced three bouts of clinical depression, lasting some six years in all. Throughout the period, my most compelling desire was to find a nice hole and crawl into it. However, despite the strength of my urge to tell the world to go away and leave me alone, my official curriculum vitae reads like a catalogue: I took three university degrees, two of them higher degrees, taught for five separate departments in schools of the university, published some scholarly papers, and otherwise earned a sort of living as part-time research assistant to my supervisor and also for a while as a freelance dogsbody and interior decorator. This is not the sort of image commonly associated with the textbook stereotype of the 'depressed patient', so you may wonder whether I could really have been depressed.

Unfortunately for the stereotype, the answer is yes. Apart from trying to kill myself, which I considered but thought better of, I had all the usual symptoms to some degree at some time: miserableness, anxiety, gloomy thoughts, fatigue, depersonalization, derealization, tearfulness alternating with feelings beyond tears, disturbed sleep and appetite, diurnal variation, loss of many former interests and of the ability to experience pleasure, loss of libido, menstrual irregularities, constipation, dry mouth, and, as I said, suicidal ideas. Not all of the symptoms were equally severe, nor were all of them present all the time, but at no time during the entire period, and for some time afterwards, when no longer formally 'depressed', was I completely free of at least a few.

The best term I have been able to find for describing the nature of my affliction is Kräupl Taylor's notion of an existential illness, an illness which is 'dependent on the continuance of a salient, exogenous and precipitating event' (Kräupl–Taylor, 1979). The event varied from time to time; the whole decade was characterized by a diabolical concatenation of depressing circumstances, one arising to replace the last. Everyone has limits, and, while I expect that my track record will establish me as fundamentally a pretty hardy sort of character, I am certainly no exception. I think the question is less why did I get depressed than how did I survive at all.

At the age of 23, having just completed a Master of Arts degree at a large

East Coast university, I arrived in London to begin my PhD and to take up a part-time post as research assistant to my supervisor. The year before, I had been awarded a Fulbright Fellowship, but had been unable to take it up, because my professor was going to be on leave that year. When I reapplied, the fellowship was, for some unknown reason, not renewed. In order to enable me to come, my professor offered me the post, the previous holder of which had left to have a baby. The fact that my thesis supervisor and boss were the same person need not in itself have constituted a problem. But within a few months of taking up the post, I discovered that, as one of my colleagues put it, my real job was to be in the wrong all the time. The bullying, they assured me, had little to do with me personally. The role of scapegoat traditionally fell upon the most vulnerable member of the department and I was 'it'.

On learning this news, my first impulse was to get the hell out of there as swiftly as possible. But when I looked around to see where else I could go, I soon realized with a sinking feeling that I was well and truly stuck. Although in theory the possibility of leaving stood open, in practice I turned out to have very few real options, and these were even less appealing than the prospect of staying on and putting up with the situation. All the alternatives had strings attached and the boss held the strings. No matter where I went – back to the States, or in search of another supervisor or another job, I'd need references. I couldn't just go away and pretend it had never happened or tell people it had all been a ghastly mistake. An official account would have to be obtained and I shuddered to think what it might say. No one would want to hear my side of the story. It is axiomatic in such situations that, whatever really happened, the underdog must be held to be at fault. With the blot of an abandoned PhD and failure to do my job satisfactorily, my past record of academic success and occupational proficiency would cease to count: as far as a future academic career was concerned, I'd be finished before I even started. I'd known several people to whom this sort of thing had happened and, having come so far already, I certainly didn't wish to lose what I'd worked so long and hard for.

On the other hand, I reasoned, if somehow I managed to stick the situation and complete my PhD, I could move on honourably, without having to give any explanations. Abhorrent as I found the prospect of an indefinite number of years of being got at, I reckoned that if I managed to survive it, the suffering would have limits, whereas the blot that protecting myself from this exploitation and abuse by leaving the situation would leave on my occupational copybook would follow me for the rest of my career – if I had one.

Given the choice between two invidious alternatives, I decided that the only 'sensible' thing to do was to look after my long-range interests, never mind the short-term costs, grit my teeth, and try to carry on with the original plan as normally as possible.

After a little over a year of subordinating my day-to-day existence to the hope of better things to come, I was ground down to flat, bleak depression.

As my sentence wore on, I became progressively disenchanted with my topic, with the whole field I was in, with the prospect of working in it for the rest of my life, and with the wisdom of the decision I had made to stay on. Yet I also knew that the longer I stayed, the worse it would look if I left without finishing what I'd started. What to do? I had to go forward, but as far as I was concerned, forward led nowhere. I hate to think how much time I wasted pondering in circles over this dilemma.

The solution, when it finally dawned upon me, was simple: keep going forward, but change direction. I had always wanted to study psychology, there just happened to be a part-time evening degree course nearby, and when I applied I was offered a place, so there seemed no time like the present. So, depressed or not, and my still unfinished thesis notwithstanding, I enrolled. To undertake the vast commitment of a part-time BSc course whilst I was already up to my ears and beyond in the PhD and my wretched job and operating on only two cylinders at the best of times may seem a pretty daft and desperate thing to do. If it hadn't worked out, it might well have been the finish of me. In the meantime, it was preferable to either doing myself in or giving up entirely.

Luckily, the plan worked, though at a cost. While starting the course did wonders for my morale and temporarily lifted my depression, it was a disaster for my already overloaded timetable. Previously, I'd been doubling up; now I was trebling. After discovering a congenital inability to be in three places at once, I got depressed again. This time I think it was more because of the unremitting exhaustion to which I was flogging myself than because I didn't like where things were headed. The exhaustion was the price I had to pay, and, given the alternatives as I saw them, I found it cheap at the price. Depressed and exhausted or not, I managed to keep myself going and finally got the PhD and BSc within a fortnight of each other, with – to my unending amazement – a First in the BSc.

The following October, after three years of this unreasonable schedule, I began a two-year course of postgraduate clinical psychology training; the course was fine in every respect but one, viz. I hadn't been able to get a grant to do it. So as far as my time-table was concerned, the next two years were a case of leaving the frying pan for the fire. I'd never before had much money, but always enough to get by on. Now most of the time I just about didn't, even with whatever work I could find to do alongside the course. In the first years, I scraped a bit together by freelancing at whatever anyone would pay me to do, a bit of translating, some indexing, but mainly weekend and evening interior decorating. The second year I taught two evening classes in outlying centres, so didn't get home till after midnight. A private student took up one evening a week, and preparation for the classes another two, so that there wasn't much time left for the course and what little there was was often eaten up by the extra demands of making ends meet. Being poor was a full-time job in itself and my unsatisfactory accommodation – a cold, windy room, without phone or bath or fridge or light in the lavatory on the landing, leaky roof and windows, and persecutory landlord – that provided the physical setting for my efforts did little to help my sense of being of any use, or interest to society. Despite all that effort, my average earnings were less than half of what I would have been getting on Social Security if I'd been unemployed. When things wore out, I couldn't replace them. I felt drab, shabby, unclean, unwanted. I kept thinking of how nice it would be to crawl into a hole somewhere and never come out.

To keep myself going, I had to keep reminding myself that this state of affairs (a) was better than the alternatives, (b) was something I'd chosen, and (c) would lead to better things. So I kept on, got my professional qualification, and accepted the first job I applied for, a full-time lectureship in psychology in one of the London colleges. But my difficulties had only just started. After a few months in the post I was offered, and foolishly accepted – the job of organizing and running the department's course for preclinical medical students, which, I soon found out, was, in common parlance, a can of worms: hostility and criticism on all sides, practically no support, and unremitting, thankless drudgery – I was right back to square one. The depression I'd brought with me from the hardship of my training dug itself in deeper. After a year of flogging myself beyond the limits of my endurance, I found that my physical health was starting to deteriorate at an alarming rate. I realized that if I stayed on any longer I'd have a complete physical and mental collapse and that once I was down I wouldn't want to get up again to face any more of what life seemed to have in store for me.

I decided to give things one more chance. If the next job wasn't a damn sight better than anything I'd had for the past 10 years, it would be the last. I'd just about had enough.

Fortunately, the next job *was* better: a lectureship in clinical psychology at the institution where I'd trained. There I found friendly, supportive, familiar people; work that could have limits set on it; a small number of very good, very highly motivated students; time to prepare my teaching; and the only bod who seemed overtly hostile to me commonly known not to have much use for psychologists and not to be taken terribly seriously for that reason. The change was unbelievable. After a month of looking for the catch, I decided there probably wan't one. I managed then to stop the antidepressants I'd been taking continuously for the past 37 months.

I'm still in that job and more or less happy to be there most of the time. Since then, I've had the odd patch of feeling put upon when nasty things have happened, which, of course, they have a residual tendency to do from time to time. But depression of any clinical significance hasn't been a further problem.

This account of my long-depressing circumstances has been long, depressing, and circumstantial, but the reader needs to know the background in order to understand the logic of the strategies for survival which I evolved over the period. If I managed to stay afloat, it was partly due to luck, to meeting the right people at the right time, but to a great extent my survival was due to a deliberate, cold-blooded effort to survive.

This effort was partly motivated by a positive hope of eventually improving my depressing circumstances. From the first, I conceived of the task before me less as that of lifting my mood in the short term than as that of managing to keep going till things got better and I no longer needed to be depressed about what was happening. But besides hope there was also fear, sheer dread of what would lie in store for me if I didn't somehow manage to keep going. I often recalled the words of one of my American professors. He had said, 'Of course it's difficult to finish your PhD thesis, but it's even harder to go through life explaining why you didn't'. Of the two, fear of a future that was worse than the present was stronger than the hope of one that would be better.

Even before I became ill, and thus before there was any question of a *psychiatric* breakdown, the distinct possibility of a social breakdown loomed before me. The blot of a failed or abandoned PhD was not something I could foresee living down, so I'd begun to entrench myself in 'getting on with what I was there to do'. But once I'd become depressed, to the threat of mucking up my occupational future was added the threat of possibly falling into the hands of the psychiatric system, which was not only horrible to contemplate in its own right but would also complicate the occupational problem further. Being a failed PhD on grounds of assumed stupidity was bad enough, but on grounds of mental instability it was pretty unthinkable.

The thought of entering hospital is repellent enough for most people; for someone with an enormous range of allergies to the foods most likely to be served there, it can be a source of unmitigated horror. Anyone with allergies knows how impossible it would be to explain one's lifelong constitutional idiosyncrasies to staff who would be likely not only to have no concept of food allergy but also to assume that patients' concerns with avoiding certain foods were symptomatic of anorexia nervosa, hypochondriasis, or paranoia. And anyone who gets migraines upon prolonged fasting realizes how invidious it might be to have to choose between eating and getting acutely ill and not eating and getting acutely ill. I just could not imagine myself coping with that sort of situation, so that, in comparison, daily life, which I could imagine myself coping with, since I'd been doing it all my life, seemed relatively easy.

The hardest thing I usually had to do on any given day was to get up and face it. The thought of the unpleasantness that might greet me at work was – apart from the thought of going into hospital – the closest I've ever come to a phobia. The difference between my dread of the office or of a hospital and a phobia was that the nastiness I anticipated finding there was objective, highly probable, and fraught with real, threatening, long-term consequences. There was no way round it: whatever I did, something nasty was bound to happen. Life was a choice between evils. Dwelling on the unhappy fact of circumstances was depressing in its own right, but I frightened myself into using it in order to get myself to face the day.

I'd have been lying there, awake but unable to move, since the early hours. When the alarm went off, I knew I'd have to move, get out of bed, queue for the loo, make breakfast, eat it, get dressed, get my things together, pack my lunch, and walk to work. Even such simple, basic tasks as getting myself up to go downstairs to pee seemed to require more effort than I could muster. But horrible as the thought of getting up and on with it was, there was at least always something worse to think about. Most mornings I would force myself to imagine how I would feel if as a result of having yielded to my desire to remain immobile and let the world go stuff itself I faced a day in which it didn't matter whether or not I got up, since there was no place in the world where my presence or absence would make the slightest difference. After a few minutes of dwelling on a future of unemployment, poverty, social isolation, and enforced dependence on the system, I'd find the energy to heave my feet over the side of the bed and let the force of gravity take over. Covert sensitization has its uses.

Once on my feet, I had a number of strategies for keeping myself moving. One was requiring myself to live only one day at a time. If things got bad, I could tell myself that all I had to do was get through till evening and remind myself I'd been doing it all my life. If I couldn't manage to convince myself, I'd force myself to go over in my mind all the difficult things I'd managed to overcome in the past and ask myself whether what I had to do now was really the most difficult thing I'd ever been faced with. If I couldn't honestly say that it was, which I couldn't, then the only sensible thing was to bloody get on with it, since if I let something that was really relatively easy get on top of me now, it would make everything I'd ever done before completely meaningless.

Another strategy was what I thought of as 'eating an elephant', based on the elephant joke. ('How do you eat an elephant?' 'With a knife and fork.') Most of the time, the thought of the enormous tasks I had to do, like finish my thesis, or, later, prepare for finals, or organize the medics' course, was enough to make me want to retreat from it all into the nearest convenient hole, or even any hole for that matter. I thought of the magnitude of the task and about how much I felt capable of doing and decided that it was a foregone conclusion that I'd never manage it. But if a large task was broken down into small enough bits, there would come a point where even in my diminished state I would lose all residual self-respect at the thought that I'd been defeated by such a puny challenge. So I would break everything I had to do down into mini-chores and then decide what order to tackle them in instead of trying to do everything all at once. I reminded myself of the old prisoners' jingle: 'Serve your sentence day by day/And do your bird the easy way'. With microscopic tasks to do, I was less likely to be a complete failure, since there would probably be at least a couple of components that would get done. Then I could tell myself I was at least making progress. 'Rome wasn't built in a day.' 'Theses are written one word at a time.' 'Many steps will take you to the top of the mountain.' I'd tell myself that if it wasn't a sensible way to be going about things, there wouldn't be so many proverbs about it. I invented the one about theses myself, so there'd be more.

In managing a day to day existence, a certain amount of planning was needed. I worked out a method that took into account the fact that although I usually managed to get my body to work by 9 a.m. I wasn't really even half awake until well into the afternoon and had to function on automatic pilot until then. My last activity of the evening, when my mind was normally more or less functioning, was to make a list of all the things I had to do the next day and place the list in my handbag. When I got to work the next morning, I'd take the list out and simply go through the day one task at a time, crossing them out when I'd finished. Any that were left undone were added to the next day's list. Besides saving me from having to rely on my memory, which was then worse than it had ever been before (or since), the daily list would give me something to fall back on at the end of the day, since, my sense of futility notwithstanding, I could remind myself by looking at all the chores I'd crossed off, that really I hadn't done *nothing*.

A related strategy was to undertake extracurricular projects which, once started, would require me to make small but regular outputs of effort. By this means I created a network of individually minor but collectively important commitments to some on going future. Thus if I joined the public library and borrowed books, I'd at least have to return them; if I bought a plant for my room, I'd be committed to watering and looking after it; if I got a roll of film, I'd have to take some pictures, put them in for developing, and go back to collect my prints. This web of purposiveness, spun over the chasm of my sense of pointlessness, served many purposes: it created a future, helped maintain appearances of normality, gave me something more interesting than my boring old thesis to talk about, and kept my toe stuck in the door of domains that lay outside the boss's sphere of influence. As long as I kept it watered, my coleus would grow, no matter what Her Ladyship said or thought or did.

But although these activities literally gave me something to look forward to, I can't say that I enjoyed them in the way I'd enjoyed such things before getting depressed and since recovering. What they afforded was not pleasure (it's no fun to find your concentration is so bad you can't even read a thriller), but at least minimal grounds for a sense of defiant satisfaction: I continued to have an existence that was independent of my identity as the boss's navvy; I could still do things that she had no say in and no control over; yah boo to you, too! Keeping some territory that was mine and had 'No Trespassing' posted on the fence was terribly important in keeping me from getting swallowed up entirely by the tempests in the department teapot.

My inability to enjoy former pleasures was one of the most noticeable ways that my clinical depression differed from earlier and subsequent bouts of ordinary dejection. In the past I'd been not only able but also keen to cheer myself up when feeling down for no particular reason. But now, with my capacity to experience pleasure, my concentration, and my memory out of action and only my sense of uselessness working overtime, most of the means I'd formerly used were simply no longer at my disposal. Under these conditions, I not only probably couldn't have cheered myself up if I'd tried, I also found I didn't really want to. What I wanted to do was not to feel better but not to feel *anything*. In the face of almost constant provocations to pain and distress, the deliberate cultivation of emotional anaesthesia had much to recommend it as a means of promoting survival.

While in my depressed state, I found that the main feelings I was able to feel just weren't worth feeling: despondency about the situation; anger at the boss for creating and exploiting it; anger at myself for having got myself into it and for letting myself be exploited; contempt at myself for the 'safe' course of action I was taking; and dread of the future. The game of feeling wasn't worth the candle. Moreover, the strength of these feelings, when I did feel them, was enormous and they disrupted my work. Interference with work would postpone my escape and was therefore to be avoided, even at the cost of improving upon the unpleasant emotional blunting that the illness brought with it. Another reason for trying not to feel anything if I could possibly help it was that if I allowed myself to feel okay about anything, I became vulnerable to the invidious contrast between the way things might have been and to the demoralizing crash of returning to despondency when the temporary aberration had passed.

In any case, the notion of 'mood' in relation to my clinical depression seemed artificial. In normal life and in ordinary depression the term was meaningful enough: I could readily tell what sort of a mood I was in and differentiate 'mood' subjectively from any one of a number of other sorts of relationship between me and life. But when I was clinically depressed, 'mood' became less distinct from the other ways in which I felt. What was normally a fairly differentiated set of complex perceptions now became a fairly undifferentiated, global apprehension. My senses all seemed to have become less acute: food was tasteless; I didn't notice smells, such as a gas leak, that I'd formerly have picked up; my fingertips seemed insensitive to textures; I was less aware of where my various extremities had got to; even my sense of pain was attenuated. Hedonic tone, or whatever mood might be called, had joined the general strike, paralysing my sensibilities; because of its decreased salience, it didn't matter all that much that the pastimes and distractions I would normally have used to improve my mood had lost most of their meaning. I thought of the line from Baudelaire: *'Le printemps adorable a perdu son odeur'*. I thought I knew what it meant.

Although I tried actively to cultivate emotional blankness, I found myself as actively fighting a pervasive cognitive blankness that was distinct from the sensory attenuation in degree if not in kind. My sensory dullness was partial and incomplete: if I burnt my hand picking up something hot, I could certainly still feel it and react with the appropriate reflex. But at times the mental blankness seemed total, a *Ganzfeld*. In the initial stages of the depression, before I'd discovered its essential difference from the everyday black moods I'd dealt with before, I tried to dispel the blankness by the usual method of distracting my attention. Now I discovered that I seemed to have no attention to distract: I wasn't focusing on a gloomy thought from which I needed to be deflected – *I simply didn't have any thoughts*. Radio silence reigned in my head. It was uncanny. About the only signs of life I could detect were physical sounds: my jaw popping, pulsebeats, eyeblinks, the odd scrunch at the back of my skull when my head turned – noises, without content, signifying nothing. The problem was now, rather, that of trying to *attract* my attention back from wherever it had gone off to and at least get it to stick to *something* so that it didn't simply disappear without a trace. This feeling of being mindless was by far the worst of the psychological deficits I experienced. The only remedy I ever found for it in all that time was to go to bed and not get up till it had gone away. When I'd wake up, I wouldn't feel particularly well rested, but at least the dreadful emptiness in my head was replaced by the usual rubbishy noise by which I recognize that I exist. I remember reflecting that one reason why depressed people try to kill themselves must surely be to test the hypothesis that they are still alive.

Fortunately, this awful blankness was pretty rare. Usually I only felt stupid and useless, which was nasty but preferable to feeling mindless. When in my usual knocked-off state, I found some use in the miscellaneous rules of thumb for dealing with depression which I had somehow managed to acquire along the way. Ever since I could recall, I'd carried them around in my head but had always just taken them for granted, like the nondescript furniture in a rented room. Now that I was living there, I began to discover uses for them. I realized belatedly, a bit like Molière's Monsieur Jourdain, that what I was doing was applying the rule, 'Try to work out what is making you depressed and do what you can about that'. I'd also applied the general formula, 'When you encounter a problem you don't know what to do about, start by finding out what you can about the nature of the problem', by reading up depression in umpteen psychiatry texts. Most of what I read was not much use in the day to day battle – so what if it's more common in women? – but it did give me a map of the battlefield and a set of public coordinates for construing my experience.

Being able to account for myself in publicly intelligible terms was of strategic importance in remaining socially viable, I realized. Other people's responses to knowing I was depressed, like anything else, would depend largely upon the way the information was presented. If my account of myself made sense to others, they'd be more inclined to regard the depression as an incidental, transient state that – for reasons well known to them – I happened, not surprisingly, to be in. Under these auspices, my depression was essentially normal, in the sense of being what people would expect to occur under the circumstances. But if I presented my sometimes quite peculiar experience in obscure and incomprehensible private terms, people's perception of me would undergo a radical shift: the me they'd known would be lost in the incomprehensibility of my report and I'd become a psychiatric leper overnight. The depression would then appear as an essence rather than as an incidental feature and that would be the end of ordinary old me. So the message had to be, 'I'm depressed, sure, but it's business as usual' and the rules I had to follow in order to support this presentation of myself were 'stick to your normal routine' and 'try and act as if you weren't feeling depressed'.

This deliberate attention to self-presentation was not something characteristic of me before my depression or since. Normally I just get on with whatever I'm doing and don't worry overmuch about the form, which usually takes care of itself and if it doesn't, well, that's tough. But during my long depression I became preternaturally aware of the effect I might have on other people and also exquisitely sensitive to what their reactions implied about their evaluation of me. The question at the back of my mind was always: do they think I'm some sort of nut or do they seem to accept me at face value? If people seemed to buy my efforts towards normalization, I'd tend to feel safe: that meant the plan was working and maybe I'd survive in the finish. But if they seemed to question the performance – and I often felt I was *impersonating myself* – I'd start to feel as though the end of the world were nigh: the plan wasn't working; I was sure to perish; there was no hope; I'd be finished, *kaputt*. It was not a nice feeling.

In view of this heightened sensitivity to what I perceived as other people's definitions of me, I was lucky that my GP, whose view of the situation was pretty crucial, went along with my efforts to carry on. His view seemed to be that it is preferable to support someone's efforts to survive as an ongoing social entity than to have to pick up the pieces if the enterprise comes unstuck. I was particularly grateful to him for allowing me to adjust my own dose of anti-depressants, which meant being able to avoid both the worst of the side effects and the awful state of having only side effects because of not having enough medication. When I saw him for my monthly refill, he was more interested in what was going right for me than in what was going wrong, though when things did go wrong he was constructively supportive. I felt that he realized how damaging it could be to imply to someone who was only just about managing that their resources were probably inadequate to see them through.

An example of the way he did things will illustrate what I mean. Once when the boss was on the warpath and I'd been declared Public Enemy Number One and was just about to go completely to bits under the onslaught of vituperation that punctuated the working day, I went to him and said I'd had enough. Instead of taking over and despatching me forthwith to the nearest bin, he asked me quite calmly what I thought it was best to do. When I recovered from the shock of still being taken seriously, I told him that if I could get out of the situation until the professorial tantrum had abated and could spend the time sleeping off the worst effects of the past 10 days or so of exposure to the constant haranguing, I might be able to get myself together.

'Right,' he said, 'how's about having "flu" for a week, then?' It was just right. So I went home to bed for a week, officially suffering from 'flu'. When I returned to work, the affray had let up enough for it to be safe for me to stay there. The extra sleep was a great help, of course, but even more so was my GP's message that, even when I was at my worst, my own methods of coping could still be relied on.

Apart from my boss, the people I worked with were always willing to add their support to my efforts to stay afloat. For a start, they tended to accept my state in a matter-of-fact way: 'You're depressed? No wonder.' People in the department would tip me off when there was extra trouble brewing, seek me out afterwards to find out how I'd fared, and, out of hours, provided many opportunities to get away from it all. They also helped in practical ways by passing on miscellaneous items of household gear that they were no longer using, which greatly improved my meagre standard of living. Later, when I was keeping the roof over my head by decorating, many former colleagues discovered rooms that just happened to want doing up, so I was never at a loss for jobs. When I was doing my training, some lent, or even gave me money to make ends meet. And when one of the consultants at the teaching hospital found out about my financial straits, he arranged for me to pay my fees over several years, which relieved a lot of pressure. The message, in many guises, was, 'You're OK; carry on'. And I really needed to hear it in order to be able to continue to do so. If everyone had adopted the boss's line of 'You're not OK; why don't you quit while you're still ahead?' I expect I really would have gone crazy, since disagreeing would have put me at odds with the majority view – and we all know what happens to people who maintain views that no one else in the world endorses.

The various couples I lodged with were also helpful. We'd often have a mutual moan when we got home from work. While preparing food in the kitchen, we'd exchange our tales of quotidien woe, commiserate, and agree that life could be very hard indeed when 'people like that' were allowed to ride roughshod over people like us. In this epic narrative of the day's hazards of fortune, the boss's behaviour could be depicted for what it was, and I, its miserable sitting target, would come off the better the worse she carried on. Retelling the tale didn't make living it appreciably easier, but at least it transformed my daily ordeal from a unique personal persecution that I was in some obscure way responsible for ('no smoke without fire') to an exemplary instance of a relatively common, recognizable syndrome ('power corrupts and absolute power corrupts absolutely') that I'd had the miserable rotten luck to get lumbered with, but which wasn't a reflection upon me. It was the people I lived with who emboldened me to hang up the phone on her when what she was saying became unfit for human consumption. I'd never have had the guts to do it otherwise. But after I'd tried it a few times, I was, as they'd predicted, gratified by a reduction in both the frequency and intensity of her dial-a-tribes. Knowing that I had sympathetic people to return to in the evening was also a source of strength when she tried having a go at me face to face. I'd distance myself from the proceedings by thinking, 'You miserable old so-and-so, if only you knew how what you're saying is going to sound when I quote you tonight, you'd shut up, you would'. I'd listen in order to be able to recall what she'd said, but that was all. I hate to think what would have happened if I'd had to take it seriously. But with the consensus of reasonable people at home to fall back on, I was spared having to entertain the notion that she might just possibly be right.

In retrospect it seems paradoxical that the only significant person who didn't contribute wholeheartedly to supporting my efforts at normalization was the psychotherapist I saw for two years. Looking back, I'm amazed that I stuck it for so long and can't really explain why. I suppose I did it because in some obscure way it was expected of me to 'do something' about the mess I was in and seeing a psychotherapist was society's idea of 'doing something'. I expect I was also trying to keep an open mind and give it a chance to prove helpful; meanwhile, it was expensive, inconvenient, and anything but what it was meant to be. I think that the main reason it didn't work out was that his goals for the intervention and mine were fundamentally incompatible. I wanted to patch myself together and keep going and he seemed to want me to break down so that I could have a radical psychic overhaul. Our versions of things rarely matched. For example, he kept insisting that the reason I was staying on in my intolerable situation was because of an unconscious need to suffer. My view was that I was choosing to put up with the suffering now in order to avoid more and worse in future: if I really wanted to suffer, and go on suffering, the ideal solution would be to let the situation get the better of me and lose everything I'd already worked so long and hard for. He wouldn't buy it. But if I'd tried to accept his view, my whole effort would have been built on quicksand.

What finally finished the therapy was my realization that what the therapist seemed to be trying to 'help' me to do was precisely the last thing on earth I wanted to do. He said that sometimes people have to accept a breakdown as part of changing. I didn't like the sound of that one bit. I asked if there were any guarantee that change following a breakdown would necessarily be for the better. When he didn't reply, I asked if *he* had had to break down in order to reap the benefits of his training analysis. The ensuing silence was pretty deafening. Then I asked, if breaking down is neither a necessary nor a sufficient condition for positive change, why the hell was he recommending it? He eventually replied that I seemed to be wanting to undermine his efforts. On the contrary, I rejoined, he seemed to be trying to undermine mine and if getting me to fall apart was what all this was in aid of, I'd be getting out while I still could.

His reply to my announcement conveyed such a total lack of insight into what I'd always understood to be the irreducible, hard, cold facts of reality that I really began to wonder which of us was meant to be daft. My desire to terminate therapy, he said, seemed to him to represent a 'flight from analysis'. If that was how he saw it, I reckoned, he was too far gone for rational argument, so I didn't bother to point out that if I were to break down completely, not only would I be unfit for analysis, I'd also be unfit to earn enough to pay for it, even if I'd wanted it, which – even more to the point – I didn't. So that was the end of psychotherapy. I guess I wasn't a very suitable patient.

The experience of formal psychotherapy left me with a profound distrust of procrustean 'therapeutic' ideologies, which, if carried to extremes, have all the attributes of a species of psychopathology in their own right. The implication that pervaded therapy, viz. that everything I did was suspect by definition because I'd done it, could have been extremely damaging if I'd allowed myself to be more influenced by it. I don't like to think of what the outcome might have been if I hadn't resisted being 'helped' in this dubious way.

Most of the remaining strategies I used during my long slog to a life that I didn't need to be depressed about are variants of the ones I've already described. Like the others, they were aimed more at maintaining my ongoing social performance than at lifting my spirits. Some, such as placing my bell alarm clock in a large metal cooking pot in order to amplify the sound so that I wouldn't over-sleep, increased my efficiency at the incidental cost of making me feel worse: the wretched pot amplified the sound of ticking as well as the alarm. At other times, I found myself *deliberately* making myself feel worse in order to function better. There was a certain level of depression at which I found I could work fairly efficiently, since I no longer gave a damn about what I was doing, so wasn't distracted by thinking of all the more interesting things I could be doing instead. Which meant that my usual boundless capacity to find things I'd rather do than all the fiddly chores I'd got to do didn't create its usual interference. If my mood showed signs of improving at critical times – like while I was swotting for exams – when I needed to be able to focus all my limited attention on the task in hand, my efforts to survive assumed the paradoxical form of rehearsing gloomy thoughts, such as what would happen if I failed, in order to make me feel that bit more depressed and enable me to get on with what I had to do. If it weren't for this technique, I'm sure I'd never have learnt any statistics, since normally the prospect of having to attend closely to anything involving lots of numbers sends me scurrying off in search of any household chores that suddenly seem in urgent need of doing. This business may sound pretty crazy, but it worked, which is all that matters.

During this time, I became a convinced pragmatist. My motto was (and still is) 'As long as it works . . .'. In any event, it finally all did work out. This period of my life is behind me now and has been for some years. As of the present, I've got a secure job that I can do and that I usually enjoy doing, a reasonable and permanent roof over my head, and intermittent rather than constant hassles at work. While I'm by no means affluent, I have more than enough to get by on. My curriculum vitae has escaped the huge messy blot that a full-scale break-down during my decade of depression would have left behind it, and I've taken many precautions in the way I've organized my new life in order to make bloody sure that everything doesn't ever get on top of me like that again. However, the protracted strain of fighting to survive has taken a heavy toll in chronic physical debilitation, which now entails further, though different sorts of, deliberate efforts to keep myself going. But that is another story.

What I learnt from my prolonged experience of surviving depression is not easy to summarize. From a personal point of view, the experience made me aware both of the limits of my endurance and of a reserve of strength and determination to endure. It was a testing ground. But while I expect I do feel somewhat more positive about myself for having come through the test, I must say that it seems to me an extravagantly wasteful means of forming character. Largely as a result of my increased physical vulnerability and decreased reserves of stamina, the experience has also led to certain deformities of character which now appear permanent. I am much more wary of possible sources of threat and damage and am inclined to take progressively fewer risks with circumstances that could turn out to be noxious. I am completely intoler-ant of situations in which people in authority start getting procrustean with me. While I no longer keep the thought in the forefront of my mind, I am never entirely free of a residual dread that somehow it could all happen again and I appraise new opportunities in terms of the likelihood of their contributing to precipitating another depression or conditions conducive to it. The loss of possibilities which erring on the side of caution must entail is a price which I accept having to pay for a life that leaves me an appreciable margin of safety. No doubt the psychotherapist would have reservations about this adjustment. But, as a confirmed pragmatist, I'm inclined to regard that as *his* problem.

As a therapist myself now, I reckon that the experience was as valuable as any which constituted a part of my formal training. Psychotherapy provided me with an excellent negative model, a personification of the kind of therapist I do not want to be. From the feedback I get in my work, I think that on the whole I succeed in building people up rather than breaking them down. From my GP's non-intrusive but sustained interest and concern, I have learnt something of the critical importance of constructively encouraging rather than undermining people's own efforts, in misplaced zeal to be 'helpful'. I also appreciate how vital it can be to have someone just go on being there and wanting to know, month after month and year after year if need be. Quite apart from the quality of the relationship, the continuity of regular contact with someone I could trust and who could still seem to relate to me as a whole and viable person when all I felt like was a heap of damaged and disconnected bits was crucial in keeping the disconnections from actually happening. In my own work I try as much as possible to bear this principle in mind. From the less intense but more extensive support I received from colleagues and friends, I've learnt how much more there is to surviving depression than the help, however invaluable, that can be provided through formal channels. The constant message of confirmation that I was still OK by them was needed to negate the disconfirmation of my worth as a person that was implicit – and sometimes writ large – in my depressing circumstances. What I learnt from my lay support network is that if certain negative and corrosive elements in a person's environment cannot for practical reasons be removed, it may at least be possible to reduce their overall impact by diluting them in the more positive medium of social support. But support is limited: others can only do so much. Then, I learnt, if you want to survive, you're on you're own: it's you who've got to do the doing, and realizing that it is up to you and you alone contains an important lesson about the crunch of living. Finally, from my chronic physical debilitation, which I now live with one day at a time, as I used to live with the depression that brought it on, I have learnt not to underestimate the possible long-term costs of 'being sensible'.

Section II   Arrivals and departures

The three chapters which make up this section share the theme of an experience of depression precipitated by the loss or birth of a family member, or, in one case, both simultaneously. As in the first section of the collection, the three writers belong to different professions – occupational therapy, nursing, and general practice, respectively – and their work and life circumstances are also very different. But their accounts of their experiences have much in common nonetheless.

Our authors describe their encounters with difficult and painful life situations: the badly handled loss of a much wanted first baby *in utero* at a time of family strain due to the death of a grandmother; the death of a father from cancer, followed by a mother's suicide, followed by the completion of a course of postgraduate study; and the birth of a first baby into an insecure marriage at a time of family strain due to a sister's illness.

Births and deaths are, of course, fundamental human experiences upon which mental health workers can claim no monopoly. But our authors' accounts suggest that some mental health workers who become depressed after these sorts of understandably depressing experiences may encounter special difficulties as a result of their professional status or circumstances.

The special burdens which depressed mental health workers may incur as a result of their depressions are not yet a part of the literature on life events and depression. To date, research seems to be confined to life-change events which precede the onset of a depressive episode. Further life changes which follow from a depression remain topics for future study in any patients, let alone mental health professionals. However, some of the findings on life events preceding depressions seem relevant to our authors' accounts. We may examine some of the main findings briefly.

Using the Social Readjustment Rating Scale (Holmes and Rahe, 1967), Thomson and Hendrie (1972), working in Manitoba, compared the overall frequency of life-change events in groups of depressed patients, polyarthritics, and hospital staff controls. They reported that the depressed patients, whether diagnosed as 'endogenous' or as 'reactive', had higher mean frequencies of events than either control group. No information about the specific content of the events was reported. But the finding that depressed patients have larger concatenations of upsetting circumstances in their backgrounds than people who are not depressed seems consistent with the complex sets of circumstances which our authors describe as preceding the onsets of their depression.

Other investigators have addressed the question of which events tend to precede depressions. Forrest, Fraser, and Priest (1965), working in Edinburgh, compared depressed patients with medically ill controls in terms of the relative frequency of selected social and medical factors in the three years prior to admission or referral. They found significantly higher rates of social isolation and loss of a social role in the depressed patients. As we shall see shortly, social isolation was certainly a factor in two of the three cases included in this section and loss of an anticipated social role, that of motherhood, was one of the precipitants in the third case.

Since the controls of Forrest *et al.* had medical illnesses – which have also been found to be associated with an increased rate of life events (Rahe, 1968; Wyler, Masuda, and Holmes, 1971), they may not have been optimal for investigating the contribution of life events to depression specifically. When Paykel and his collaborators at Yale University in New Haven conducted their study of the role of life events in female depressed patients, they used a control sample drawn from the same local community as the patients (Paykel, Myers, Dienelt, Klerman, Lindenthal, and Pepper, 1969). They found that the depressed patients reported nearly three times as many significant life events in the spheres of employment, health, and marital relations during the six-month period prior to their depressive episode as the controls reported for a comparable period. A raised incidence of events regarded as undesirable was also found for the patients. Finally, when events designated as 'entrances' (engagement, marriage, birth of child, new person in home) and 'exits' (death of close family member, separation, divorce, family member leaves home, child married, son drafted) were compared for the two groups, 'entrances' were not found to be significantly more common in patients, but nearly twice as many patients as controls reported 'exits' and the difference was statistically significant. The finding of a raised incidence of 'exits' seems relevant to our authors' experiences, as two of the three (as well as others whose work appears elsewhere in the collection) describe depressions occurring after exits and the third describes an exit occurring subsequently and precipitating further depression.

The work of Brown (1974) in London confirms the general conclusion that depressed patients, women at least, have an excess of upsetting life events in their background. He compared the rate of life events, differentiated according to degree of judged severity, in depressed female patients and community-based controls. In the 38-week period before onset of depression, the patients reported significantly higher rates of markedly and moderately severe events, but events of lesser severity were not more common. Overall, some 61% of patients had at least one severe life event during the study period, as compared to 21% of controls.

Brown's chief contribution in this area is not, however, the finding of a raised rate of severe life events amongst depressed women but rather his demonstration that certain historical and social factors increase the risk of becoming depressed when severe life events occur but do not have obvious effects in the absence of such events. In the introduction to the previous section, we have already considered one of these 'vulnerability factors', namely holding a job outside the home. The other identified factors are loss of mother in childhood (which applies to the author of 'Hitting rock bottom' in Section I), having three or more children under age 14 living at home, and lack of a confiding relationship (Brown, Ní Bhrolcháin and Harris, 1975).

This last-mentioned vulnerability factor is relevant to the accounts of two of our three authors, who describe upsetting events occurring at a time when they lacked a confiding relationship with a significant other. The psychiatric-nurse-turned-health-visitor author of 'In the wilderness' (Chapter 5) describes turning to the casualty department of a London teaching hospital when he became depressed after his mother's suicide and the completion of his course. He does not actually say that he had no one else to turn to, but he implies as much in describing himself as lonely at this time. The general practitioner author of 'Hope is the key' (Chapter 6) is more explicit about the exceptional degree of social isolation she experienced at the time of her first pregnancy. She notes that she was too busy working to make new friends in the new neighbourhood to which she and her husband had recently moved; they came to realize how little they understood one another and knew of no one they could trust to discuss their anxieties with. Moreover, neither her own family nor her in-laws could offer support at this time.

These two writers' isolation at the time of their troubles contrasts with the more fortunate situation of the occupational therapist author of 'It couldn't happen to me, could it?' (Chapter 4). She did have a confiding relationship with her husband, but it was apparently not enough to make her invulnerable to depression after the loss of her baby. From her report, it appears that the loss was handled very unsympathetically by her consultant, by hospital paramedical staff, and, subsequently, by her supervisor at work – which may have gone some way towards offsetting the effects of her good relationship with her husband.

The insensitive treatment our occupational therapist received at a time of tremendous personal stress represents a common theme running through these three chapters. All three authors point to potential sources of support and comfort which they were disappointed to find unavailable at their time of troubles. Our occupational therapist describes how she wished to return to her old job, as she felt she 'needed the security of the familiar routine' and anticipated that her colleagues would be patient with her. But 'for her own good', she was summarily transferred to a new post, so that in addition to losing her baby, she also lost her job. In addition, she reports finding that neither many of her friends nor even many of her colleagues could be counted upon to deal sensibly with her.

Her experience of finding potential support not there when it was needed is echoed in 'In the wilderness'. The author describes the tactless comments of some of his hospital visitors, the hostile reaction of his head of nursing after his return to work, unsympathetic attitudes of general hospital staff after his overdose, further unsympathetic reactions from an interviewer on the professional register, and rejection by most of his relatives when he revealed to them that he is a homosexual. Similarly, the author of 'Hope is the key' notes that during her stay in hospital for the birth of her baby, she felt very alone. Her family was preoccupied with her sister's ill-health and ward staff appeared to withhold help and advice about infant feeding 'as I was a doctor and was supposed to know all the answers'. Subsequently, she describes meeting a similar attitude from her GP, presumably for the same reason. At the same time, the professional pride that we discussed in the introduction to Section I also rears its head in her account: she reports that she, too, was too proud to seek medical help for her puerperal depression.

Some of these instances of non-support by the social environment are presumably generic and could happen to anyone. But some of them do seem to represent additional hardships for depressed mental health workers specifically, extra burdens which they come to bear not so much because of their own failure in coping but rather more because of failures in their colleagues and medical advisors' efforts to cope with them in their distress. Our occupational therapist remarks of some of her colleagues that she 'found it very disturbing that someone who had worked for so many years in psychiatry was so inept at dealing' with her. We are inclined to share her disquiet.

Wounded Healers
Edited by V. Rippere and R. Williams
© 1985 John Wiley & Sons Ltd.

4   It couldn't happen to me – could it?

By an Occupational Therapist

The summer of 1979 was a time of decision-making. I had worked for a number of years as an OT, initially in the field of physical rehabilitation but more recently in psychiatry. I had also been married for four years. At the start of our marriage, I had been the breadwinner while my husband worked on his doctoral thesis. But by the summer of 1979 he had settled into his job as a scientific civil servant, we had become owner-occupiers of a three-bedroomed semi, and we had bought the basic essentials to make life comfortable. The time seemed ripe for starting a family. This decision was prompted by my own waning interest in my career (because of my husband, I was tied to an area where there were few future prospects that really appealed) and by a past gynaecological problem which could possibly have meant difficulty in conceiving.

Thus, at the beginning of that August, my husband and I decided to start trying for a family. Five weeks later I was almost sure I was pregnant but, to my amazement, six weeks after my last period I started to haemorrhage. The bleeding, however, was much lighter than usual and only lasted a couple of days. I still continued to feel sick and tired so the next week I went to the occupational health sister at work for a pregnancy test. It was negative. She advised me to return, however, if I missed my next period. I returned five weeks later: this time the result was positive.

The first few months of pregnancy were, I suppose, fairly typical of those of most first-time mothers. I experienced alternating periods of elation and then apprehension. Gradually the developing embryo became the central theme to my life as my waist enlarged and the nausea subsided. A couple of other people at work were also pregnant and we spent many lunch-hours discussing knitting patterns, the price of nappies, and the pros and cons of maternity leave.

After my first antenatal appointment with the GP, it was decided to put me down for the GP unit. He decided to consider my pregnancy as dating from that last menstruation in early September: the baby was therefore expected in early June.

The first untoward sign happened at my monthly visit to the GP in the week before Christmas. After the initial examination, he said to me, 'I don't think you can be only 15 weeks. I would say you were at least 19 – I'd like you to see the consultant and have a scan'. I was not unduly concerned by this as I'd always thought that I'd conceived in August.

My visit to the consultant in early January merely reaffirmed the GP's feelings. At the end of January, I arrived in the scan room of the radiography department. The scan, however, did not prove helpful in settling my dates. At the end of January I thought I was either 21 or 25 weeks pregnant. The scan, however, showed me to be only 17½ weeks pregnant. When I queried this with my GP, he said that the scan must be right and probably it was just because of scarring from a previous laparotomy that there was a discrepancy in uterus height. This opinion was repeated by the consultant when I saw him on the 20th of February and he bade me a jovial goodbye.

The following weekend, I noticed that I had developed a raging thirst. By Wednesday evening, I had a pair of nicely swollen ankles which continued to enlarge all day Thursday. Although I knew pregnant women often had swollen ankles and I had spent most of my time at work on my feet, I decided to see my GP the next day. On Friday when I got up, I weighed myself and to my horror discovered that I had put on 1 stone 3 lbs in a week. I went post-haste to the doctor and was immediately sent home to bed. That evening we heard that my husband's grandmother had died.

She had been ill for some time and had proved to be a considerable strain on my mother-in-law, who had nursed her. I mentioned to my mother-in-law that I was not so well and she replied, 'Now my mother has died, my first grandchild is the only thing I have to look forward to. If anything happens to it, I'll never forgive you'. Although she was at the time extremely shocked and exhausted, her comment totally shook me, since I was already starting to be worried.

I spent the next few days resting and worrying. Avidly I read all the books I could lay my hands on, trying to decide what was wrong. I visited the GP again the next Tuesday. He examined me carefully and I mentioned that I hadn't noticed any foetal movements recently. (To be honest, I had never experienced strong foetal movements but as I had never been pregnant before, I had nothing to compare with.) The GP decided I must see the consultant again urgently and made an appointment for me on the Thursday.

The next day dragged. I had not been able to bring myself to ask the GP what was really wrong, as I dreaded the answer. I did, however, look up his diagnosis, which had been on my sickness benefit certificate – polyhydramnios. Generally, the causes of this are general deformity of the foetus, or sometimes twins. Alone at home, I became totally distraught and at times just cried for long periods. I felt angry and frustrated with myself – perhaps I was just being an hysterical woman making mountains out of molehills.

The visit to the consultant did nothing to allay or quell my growing anxiety; it merely served to confuse me further. This examination of me was terse and abrupt and unlike previous visits he seemed disinclined to discuss my problems with me. He spent several minutes scanning my stomach with an ultrasonic scanner, trying to pick up a heartbeat. I strained to hear one too but I couldn't hear anything. ('Perhaps it takes an experienced ear to detect a foetal heartbeat?' I rationalized desperately to myself, not caring to think of the other alternative.) The consultant then turned to me and said, 'You don't want to come into hospital, do you'?

'No', I replied. 'What an odd question', I thought. But spurred on by this seemingly hopeful comment, I asked, 'What is wrong?'

He tried to ignore me and then said brusquely, 'Nothing much, but I think you should have another scan'.

I had one already arranged for the following Monday as a follow-up appointment. So it was agreed that I should keep this appointment and then return to see the consultant on the next Wednesday.

I spent the weekend in a state of complete turmoil. I was sure there was something seriously wrong and yet why hadn't I been admitted to hospital? Why did I have to wait four days for a scan? Why couldn't I feel any movements? And surely a foetal heartbeat is recognizable even to a layman? I was unable to concentrate. I felt restless and yet exhausted. I could not make the simplest decision. As I approached Monday afternoon, my anxiety level became unbearable and I paced round the house. My husband had gone to work as usual because he had already taken time off to take me to the doctor's and for his grandmother's funeral. The previous week I had assured him I was really all right, as I wasn't sure if I wasn't just making a fuss about nothing. The scan was a nightmare. It was blatantly obvious that something was very wrong. I had seen scans before, including my own previous one. But I could not make head or tail of this one. I questioned the radiographer closely, 'Is that the baby's head?' 'How big is the baby now?' She ignored all my questions and instead repeated the scan. She then asked her colleague to take some pictures. They both then disappeared with the films to see the radiologist. On their return they told me to get dressed and that I would not require another scan in the future. I then asked the most difficult question, 'Is the baby all right?'

At first she ignored me but then replied, 'I am afraid we cannot diagnose. We only take the pictures. You must discuss it with your consultant.'

I knew then the baby was dead. How often had I heard other paramedics use similar tactics when trying to avoid a patient's probing questions.

The next few days, surprisingly, I coped fairly well. It was as if I were totally unfeeling and had no emotions. I did cry a bit but in a sense I felt relieved – at least I knew the truth and was no longer left in ghastly suspense. My husband rang the GP, who chased up the report and confirmed that the baby had died.

My mother arrived and I visited the consultant again. He made arrangements for me to come into hospital a couple of days later to have labour induced. He told me that he had known from the previous visit that the baby was dead. (At that time I just accepted this news, but later I felt very angry that he had allowed me to spend four days in a state of constant anxiety and apprehension.) I even went with my husband and booked a holiday for later in the summer.

On Friday the 14th of March, I was admitted to a gynaecology ward to have labour induced. By Saturday afternoon my calm was shattered, as I was in a private room on my own and I still had not been seen by a doctor. Eventually, an SHO arrived and after a rather heated discussion with my husband, a pessary was inserted and labour began. The labour was not an easy one, as the pessaries made me feel ill and finally everything happened so fast that there was no time to administer any pain-killers. I also became severely dehydrated, thus necessitating a saline drip. After giving birth, a feeling of immense relief came over me that it was all over. This feeling of elation remained until I was discharged on Monday following a D&C. I then went to stay at my mother-in-law's for a couple of weeks with my husband. He commuted to work from there and I spent the fortnight helping my mother-in-law about the house and visiting a couple of friends who lived locally. My feelings at this time can perhaps be compared to the return of sensations in your jaw after a local anaesthetic given by the dentist. At times I felt totally devoid of feeling, at others I was utterly distraught. I discovered, however, that my mother-in-law, although caring in many ways, was totally unable to cope with my floods of tears and would rush off and make me a cup of tea. So I forced myself to put on a brave face for her and kept my feelings to myself and my husband.

As the fortnight passed, I began to dread returning home and having to be alone with my thoughts. My husband contacted an old schoolfriend of mine who is a teacher (and would therefore be on holiday) and asked her to stay with us for a while. She refused, saying she had a lot of schoolwork to catch up on. This may well have been true, but at this vulnerable time I felt utterly rejected.

My fears were confirmed on my return home. On the Tuesday before Easter, I hit an all-time low, no longer able to cry and angry with myself for not being able to overcome my misery for a baby I had never even had. I felt completely desolate. I sat for about two hours fighting an overwhelming desire to take a massive overdose. It was only the love I felt for my husband and the few friends who had really stood by me that prevented it.

Gradually, though, I began to climb out of that feeling of total and absolute blackness. I began to think about returning to work. After much heart-searching, I decided to return to my old job for the time being (I had been on sick leave all this time) as I felt I needed the security of the familiar routine and also anticipated that all the staff in my department would be patient with me.

The Thursday after Easter I went to see the District OT to say I intended to return to work the following Monday. To my absolute horror, I was informed that I was to be transferred from my post as Senior OT in charge of acute admission psychiatry to another hospital which specialized in long-stay and psychogeriatric patients.

Despite pleas that I should be allowed to return, at least for the time being, to my old job I was told that the change was for my own good and that I was to report to the new job on Monday. It was like being stabbed in the back by a friend. Within four weeks, I had lost not only my baby but also my job. My life had just fallen to pieces.

Fortunately, my husband supported me during this very difficult time and I had a great deal of help from a neighbouring District OT, who offered me a senior post in a psychiatric day hospital. It restored some of my confidence to be able to hand in my notice and the new job has been a considerable improvement over my last one, so I feel retrospectively that maybe my old District OT inadvertently did me a favour by forcing me to look for a new job.

These experiences have had a profound effect upon me both as a person and as a therapist.

Firstly, I have discovered that although I am once again functioning with a modicum of efficiency, I still feel very vulnerable and I am liable to be upset by fairly minor events. Secondly, comments like 'pull yourself together' are not at all helpful; in fact the reverse is true.

Generally, it was interesting to note other people's reactions to me. Some friends were so caring, visting me regularly, ringing me, taking me out. My husband, in particular, had tried desperately hard to comfort me. But I also found that I became guilty because I knew it distressed him that he could not alleviate my misery and unhappiness. Talking to more objective friends was often easier. Some friends, however, I discovered were afraid of seeing me. It is very hard to tell people your baby has died and on one occasion the friend I was ringing just hung up on me. People seemed to think that somehow I had become a terrible monster or else that I would dissolve into hysterics as soon as I saw them.

The way to cope with this, I felt in the end, was for me to take the initiative and contact them. I also found that if I mentioned my feelings in conversation, people would usually then relax but if I did not mention my loss, then they would talk to me as if I were some distant acquaintance rather than a friend.

As my depression started to lift, I found my mood fluctuated considerably. At times I would be quite composed and cheerful, looking forward to the future and planning various activities with friends. Other times I would become apathetic and withdrawn, unable to find any enthusiasm for anything, totally preoccupied and self-oriented. I also experienced feelings of agitation and anxiety when approaching activities, mainly, I think, because I feared failure and rejection. I became hesitant in looking forward to events in case I was disappointed.

During this time, my GP was a great support. I visited him weekly and he would just sit and let me talk. Initially he prescribed some Librium to help me sleep at night. (I had trouble with early morning waking.) I only took two and then decided that really my grief was something I had to come to terms with by myself, without pharmaceutical aid.

One of the biggest problems I encountered with my depression was the feeling of guilt and frustration with myself. I felt very much that I should be able to pull myself together and not let things get on top of me. I also felt ashamed that I, a therapist, had become a patient. This really struck home when my GP said to me, 'You are suicidal, aren't you?' I was horrified that he had guessed how I felt when I had been trying to say that I was coping. The recognition also made me feel guilty; after all, I've been telling people for years that anyone could have a psychiatric illness.

I found that although when in the depths of depression I was totally unable to do anything, once it started to lift, activities that provided scope for me to achieve boosted my confidence. Although talking about my feelings was important, I found it was also good to forget about my problems for a while and devote my attentions instead to something I enjoy, which helped me to feel useful and an achiever again.

Also, as my depression lifted, I found myself becoming very angry and searching for someone or something to blame for my misfortune. Certainly I found several targets for my anger, including the consultant and the District OT.

I feel that as a therapist I now have a lot more understanding and empathy for my patients. When they say, 'It's all right for you, you've never been through it', I can say to them that I have experienced similar feelings to theirs and this revelation often seems to help them to relate better to me. I also feel that, as I know from my own experience, useful activity can be therapeutic in coping with depression. I have added conviction in trying to help my patients attempt tasks and take up new hobbies and interests.

Finally, I found it very enlightening to study the reaction of my colleagues. In some cases, I found it very disturbing that someone who had worked for so many years in psychiatry was so inept at dealing with me. Other colleagues were very sympathetic and my dealings with the consultant and radiographers in the general hospital have confirmed my feelings that it is of the utmost importance to communicate with the patient and realize that he is a human being with feelings and not just a broken-down machine needing a service.

Wounded Healers
Edited by V. Rippere and R. Williams
© 1985 John Wiley & Sons Ltd.

5   In the wilderness

By a Health Visitor

I come from a Merseyside working-class background. I was brought up in the
1940s. Circumstances were poor and opportunity poorer, surrounded by the
ravages of World War II. My mother, very neurotic, had excellent aspirations
but under the circumstances was forced to recognize her total inability to bring
them to fruition. My father, silent and – on reflection – very depressed, was the
eldest of 12 children. He had experienced extreme poverty. A bitter and
frustrated man, he was very intelligent but obstructed by circumstances.
Because he was completely unable to communicate with his children, my
mother took the role of husband/wife. My brother – a non-identical twin – and I
were the only children of the marriage. In childhood we were very close and
used to walk around holding hands: Freud, eat your heart out! I was also
extremely close to my mother. Although I did not understand it at the time, I
can see in retrospect that our relationship was pathological. Before my illness I
would describe my personality as extremely hypersensitive, obsessional, tidy,
punctilious, rigid, and possessed of high standards. One positive attribute is an
excellent sense of humour.

It is very difficult to describe an event that happened over 10 years ago. They
say that 'distance lends enchantment to the view'. But I will try to describe the
events leading up to and surrounding my depression and to reflect upon what
the experience has taught me.

I left home at 18 to do my national service and afterwards trained as a nurse.
When my father died of cancer in 1965, my mother was quite overwhelmed.
Even though their relationship had not been good – they were two totally
incompatible human beings – her grief was genuine up to a point. She feared
loneliness and wanted me to return home, which I refused to do.

In 1968 while I was doing a Diploma Admin course, my mother committed
suicide. I suppressed my guilt and grief for a year and qualified in 1969. Then
the whole world began to collapse about my ears. My first feelings prior to the
breakdown were darkness and loneliness. My outlook was hopeless. I felt I had
nothing to live for, only an appalling sense of disaster and panic. Instead of
returning to duty at the mental hospital after my years on the course, I walked
into the casualty department of a London teaching hospital one afternoon
sobbing my heart out and admitted that I wished to kill myself. I could think
only of death and escape.

I was admitted to the X Clinic, where I was to stay for nine months. My first few days in the psychiatric unit were filled with apprehension. I was given a single room and didn't leave it for five months. I had not the slightest wish to mix with the other patients. I heard a nurse say one morning that someone was very ill so could the patient playing the guitar move somewhere else. I felt sorry for the very ill patient, not knowing they were referring to me.

My depression increased. I started to have terrible nightmares. Although I never lost my appetite, I had only small portions of food, which tasted like cardboard (no reflection on the cooking). I saw absolutely no future ahead of me, just a black wall of utter despair. I developed panic attacks. I walked up and down my room, wringing my hands and sobbing inconsolably. Eventually I had to be sedated.

My medication was quite heavy. It made me feel like a walking zombie. Constipation became a problem. Although the antidepressants made it difficult for me to focus my eyes, I read quite a lot. I used to fly to the toilet, talking to nobody, run back to my room and close the door. It became a way of life. I couldn't ever see myself getting better and didn't really want to.

I coped badly with all my symptoms. I couldn't believe it was happening to me. I became introverted and hypochondriacal, hyperventilated often, and hoped to die. So great was the coldness, the loneliness of my depression, I felt that I was standing in the Antarctic. I felt completely alienated from everyone.

My depression finally reached a pitch of despair. When I attempted suicide, I was having psychotherapy plus sedation. One night I slashed open my arms with a razor blade, stopping the circulation in both of them. As soon as I had done it I rang my room bell and was rushed to the theatre. Following the suicide attempt, I was given a course of ECT, 16 sessions in all. When the psychiatrist suggested it to me, I was filled with horror at the prospect and wept for a day.

The staff at the clinic were at all times patient, understanding, sympathetic, and loving in the true sense. They tried to give me back my self-esteem and bolster my confidence. They would sit in my room and talk and, perhaps more importantly, listen. They eventually persuaded me to come out of my room and visit the Occupational Therapy Department. Until then I had done OT in my room. Once I began to mix with them, I eventually identified with the patients and benefitted enormously from their warmth and friendship. I can only recall two instances where staff were less than helpful. One nurse commented, 'He is only suffering from depression', and a workman on the ward remarked, 'They are all nutters in this clinic'. Otherwise I can't think of any.

Others with whom I came into contact during my stay in hospital displayed a range of reactions. Particularly at the beginning, I was overwhelmed with visitors from my parent hospital where I had been employed as a psychiatric charge nurse. Finally the staff had to stop the flow because I was too ill to manage them all. Also it was felt that they might go back and convey a very bad impression of my 'mad' state to all concerned, including my employers, who, be it said, did not visit me at all. Visitors often came out with remarks like 'You of all people', 'Everyone at the hospital is amazed that you have had a breakdown', 'You've studied too much, you were never up to it', 'I'm not surprised, I always thought you had a weakness, you were far too proud', and, rather chillingly, 'What are you going to do now? You can't ever nurse again', and so forth. By contrast, my true friends were superb. They came and sat with me for hours, often making long journeys to do so, listened to my ramblings and self-pity, and never wavered in their support for my cause. At all times I was looking for a mast to stick my flag on and they provided it in full measure, and I will never forget them. Not so the relative who came down from Liverpool and suggested that I should pull myself together. 'Don't go like your mother, you know what happened to her', he said. 'Marriage is what you need'. Finally I threw a Gideon Bible at him and he departed.

As my illness progressed it became quite apparent to everyone but me that I would have to give up my post as a charge nurse. Shortly after I was discharged from the clinic, I returned to my place of work and walked into a very hostile reception. The Head of Nursing told me that I had behaved disgracefully and let the hospital down and everyone in it and what the hell did I think I was playing at. After that blistering attack, I went to see the Medical Super-intendent. He was charming and told me to take a month's holiday. I went home and stayed with an aunt and uncle, who were marvellous. The rest of the family had disowned me, because during my acute depressive phase I had told them that I was homosexual. But my aunt and uncle gave me love, endless patience, and support. I went to bed at 5.30 every night and would sleep and sleep. They used to leave a flask of tea and a nightlight on the bedtable for when I would wake in the night.

When I returned from my leave, I wrote a long letter to the Nursing Chief and promptly took a large overdose of Tuinal tablets. When I woke up five days later in an intensive care unit, I think I knew then that it was all over with my past life and occupation. The general hospital staff were most unsympathetic; they took the view that I had wasted their time. I had a severe attack of inhalation pneumonia. An officious ward sister told me that I was stupid and deserved to finish up in a large lunatic asylum. I told her to fuck off.

I was returned to the London teaching hospital with a large indwelling catheter in my penis. It was a long journey from Surrey to London on that cold day in February. It was late afternoon, the sun was dying, all the trees were bare. I have never felt so completely abandoned or such despair. But the ambulance men were marvellous, kind and understanding. They kept saying, 'You'll be all right, mate', 'Every cloud has a silver lining'.

Once back 'home', out came the catheter. Three pots of hot tea and I was voiding like a demented elephant. End of bladder problem. I remember the ward sister – one of the 'old school' – saying, 'All you need, George, is a good dose of mental nursing'. I stayed at the clinic for a further three months, during which time I had to resign my post. I did this under pressure from my boss: resign or be sacked was the ultimatum. The psychiatrist had a long chat with me. He told me that I had lost the lot: my home when my mother killed herself, my family through the 'gay revelation' (except the aunt and uncle who stuck by me all the way along the road and are with me even today), and my job. He put it to me in a matter of fact way that I would have to start all over again and that it would not be easy. How true.

With the help of the very supportive social worker, I set about finding a bed-sit. Eventually I found one in Hampstead and left the clinic. My first impressions of the place, a medium-sized room, were not good. I arrived on a cold afternoon in April, the Friday after Easter. After so long in hospital, where everything was done for me, I found that the thought of doing everything for myself was pretty overwhelming. My feelings as I put my case on the bed were horror, alienation, utter loneliness, and bewilderment. However, I soon discovered that the room was in a very friendly house. The tenants were quite friendly and an elderly couple soon 'adopted' me as the son they had never had. I learnt to cook for myself, shop, wash my clothes, etc. Although the experience was new to me, bed-sit life was to become a way of life for me.

Nonetheless, it was a very lonely existence. I visited the hospital weekly for support from the social worker. Meanwhile, I told the people at the house that the reason I didn't work was that I was doing a research project. But the old couple soon spotted the DHSS cheques and gently quizzed me. I also used to visit my former place of work, to see the housekeeper in the male nurses' home. She was my 'second mother'. On occasions I met staff who would look at me with despair in their eyes. I always said that I was fine and would get back into the nursing profession soon. In reality, my fight to achieve this aim lacked power and will. I still felt appalling and my outlook was totally nihilistic.

I had many interviews; all failed. One day in August I applied to be seen at a special department that dealt with professional people. It was a disaster. At one interview for a job, I had told them that I had three qualifications. They promptly informed me that with my mental history I could never again expect to be employed in the Health Service: 'You know, with your history, we couldn't be certain, could we?' Good afternoon. I mentioned my difficulties to the woman who was interviewing me. She said that her great delight at the end of the day was to escape to her flat in Maida Vale and get away from people and their problems. I told her to stuff herself, walked out, and cried all the way down the street. So much for official sources of help for the distressed professional.

I then went to an employment agency. They offered me three jobs: a sweet shop attendant, a butcher's assistant, and a runner for a bank in the City (plenty of fresh air). I walked out. Then I walked the streets of London for months, sat and watched the Thames go by, visited Salvation Army hostels for tea, etc., etc. That Christmas I attempted to gas myself, but it was a feeble attempt. I soon remembered that we had changed to North Sea gas. After that I became a day patient at the clinic and found it most helpful.

The following March, I applied to a London borough council for a job, as an assistant at the old people's home. I was seen by a charming Principal Nursing Officer, who listened to my story for an hour. I was then sent for an interview and in the space of an afternoon found myself employed as a geriatric visitor and research assistant at the University of London. I left the interview petrified at the prospect of working again.

The Principal Nursing Officer asked me if I would like to join a group practice. I did the research project from there. I joined them and set up their first Geriatric Visiting Service. The project turned out to be a superb experience. The people I worked with heard my story and provided support. It might be more accurate to say that we all supported each other – which at the time was particularly good for my morale.

In 1975 I went off to college to do obstetrics and combined it with the Health Visitors' Course. It was during this course that I had a further bout of depression. I went to a London teaching hospital near my bed-sit. It wasn't a severe bout. I was only in there for a month and the staff treated me very well indeed. My tutors came to see me frequently. They were very kind and understanding. My new friends all rallied round and took it in turns to take me out for car drives. The reaction of my new employers was completely different this time than my first experience had been. They came bearing gifts – fruit, flowers, books. It was quite overwhelming. On her first visit, the Principal Nursing Officer took pains to tell me that my job was absolutely safe. She said, 'If I sacked all the staff who suffer from depression, I wouldn't have any staff left'.

Since 1976 I have been free from depression and tablets and I think I am working on all cylinders.

So the two blackest years of my life remain the period from August 1969 until April 1971. Thereafter I went though a period of 'why me?' introspection, self-pity, told my story constantly, and became very boring. Then one day I woke up and decided to 'get my finger out'. I joined the local church group, met many new and firm friends, started to socialize and to regain my self-respect. My family situation has improved dramatically in the past five years. Apologies have been received and rifts healed with understanding and sympathy. Now life is very much worth living and all that I lost has been returned to me in abundance. Although I would like a council flat, I remain in a bed-sit. I moved rooms some years ago in the same house. The room is very comfortable but not my own. One day, perhaps, I will get my own front door. I keep sending poems and letters to the Council.

How did my experience help me to help others?

I now manage a very busy clinic in a deprived area of London, one with many social and health problems. Before my breakdown I was a very pompous, overbearing, ruthlessly ambitious person. All my qualifications had to be firsts, silver medals, nurse of the year, etc. In other words, I was a right little creep-arse. The experience has mellowed me. I now consider other people. I try not to judge any more. I have, dare I say, a fair measure of humility and *I listen*. My ambition has been tempered with wisdom and acceptance. I see my patients and staff as human beings with human frailties, as I possess them myself. I can put myself in their position, but not in a patronizing sense. One can never say, 'I know how you feel'. That is impertinent in the extreme. But you can say to yourself, 'Yes, I have been there and come through', and to the person, 'How can I help you?'

As a manager I listen to problems from my staff and offer advice. I do not judge. I am sympathetic to illness and offer help and guidance. I hope that with my training I can spot a manipulative situation and ask the question 'why'? before embarking on criticism of that behaviour. Yes, my illness has taught me a lot, and I hope in subtle ways it can help others.

Wounded Healers
Edited by V. Rippere and R. Williams
© 1985 John Wiley & Sons Ltd.

6 *Hope is the key*

By a General Practitioner

I was married while I was still a medical student with 18 months to go before I qualified. I had known my husband for four years and we seemed to be well suited. All predicted a happy future for us both, yet we ourselves soon became uncertain about the wisdom of our choice. We had married because we were lonely and in need of affection. My husband had been passing through a period of uncertainty in many respects and I had appeared as someone who had definite views on most subjects and knew what I was aiming for. John had needed this stability but quickly found his own feet with the security that marriage provided. I was left to recover from the shock of this transformation, while John left the vicinity of my college to do a teacher training course 300 miles away. I completed my medical training with an apprehensive heart, then arranged to do my pre-registration house jobs near his college.

We both began to realize that our marriage would need considerable effort and adjustment if it were to survive, but we did not consider the possibility of divorce, as we had made solemn vows and intended marriage to be for life.

Because I only saw my husband infrequently while I worked in hospital, our relationship improved sufficiently for us to consider starting a family. My husband got a good teaching job and we bought a sound but dilapidated house which had been vacant for over a year. By this time a baby was on the way and I felt generally unwell. I got an almost full-time job in order to give us enough money to furnish two rooms and have a little put by for the baby's arrival. I was also doing the housework and cooking and helping my husband with repairs. It was a shocking winter and I remember that we had two floods in the bathroom after the pipes burst. These were major disasters to us at the time. I was too busy to make new friends and worked long after the recommended 28 weeks in pregnancy. When we did have a few moments together, my husband and I recognized how little we understood each other and feared for the future of our marriage, for the baby about to be born, and for the world, which was seemingly on the edge of a nuclear war. We knew of no one we could trust to discuss our anxieties with. My husband's family were preoccupied with their own problems and my sister was ill in hospital, so this seemed enough burden for my own family.

In this atmosphere of uncertainty, fear, and isolation, I became depressed and spent many sleepless nights wandering the house while the baby kicked under my ribs as a constant reminder that I would soon have responsibilities for another's well-being, when I felt I could barely cope with my own.

I finished working when 36 weeks pregnant and turned to the preparation of a room for the new baby. After two days of stripping paper off walls, I developed severe abdominal pains. Eventually I realized that I must be in labour and aroused a very disbelieving husband to take me into hospital. The baby was born shortly after my arrival there, but my husband did not know until the following morning, so firm was his belief that I was exaggerating my pains.

I felt so alone during those eight days in hospital. My husband was not pleased that the baby had arrived before we were prepared for it. My parents were more concerned about my sick sister, and, to crown it all, the baby, being a little premature, was rather sleepy and difficult to feed. I received very little help or advice from the staff on the subject of feeding, as I was a doctor and was supposed to know all the answers.

When I returned home, the baby became even more difficult to feed and started to vomit. Because of this, she required more feeds and I was often up half the night trying to get enough fluid into her. By the age of one month, she had still not regained her birth weight, so the midwife suggested that it was about time I took her to see my GP. My GP considered treatment for the diarrhoea she was now having, but then he went away on holiday. How I inwardly wished that someone would admit the baby to hospital for observation. I was reluctant to suggest admission myself, because I did not wish to appear over-anxious, but I was naturally very concerned about the situation and was rapidly becoming exhausted with all the washing that such a sickly baby involved, not to mention the frequent feeding. Unfortunately, I think because I was a doctor, everyone just patted me on the head and told me how well I was coping. They just didn't know that I would lie half the night on the floor, sobbing and wondering what sort of happiness I and my child could ever hope to have in life.

In retrospect, I suppose it would be true to say that I had a classical puerperal depression. I was too proud to seek medical help and did not think that psychiatrists or pills could alter my life situation, which I recognized as the main problem. Although I considered suicide for myself and the baby, through it all I was able to cling to the belief that there was a God who cared and that he must have a plan and purpose for my life, even in this suffering. As I lay, night after night, sobbing my heart out, my crying would gradually turn to prayer. Slowly a calmness would follow, in the assurance that I could draw on God for the strength I did not have and that He was able to understand and share my need, whatever it might be.

This dreadful situation continued for about six months. The baby continued to remain well below weight for her age. I suppose that my general anxiety and tension must have contributed to her vomiting, because when I decided to return to part-time work and employed a mother's help, the situation eased considerably and the baby began to feed much better. I was happier too, because I was back in a situation where I felt I had something to give and where I was not constantly made to feel a failure.

Through the long years of struggle in marriage that followed, I always found that practising medicine was a relief to me. Children are a delight to have, but your reward in their care is to see them well adjusted and looked after. If you are not really the 'ideal wife' for your husband, you may make every effort to adapt yourself to his needs, but the inward sense of rejection remains. In medicine, however, I was fortunate to have a job I was well suited to and a constant challenge, which I found stimulating. In general practice, which I ended up doing, I am also privileged to share people's joys and sorrows, which has enabled me to get a better perspective on my own.

I suppose it would be true to admit that I have probably received as much help from my patients as they have received from me. For example, in the next crisis I had to face in my marriage, when my husband nearly left me for another woman, I was having to support a patient whose wife had just deserted him, leaving four small children behind. His initial despair turned to a firm resolve to live for the sake of his children and his resolution made me resolve to do likewise.

In the event, my husband decided to stay 'for the sake of the children'. I felt rejected more than ever and determined to work even harder at trying to please him. I gave up general practice, which was giving me so much satisfaction, and, instead, concentrated on 'the simple life' of being a good wife and mother.

I suppose one has to have a fairly conscientious type of personality to be a good doctor. It is a caring and painstaking approach which endears doctors to their patients. The problem is that this same personality can make a person very conscious of failure, which in turn leads to depression. I also found that my sensitive nature, which fitted me so well for my profession, caused me to feel hurt over matters I have seen others shrug off without apparent injury. I was suicidal at only two periods of my married life, but I was depressed most of the time. The sense of failure was forever with me and at times I lost hope for a better future.

While I was able to cling to hope I found that life was bearable. I believe sincerely in a God who does not allow us to have burdens too great to be borne. However, the Slough of Despond is a very easy quagmire to slip into and is difficult to climb out of. After 10 years of persevering, I found myself in a marriage where I wasn't wanted, with three dependent children, and no hope of returning to my old Practice. A replacement partner had been found and I had given an agreement not to practice within a five mile radius for a specified number of years. My husband again began to seek happiness elsewhere. I knew I had made every effort to be the wife he wanted and I had failed. Although I could see no freedom ahead for myself – apart from the relief of no longer trying to fit into the wrong hole – I felt the most loving thing I could do was to release him from the marriage.

A solicitor advised me not to move out of the matrimonial home. The next four months while my husband was househunting were pure hell. We had decided not to tell family or children what was going to happen until the children could be introduced to my husband's new abode as a place where Daddy was going to live and where they would always be welcome. We wished to avoid the strain of our children trying to patch up the marriage or taking sides. What we both had not bargained for was the strain of living under the same roof with nothing but concern for the children to hold us together. Whatever material advantages there were in my staying, I'm afraid the emotional strain was almost more than I could bear. I would never recommend our course of action to anyone. My husband went as far as threatening to drive into the country and connect the exhaust into the car to kill himself when it looked as though he might not be granted a mortgage. How I managed to go out and do my part-time job in a geriatric day hospital I really do not know, for those four months were the most demanding I can ever imagine experiencing. I used to think that solitary confinement would have been preferable.

At last we separated and I began the painful job of informing family, neighbours, friends, and schoolteachers. Fortunately, I belonged to a group at my church, called the 'Prayer and Share Group'. It was the love, concern, and prayers of this group which helped me through those long, dark days. At times I was again tempted to consider taking a lethal overdose, but the remembrance of that caring group dissuaded me.

It is now five years since my marriage broke up. The children have flourished and done well at school. Their father has remarried but has kept in good contact with them. I was able to re-enter general practice in a new town and have settled well after the initial effort of getting to know a whole new lot of patients. My experiences have certainly made me a more understanding GP, especially with those involved in the breakdown of their marriage. There are, unfortunately, many of these.

My experience has taught me that depression is no respecter of persons. If anyone gets into a life situation which seems impossible to resolve, then he or she will tend to despair and think of suicide. I have also noticed that tiredness and depression go hand in hand. I think that tiredness is often a greater factor in puerperal depression than is commonly realized. In my own case, I have often found that a good night's sleep will lighten my mood considerably.

Although I often prescribe tablets for depression, I did not turn to them myself, except for relieving migraines, which at one stage I was getting every day. Tablets do not alter life situations; they only help a person to cope with them better. I think a chat with a friend or an understanding person is often much more therapeutic; it can restore the sense of being valued that so many depressed people lack. If there is no human being whom we feel we can trust enough to turn to, I believe we can turn to a God who has entered our suffering humanity and is therefore able to understand our problems. I do not preach this way to my NHS patients, though I will sometimes tell them if I think they are in need of spiritual help. This need is often something they will recognize themselves. I must, however, conclude by testifying that it was my faith in God's ultimate goodness which provided the 'light at the end of the tunnel' for me and which kept me from destroying the life He gave.

Section III   Women and depression

The three chapters forming this section are all written by women – a general practitioner, a clinical psychologist, and a psychiatric social worker – and all three describe experiences of depression precipitated by bankruptcy of the writer's attempts to conform to contemporary cultural stereotypes of feminity, wifeliness, and domesticity. Eventually, all three writers were able to read the signals correctly and to find a way out of their personal impasse. They all depict their depression as a turning point in their lives – the point at which they stopped subordinating themselves to other people's expectations and began to take responsibility for deciding what they wanted for themselves.

The stories they tell are highly similar in many respects, from the evocative titles – 'Learning to live', 'Metamorphosis', and 'Beginning to live' – down to individual turns of phrase. Yet the backgrounds they come from and the people they have become are all highly individual. Only the conflict between other people's stifling expectations and the need to be a person in one's own right is the same.

It is probably no coincidence that the three contributors who have construed their experience of depression most explicitly in these terms have all participated in the women's movement. Their accounts may be seen as belonging to the feminist tradition. Stanley and Wise (1983) have noted that there are three themes which characterize the thinking of contemporary feminists. The first is the assumption that women in our society are oppressed. The common acceptance of this presupposition arises from personal experience and from sharing of personal experience with other women. The second key theme, they note, 'is concerned with the nature of this experience as it is shared and understood in terms of "the personal" ' (Stanley and Wise, 1983, p. 52). Although experiences are discussed in individual, personal terms, they must also be seen to have a significant political dimension:

> 'The emphasis on the personal within feminism is summed up in the statement "the personal is the political". This argues that power and its use can be examined within personal life and, indeed, in some sense that the political *must* be examined in this way It also emphasized that "the system" is experienced *in* everyday life, and isn't separate from it. And so feminism argues that systems and social structures, whether concerned with the economy, the family, or the oppression of women more generally, can best be examined and understood through an exploration of relationships and experiences within everyday life' (Stanley and Wise, 1983, p. 53).

The exploration of the 'world in the grain of sand' of individual experience is thought to be the most readily done through the process of women coming together and talking in small 'consciousness-raising' groups. The third key theme of feminism 'concerns the new understanding that women gain through consciousness-raising activities' (Stanley and Wise, 1983, p. 54). Specifically, Stanley and Wise argue that what emerges from these discussions is a 'double vision' of reality, a vision which incorporates seeing everyday reality in both the 'old' and in a 'new' way simultaneously, so that the multiple contradictions inherent in everyday reality become manifest. The woman who has acquired 'feminist consciousness' develops a vision of reality which is considerably more complex and open-ended than the one with which she came to the women's movement. This new consciousness is a precursor and a prerequisite of working to change her life by assuming personal control of herself and her expectations.

These key themes of feminism are represented in the three chapters we are considering here. Oppression is implicit in the need, described by all three authors, to gain personal control of their lives and aspirations, to live for themselves rather than to live up to others' expectations. All three, likewise, allude to or overtly describe the political dimensions which they discovered to be inherent in their personal lives. The issues of subordination, responsibility, and control loom large in their accounts. And finally, all three have emerged from their experiences with a vision that is consonant with the notion of 'feminist consciousness', specifically in relation to depression. The author of 'Learning to live' (Chapter 7) closes her account by noting that 'Trying to understand the pain of depression, mine and others', and searching for a positive way out is part of the struggle 'of people taking power in their own lives'. 'Conditions, even anorexia and depression, create consciousness, and conciousness leads to change.' The author of 'Metamorphosis' (Chapter 8) notes, with feminist writer Phyllis Chesler (1973), that 'depression can be seen as an intensification of some commonly ascribed "feminine" characteristics. These include helplessness, passivity, dependence, indecisiveness and so on. Depression becomes a protest position for those forced into it by social pressures . . . .' And, finally, the author of 'Beginning to live' (Chapter 9) observes that her experience of depression led her to change the way she works with depressed women clients. Whereas previously she would have tried to help them find ways of adjusting to others' expectations, she now tries

'to help the woman to work out a more satisfactory role according to what she wants for herself. I try to help her to recognize the conditions which have led to her depression, to understand that it is not individual inadequacy or failure which have made her depressed, but the situation in which she and most other mothers find themselves.'

Thus the concept of depression found in these chapters is one which is transformed by feminist consciousness from a state of individual psychopathology to a source of information about the conventional role of women in our society and the pressures which this role exerts upon individuals.

These accounts add to the list of psychosocial pathogens contributing to depression, what the author of 'Metamorphosis' calls 'the housewife thing'. 'The housewife thing' contains elements of both the themes we have examined in the introductions to the preceding sections. The author of 'Metamorphosis' in particular describes the salutary effect on her self-esteem of obtaining employment outside the home and thus ceasing to be a full-time housewife. The author of 'Beginning to live' notes that, as her marriage deteriorated, 'going to work was something of an escape from an insoluble situation because that was the one area in which I still felt reasonably competent and valued'. And the author of 'Learning to live' contrasts her life as a GP in a small country town where she lived and worked with her (male) friend: 'It was a caricature of a dream come true. Home every night to cook the tea, watch TV and go for a pint. Lots of cleaning and washing (his as well as mine) and mending, while he dismantled cars in the yard. So cosy.' Retrospectively, she realized that this sort of happily-ever-after life was 'the antithesis of *me*'. Her rebirth occurred after she decided to go her own way and took a hospital job where she could see herself as 'a whole person doing a responsible job'.

These excerpts suggest that 'the housewife thing' is pernicious to women's mental health not only because it precludes the exercise of certain complex and valued skills but also because it involves little opportunity for the individual woman's value as a person in her own right to be acknowledged. Both of these features are prominent characteristics of professional career roles. These observations point to the second way in which 'the housewife thing' amplifies themes we have encountered earlier, namely the theme of loss as a precipitant of depression. Although all these accounts refer to losses of loved ones by death or marital break-up as immediate precipitants of depressive episodes, we should like to consider here the more subtle kind of loss sustained through lack of opportunity to fulfil what one sees as one's human potential.

Losses need not be acute nor concern significant others in order to contribute to the genesis of depression. In her seminal book, *The Feminine Mystique*, Betty Friedan (1963) devotes a chapter to the theme of 'the forfeited self'. By this evocative phrase, Friedan refers to the broad tradition of 20th century psychological thought concerned with what makes men (and women) human. According to this humanist–existentialist tradition, neurosis is defined 'in terms of that which destroys man's capacity to fulfill his own being' (Friedan, 1983, p. 269). Within this frame of reference 'the housewife thing' may be seen as forfeiture of a woman's opportunity to fulfil some aspects of her human potential. As Friedan puts it, women who adjust to the feminine mystique adjust 'to an image that does not permit them to become what they now can be' (Friedan, 1983, p. 270). The outcome of these efforts to adjust is a familiar state of dysphoria, dissatisfaction, and low self-esteem in the midst of apparent womanly fulfilment.

In highlighting the experiences that led them to reject this image, our authors contribute to an understanding of the psychology of contemporary women and of the ways in which our society's expectations of women can make them ill. These chapters also contribute to our understanding of depression in mental health workers. The authors' 'women's problems' interacted with their professional careers in different ways. In all three, recovery from the depression provoked by their efforts to adjust to others' expectations led to career changes — entry into a mental health career, promotion within one, or a change of work settings. The two who were already working in the field at the time of their depressions do not report the sorts of professional harrassment that some of our other authors have mentioned, but one of them does report having experienced qualms about seeking help in a place where she was known professionally. Her question, 'Where do professional helpers go when they need help themselves?' is pertinent to some of our other authors' experiences.

7 Learning to live

By a General Practitioner

I first wrote this account two years ago for myself primarily, but having been strengthened by sharing the experiences of others I now feel able to share it.

It has been most difficult to write about my feelings in the depths of depression, partly because the pain was such that I shut out many memories and feelings . . . there are large gaps for which I have no memory . . . and partly because of the fear of having to face up to and deal with similar feelings, on occasion, throughout the rest of my life. Recently I was ill with what proved to be a virus infection, but it made me feel nauseated, and I was so frightened that it might be psychological, that I had 'lost control', and that my body was playing tricks on me, that despair set in, and by the time I recovered, six weeks later, a great deal of damage to friends and relationships had already been done.

I am learning after 30 years to cope with my own despair and to be strong 'for myself' but I still have a long way to go to enable those who come close to me to trust in my strength. Therein lies the future. Most of the time it is a positive one.

I feel I was almost born depressed. While pregnant with me my mother thought she was in the menopause until it was too late to have an abortion, legal or illegal, and was horrified when she learnt the truth. My parents' marriage was collapsing after 20 years of respectable silence about their total indifference to each other. My arrival finally provoked my mother to leave, which filled my father with rage and bewilderment. Even years later, when married again, he could not forgive her. His property, which he had acquired for life, had suddenly removed itself! My overriding feeling about my childhood is relief that it is over. I seemed to turn in on myself and felt terrified of contact with others, running home from school, parties, friends' houses and being scared of telephones, shops, and buses. My first bus ride alone was when I was 13. Food was a comfort right from the start, when I would only eat scrambled egg and refused to eat in strange houses or away from home. I discovered secret eating and raided the larder regularly. Feeding myself secretly gave me the security that I lacked everywhere else.

At nine I was sent into the bizarre, 'be tough' world of a girls' public boarding school. It may have been an improvement on the continual oscillation between parents that had been going on since I was three, but I was devastated, lonely, and powerless, in the face of regimented discipline and cold east winds. Every

69

minute of every school day was spent with others who thought me 'a drip' and gave me a longing for time and space of my own which is still immensely strong.

Gradually I realized that one way to gain control over myself and others was by being an academic success. I was a misfit at school and socially: my stockings were always in holes and I never could be the neat, tidy young lady, building up her muscles by day on the hockey field, that I was supposed to be. Later my lipstick was to smudge and my makeup run down my face at parties, which only confirmed the image. My mother, meanwhile, remarried and my step-father, who in many ways was the love of my life, further ingrained in me the work ethic, spending endless hours in his study poring over papers.

Events took a downward turn with the appearance of my stepmother when I was 12. She abandoned a successful job in an entirely man's world to marry my father. She needed power to replace what she had lost and since she could not entirely control my father she decided to control me. I still feel enormous anger at her attempts to take over my life and rearrange it according to her wishes. This involved ruthless discarding of some of my best friends, control over clothes, relationships, and lifestyle, and relentless condemnation of my mother and stepfather which left me angry, defensive, and doubting about everyone, especially myself. I spent days and months longing for those rare occasions when I could experiment at 'being myself'. My only real escape was work and books, a substitute for the real world. Loneliness and fantasy have almost become a habit, which is with me still when times are bad.

Another form of torture my stepmother used was inconsistency. Every day was a double bind: I never knew what I might have done wrong, and what was wrong one day was right the next, leaving me constantly anxious. Reading R. D. Laing years later was a revelation. It was the first time I discovered that I was not alone and that family life could create such situations.

In desperation one day after lunch at school, when I was supposed to be practising the piano, I cut my wrists with my compass points. I did not know much about arteries and veins and all that resulted was a mess, a septic wrist, and a slight scandal. This was my only 'suicidal gesture', a phrase I hate because it is full of patronizing assumptions about a tragic situation. It also seeks to hide all the anger and guilt that others feel when someone close to them chooses to deal with the world and their relationships in this way. Recently I found out that during this time my mother had been in constant touch with her lawyer about gaining the legal rights to take me away from school and my stepmother, but that she and my stepfather were too frightened of causing more upset, and maybe losing me altogether. Both regretted later that they did not act more forcefully and I too feel anger, both at them and at myself, for being so passive and seeing no positive way out.

Bargaining went on constantly between my parents about how many hours and minutes I was to spend with one or the other. In all this I was nowhere and nothing: just a ping-pong ball – a symbol of a nice, respectable (if divorced) family. Ironically my role as a status symbol provided a possible escape. If I were an academic success I could cast off my family and sail into the sunset leaving a trail of qualifications behind to be exhibited instead of me. The only other alternative was Prince Charming . . . every young girl's dream of escaping from one control into the arms of another.

The way I felt, helpless and out of control, has its positive side. Now I can tune in easily to this kind of situation when it is going on in my patients' families, and indeed in my own. The negative side is that in some ways 'learned helplessness', which is how Seligman describes depression, can become a way of life, a way of responding to situations which is hard to change.

I began to diet and to take increasing amounts of laxatives. It seemed as if I were trying to get rid of all the pain and badness by gradually getting rid of myself altogether: like Alice in *Alice in Wonderland*, only there was no wise caterpillar to give me advice. Laxatives were easy. I had been brought up on syrup of figs, and to believe I was constipated because none of our family goes to the loo more than once a week without artificial aid. The results of my mother's nightly purge are still audible every morning. Several times I overdid it and simply passed out in a pool of shit. Nobody apparently noticed, though I think at school they had their suspicions. I was actually quite large at the time, larger than I am now, and many of my friends were on diets, trying to be one of those beautiful slim girls that supposedly attracted men like flies. My father and stepmother were rapidly expanding under my stepmother's regime of forced feeding: delicious but deadly. With them food was a constant topic of conversation and there was no way she was going to let me get thin while they got fat. I used laxatives on the basis that food that did not stay inside a long time could not make me fat, and also for the glorious feeling of release and emptiness. I got to eight or nine Senokot a day plus anything else that was going and took that number regularly for nearly 10 years. Food and work became the focus of my life. I was obsessed with eating as little as I could in between secret binges on apple crumble which left me guilty and depressed. Food was my best friend and my worst enemy, and all the problems in my life condensed themselves into how to get thin. Fear of being large overwhelmed me along with a sense of triumph. This was *my* adventure: I was taking control of my life. I never realized that I had been fooled and was really indulging in self-punishment of a vicious kind.

On leaving school, despite, or maybe because of, getting into Cambridge, I became unable to eat at all. A day came when I could not eat one fish finger, having eaten nothing at all all day. My mother cried but I could not understand why. Suddenly, too, everyone seemed to be looking at me, and I relapsed into isolation and fear of buses and crowds, feeling everyone was talking about me, saying how large I was. I now realize that this distortion of reality is just a part of being so thin . . . a kind of anorexia of the brain.

By this time I weighed less than six stone and my family were showing signs of alarm. At last they seemed to be interested in *me* but I was almost past noticing. I was taken to a private specialist who did not talk with me but X-rayed everything instead. He decided I had 'spastic colon', a get-out of a diagnosis if ever there was one. Fortunately, at this point, my GP intervened and said that I must get away from my family, and I went to Spain for four months. I stayed with a family who ate oranges with a knife and fork while armed police searched us on our way into class at the university. The contradictions, plus being away and on my own, began to shake me into eating.

It still took three years of university to finally convince me that I could not and did not want to be what my stepmother wanted, so powerful was she. To really try to discover *me* was very scary. I am sure this is why so many people escape from intolerable situations with great determination only to collapse later, and why autonomy is so difficult to achieve.

In my final year at university I decided to do medicine, perhaps because it seemed an impossible thing to do, the ultimate challenge. I feel in some ways as if I still use general practice as a way of closing the door on real closeness. The doctor–patient relationship, however good, is a substitute for the real thing. I became very involved with a man in my final year at university. I remember being very anxious about sleeping with him in case I became dependent, and I did: immersed completely at once! Eventually he simply removed himself by going away for the summer and transferring medical schools so that we would no longer be together . . . without telling me. Anger did not prevent me from wondering what was so awful about *me* to drive him away (depressive thinking). Medical school, with its bizarre, rugby-playing, sexist, beer-drinking atmosphere was so astonishing that it saved me from a nose dive for the time being.

Most of my close relationships at this time were with men, and in the background always was my stepfather. I was also trying to be 'one of the lads' as, both at university and medical school: it was definitely a man's world.

Living in a communal house, I gradually began to crawl out of my eating problems. I stopped hiding food under the table at meals and became less terrified of eating with others, mainly because the people in my house did not put any pressure on me to eat, they just accepted me as me. I still mainly ate secretly and on my own and it is only in the last two years that I have been able to go to a restaurant without being crippled with guilt and anxiety for a week afterwards. I felt, though, that I was making headway . . . little did I realize that worse was yet to come.

My pre-registration year, being on duty more often than not, and at the bottom of the hierarchy, proved a strain 'until I discovered Valium' of which my predecessor had left a vast supply in his hospital room, demonstrating how he coped with the job! When admissions were piling up, I was exhausted, and still had the weekend to go, Valium made me feel almost human again. I was soon hooked. There is not a lot of difference between the addiction to Valium and to heroin, except in degree. The need to blot out the realities of life is what gets people. Happily for me, at this time, I became involved with local community groups working on women and health and access to health care. It soon became clear why women in particular are so easily given drugs like Valium. Of course doctors are not wicked and dreadful and often want to 'help', but faced with the demand for magic solutions to apparently insoluble problems and an average of six minutes consultation time, Valium is the easy way out. Recognizing this helped me to stop taking Valium at the end of the year, but I still have to take one occasionally when I am 'over the top' and surgery must be got through, or when I am in a non-sleeping phase. I resent every single pill. I also admit to prescribing tranquillizers on occasion, and, if possible, for short-term use only, because when faced with an acute situation the correct political solution is not always the most human one.

I needed to leave London, to break out on my own finally, so I thought. A close relationship was breaking up because I kept struggling for time and space and couldn't reconcile *me* with *us*. Instead of forging ahead to autonomy I immediately fell into the arms of everything I had been trying for years to escape from! It was a sudden desperate scramble for 'love', 'security', and 'respectability'. The arms belonged to a gentle and kind man who was dying to love and protect me. I remember going to a friend's wedding with him: beautiful trees, white lace, and sun, and thinking 'This could be me'. I know now that this was the antithesis of *me*.

My friend, doctor's son, gallant, respectable, chauvinist, and completely disorganized, and I became GPs in a small country town. I loved it . . . or did I? It was a caricature of a dream come true. Home every night to cook the tea, watch TV and go for a pint. Lots of cleaning and washing (his as well as mine) and mending, while he dismantled cars in the yard. So cosy.

Suddenly my stepfather died. My mother was prepared, as he had had high blood pressure for years, but I had felt somehow he would live for ever, and never thought realistically about the possibility of his death. I raced home and efficiently organized funerals, relatives, death certificates, etc. while my mum drank endless cups of tea. In front of others she never gave way to grief and has not done since. I never before realized how strong she was.

As it was, I, not she, collapsed over the next few months. My stepfather for many years had been the rock in the background against which I took soundings and orientated myself in the world. He was bound up in my decision to do medicine and was in my life in many subtle ways. Loving him helped assuage the guilt I felt at abandoning my father, which I had to do in order to survive.

All the sadness in my life seemed to come to the surface like an enormous boil. Over a few weeks I became lifeless. I breathed and moved but felt alive only in the sense that I was too apathetic to die. I had started to cry increasingly even before my stepfather's death but had not taken much notice as I have always cried a lot, especially before periods, and mainly on my own late at night. This was different. I cried my way through surgeries and visits, so blinded by tears that I could hardly find my way to patient's houses. As soon as I opened my eyes in the morning tears came out. I didn't even have time to breathe or take things in hand before they came. I clammed up, and often had to curl up in a ball, unable to speak, trying to control the pain inside, trying, but unable to fight. For hours I could not speak, and certainly could not communicate 'the problem' because I did not know what it was. I stopped eating except for the occasional binge when I felt completely out of control and sickened at myself.

The most devastating experience was early morning wakening. I experience a stomach lurch when people tell me about this in the surgery today. It is, of course, a useful symptom of physiological depression to 'elicit' from a patient, but experientially it is soul-destroying. It felt like my own private torture chamber, devised to undermine every ounce of strength, and drive me under completely. Night after night, month after month, I woke at two or three and felt lonely and hopeless, hour after hour, wishing that someone else was awake just to be alive and human, getting up quietly to cry in the other room so as not to disturb my friend, and worst, knowing that neither he nor anyone else could help, that I was cut off, removed from the world. Endless thoughts going round in circles, advancing nowhere, on top of this came panic about how I would survive the next day and the exhaustion of night after night with no sleep. I dragged myself to work in the day, too tired and too scared to do anything after work except blot out my mind with old movies on TV.

When, rarely, my mind made contact with the external world I thought about my friend and the horror of living closely with someone who is dissolving before your eyes and whom you cannot reach, cannot understand, and cannot apparently help. He had never been depressed and later said that he could no longer live with me because he could not face the possibility of going through that experience again. I can quite understand.

I knew also that our relationship had something, probably a great deal, to do with my being depressed but I was too scared to face it. I could see his helplessness and could do nothing. I just wanted the world and him to vanish. I realize now how much support those close to a depressed person need in order themselves to stay in control and not give way to anger and despair. It is something we are not, as doctors, conscious enough about.

Looking back, it seems impossible that I could have felt so bad, living in such a beautiful place with a secure job and on the surface a secure and loving relationship. But it was the climax of all the anger building up over the years at the world and at myself for finally not being able to take control and being so helpless. In fact this is what happens to so many women . . . indeed we say 'I am depressed', as if we are being 'done to' and remain passive, too scared to face our own anger.

Not to say that I do not believe that biochemistry and genes play some part in who becomes depressed. I have several relatives who have themselves been depressed and a cousin who cut himself up with an axe after years of gloom. For me also clearly grief played a big part. There is, however, a point at which the process of depression fills not only one's mind but also one's body and it seems as if one's whole body is grinding to a halt. Appetite vanishes, bowels cease to function, interest and energy drain away.

I would never wish to go through such an experience again. For some time I thought 'if I ever get this bad again I will kill myself', but I have come to be less 'anti-drugs', have seen the value of antidepressants in practice, and feel that if I were on my way down again I would take antidepressants. I am sure that, at the

time, had they been suggested and had I been willing to take them they would
have helped. They can, on occasions be life-saving, and help, even if only to
speed recovery, people who have gone beyond the stage of simply feeling
'down' to experiencing early morning wakening and the other 'physiological'
symptoms of depression. They *can* be used in a positive way to enable a person
to begin to tackle the problems which precipitate the depression in the first
place and the changes that may be necessary to prevent recurrence. It is useless
to ask people who are beyond words, and beyond reach, to look at themselves,
at their relationships, and at society and to begin to make revolutionary changes.
Sadly doctors, themselves under pressure, may misuse antidepressants, in an
attempt to contain misery, anger, and grief, or to 'cure' depression without
looking at the persons, their situations, and the possibilities of change.

Doctors who are depressed have a problem. The experience, by its nature,
paralyses one and makes active steps to combat it extremely difficult. Meanwhile, engaged with survival, and getting to the top and 'coping', the medical
profession tends to ignore signs of non-coping within itself. Fortunately I was
not ignored for too long, partly because I could no longer work and partly
because, only a few months previously, a doctor in the practice had killed
himself a week after resigning. He had always worked efficiently, despite many
problems, and killed himself in the same efficient way with an overdose of
antidepressants. The practice arranged for me to see a psychiatrist, who has
since become a friend and to whom I shall always be grateful. He was able to
make contact in a practical way. First, he was not surprised that I was depressed
and did not condemn me, which I was afraid of. Second he told me that since I
was reluctant to take drugs, and things already being so bad, if I did not improve
soon I might have to go into hospital. Despite the nightmare of life as it was, I
knew I did not want to go into hospital, and, almost as if I had been given an
excuse, from that moment on I began to come back to life. Of course, looking
back at the time scale, it may have been that this was the natural course of
events, and even then it was no miracle cure. It was at least a year before I can
say I was out of it.

Meanwhile, an abortion bill came and went, and I, formerly a vigorous
campaigner for a woman's right to choose, never noticed. Spring arrived, with
all its beauty, and the sun and the trees seemed to mock me and sent me
scurrying indoors to curl up in bed, which was the only safe place. The more
sun, the more green grass, and country smells and noises, the worse I felt. After
two weeks I went back to work, determined to 'start again'. I applied for, and
got, a busy, challenging job on the South Coast, far from people who 'knew' the
truth. I left general practice and my friend: the only solution for both of us. He
was relieved, and fortunately trusted me enough to let me go.

Beginning to feel better was like being born again. In a sense it was just that
because the whole experience left scars that remain and was a turning point in
my life. I knew there was no going back to there. The whole year, spent by the
sea and including the best summer of the 1970s, was a rebirth experience. The
fact that no one there knew what I had been through meant that I could start

again and people would just accept me from scratch. Early morning waking went on for many months and some desperate nights were only relieved by cups of tea from the hospital switchboard, where I lived and worked, but in the morning I was a whole person doing a responsible job which I loved. Strangely, it was only then that I thought seriously about suicide. Before I had only thought passively about having a car accident, which was an easy way out . . . no responsibility . . . a cop out . . . very selfish. Now I had to make a decision, it had to be all or nothing. Even the means was there. I lived on the eighth floor.

I would like to be able to say that it was entirely a political decision not to jump, because suicide is the final rejection of a united struggle for a better life, but I know the sun, the sea, and the job made life good enough not to leave. It was the fear, voiced time and again by people I talk with, who have gone through the experience of being depressed, of slipping back and down again, that made me think of suicide. It is a fear that is present, if remote, as time passes in all who have been depressed, and for which there is no easy reassurance.

As I climbed slowly out of the depths I began to turn myself and my anger outwards, the anger which had almost destroyed me. Since then my life has been a continual struggle for change, not only in myself but fighting for a society which encourages people to have control and participate in their lives, that encourages choice, that encourages people not to have to possess others because they feel helpless themselves. Of course, this includes having the material basis for choice. It has not been easy, but I have chosen, and survived inner city general practice, where, although the problems are great, the challenge is infinite.

Getting to know and trust women, through involvement in the women's movement over the last few years, has helped me maintain this struggle, despite many negative moments, and has been very exciting, part of being born again. Hangovers from the past remain: I still harbour guilt about my stepmother, though I never see her now; I am still terrified about getting really close to someone, although less so, gradually; and I still do not have real choice about having children because of fears of my own childhood.

I know my experience has helped me enormously as a doctor. My antennae are very sensitive, and most of the time I can distance myself enough from the person's situation to detect their feelings, wants, needs, and try to respond. Knowing that I have 'been there too' enables me to get into others' feelings with a degree of ease. It is not easy, however, when I am in a bad patch, when my own doubts and feelings tend to blot out everything else. This can be very destructive, both in the surgery and outside, and I am aware that should I feel like this for a prolonged period it would not be fair to struggle on with the job. Fortunately this has not occurred to date.

We hear a lot today about the power of the medical profession. I am concerned with people taking power in their own lives. Occasionally as doctors we are in a position to help people do this. Every day, all of us as people can work towards this. Trying to understand the pain of depression, mine and others', and searching for a positive way out is part of the struggle. Conditions, even anorexia and depression, create consciousness, and consciousness leads to change.

Katy
1979–81

8 Metamorphosis

By a Clinical Psychologist

When I was first diagnosed as being clinically depressed, I was about as far away as I could be from being any sort of professional. It happened when I was about 30, and on looking back I'm only surprised that it didn't occur much earlier. For as long as I could remember I had thought of myself as a misfit. I had done as badly at school as anyone could, and always saw myself as a failure. I was a lonely and unhappy child, and unquestioningly accepted this as my lot in life. Other people were happy; other people had friends; other people were bright and pretty. I spent almost 30 years of my life with my nose up against the lollyshop window.

As a child I was known as a daydreamer, and lived largely in a fantasy world. This was peopled by colourful beings, among whom were my glamorous 'real' parents. My actual father was domineering, and my mother too timorous to be able to protect me from him. Father was aggressively 'working class', mother apologetically but stubbornly 'middle class'. Differences in tastes and values confused me, but I had chosen my mother's. I was much attached to my father, but was afraid of him and aware that he didn't like me much. He kept my mother and me in a state of subjection. We were both convinced we were stupid, and that our interests were to be despised.

The general state of affairs didn't change much over the years. I married at 20, and over the next eight years had four children without really thinking about what I was doing. I still saw myself as a failure, and was desperately lonely. Added to the loneliness was guilt over what I saw as my dreadful shortcomings as a wife and mother. I imagined that any woman should be able to bring up a family more or less by instinct, and there was something terribly wrong with me because I couldn't. I was unable to share with anyone the resulting feelings of despair. I wasn't completely useless: I was a good cook, and enjoyed making all our clothes. I was good at most things I could do with my hands, and derived pleasure from doing them. I sang reasonably well, and joined various choirs over the years, but never had enough confidence to do more than hang around on the edges of them.

We moved to a new area. One of my neighbours was a fanatically house-proud lady who had never had any children, and who complained constantly and at length about various aspects of our children's behaviour. In her rigid

79

meticulousness I read implied criticisms of what I saw as my sloppy house-
keeping, and blamed myself for my 'laziness'. The overall situation was
exacerbated by the children's and my minor illnesses. One of us was always at
the surgery. My three-year-old daughter became seriously ill, and there was
doubt for a time about whether she would recover.

Desperate by now, and looking for answers to my manifold problems, I
became involved in a local church group. I felt like a failure even here.
Everyone else seemed imbued with 'faith', whatever that meant. The charismatic preacher assured me that I could have it too; all I had to do was to act 'as
if' I had faith, and it would come. I had no such luck, in spite of being baptised in
the arms of the charming charismatic. 'Faith' continued to elude my heart, and
belief my head. My guilt feelings increased a hundredfold. If God, who loved
everyone, found me unacceptable, I must indeed be worthless. I began reading.
I knew I had to find answers somewhere, or that if there weren't any then I must
be crazy. I read through the local library's stock of theology, philosophy,
biography, and psychology. My interest in psychology, particularly abnormal
psychology, worried my mother. When I did eventually crack up, she attributed
it to my reading 'all those morbid books'.

That winter I had a bad attack of influenza, and didn't get better when I
might reasonably have expected to. The fever went, but I remained ill, and
became more and more depressed. The general practitioner was helpful as far
as he could be, but nothing made any difference. I remained very depressed and
quite hopeless, sitting or lying around for hours, or just standing, at the sink,
over the washing machine, or in the shower, tears running down my face. My
internal clock was running so slowly that I never caught up with outside time.
Feeding people and washing clothes seemed to fill my whole day. I went out less
and less, and didn't want to see people. I pretended not to be home if anyone
called. I couldn't bring myself to go outside to hang out the washing. I found it
difficult to eat, and lost weight. My former activities no longer interested me,
and housework became quite beyond me. Everything had to be very quiet. I
had no sleeping problems: I fell into bed dead tired every night, and could sleep
half the next day too. I castigated myself for my 'laziness'.

I began to think about killing myself – and the two younger children. To me,
the logic of this plan was beyond argument: it was obvious that the rest of the
family would be better without me. I was unable to believe that I would ever
feel any better. I couldn't see that I had been happy at any time in the past, or
that I could be at any time in the future. My life was hopeless. Clearly there was
no point in my going on. On the other hand, children as young as mine were
couldn't be left without a mother: we all had to go together. I began stealing
sodium amytal capsules from my mother. All I wanted to do was to sleep for
ever – to be free of responsibility, free of the demands of people around me,
free from having to keep up some semblance of 'normality'. I avoided other
people, having attached the label of outcast to myself, but I knew that my
withdrawal was seen as 'queer', and that I was no longer passing as 'normal'. At
the same time, I could observe a cynical, split-off part of me observing the

world and the rest of me. It seemed amused by our struggles to avoid an inevitable and unenviable fate. This self told me there was no point in looking for answers, trying to work things through – everything was futile.

I didn't bother to argue when the GP suggested I go to a receiving home. This was my release from responsibility, my chance to hide from the world. After admission formalities, I was allotted a bed in a dormitory, and on my first night was terrified to find myself securely locked in with 11 other 'crazy' women, and no staff. Most of the staff seemed to think the less we were told, the less trouble we would be. Hospital procedures were rarely explained, and it took time to work out what was likely to happen, what we could expect, and what was expected of us. For most of the first month I wandered around like a newly-blind person, bumping into the walls of other people's expectations. It didn't occur to me to complain about anything. I was unaware of my rights as a voluntary patient: nobody ever told me I had any. The idea of leaving the hospital didn't enter my head.

It was decided I was suffering from 'endogenous' depression and would benefit from electroconvulsive therapy. The first thing I knew about my 'treat-ment' was being told one morning I was to have no breakfast. Those of us for ECT were lined up and led to the treatment rooms. I asked whether I was to have an anaesthetic, and was told 'No'. I had no idea what was likely to happen, and was hiding in the bathroom, hysterical, by the time the medical officer arrived. I was given an anaesthetic. I was soon disabused of the idea that hospital was a rest-cure. We were not permitted to lie down during the day, and were hounded to meals and to occupational therapy. Part of our OT was to make our beds and to wash the dishes. In the main I did as I was told. I never did come to terms with the psychiatrist to whom I was assigned. He either bullied me or ignored me.

Overall there was a certain security about being in hospital. While 'craziness' may not have been tolerated there it was certainly expected. The status of 'patient' therefore conferred a certain immunity from having to act 'normally'. It had its disadvantages too, in that we were not expected to be rational, so that when I voiced concern about my children and their welfare I was said to be avoiding my own problem. When I refused to take the hospital's brand of oral contraceptive, which nauseated me, I was told this was a subconscious way of avoiding responsibility. Once I accepted that this was what hospital was like, that this was the price I was prepared to pay for a kind of security, I became very calm. It was as though I were in the eye of a whirlwind, very still, and watching the more or less devastating effects of the whirlwind on people about me, I felt so detached from all this, I wondered if I were faking. Loneliness, desperation, hopelessness were all gone. It seemed there was nothing left. This empty state was serenity for me. Most people stopped coming to see me. The family still came. My parents used to bring the two younger children. I could have enjoyed the children's company but my parents pressured me: 'It's time to pull yourself together, dear . . . all mothers of young children get tired – it's normal . . . you've had a rest now'.

After five months in hospital I asked to go home. I was told I wasn't yet ready, but nothing was attempted to make me more 'ready'. After more visits by tensely strained parents and unhappy children, I simply announced that I was going home. I learned afterwards that the medical officer had spoken to my husband to see whether he were prepared to have me there, that he would have to watch me closely, to expect suicide attempts or harm to the children, and that in any case I would very likely be back in hospital within a week or two. It seems that without the determination I had to stay out, I could have easily been left to deteriorate in a back ward forever. In a way, 'they' were right: I hadn't recovered, but I had acquired a hardened resolve. I determined that the only way I could survive was never to take account of my emotions again. I lived inside a hard, thick shell, wanting to survive just long enough to bring up my children. I had been issued with a small supply of pills and instructions to visit the out-patients' department. The few visits I did make revealed this as a pretty pointless activity. There were so many people, so little time, and the psychiatrist seemed interested only in the fact that I had combed my hair, or perhaps made my clothes.

One of the first things that happened after I came home was moving house. The new house was bigger, with an enormous garden where the children could play without disturbing anyone. I began to meet the neighbours, who hadn't known me before, and could see that they accepted me. Life was beginning to improve in small ways. The GP suggested I take a job – the first in 12 years of marriage. I applied at the local employment office and was soon offered work with a government department. This involved helping to carry out a public survey and lasted for several months. I was afraid I wouldn't be able to cope, but, to my surprise, managed it successfully. In my own eyes I was acting the part of an efficient worker, covering up inner chaos. The department decided to make a brief television documentary to publicize the survey, and I was chosen as the subject to be filmed going about her work. This was proof to me that I was putting on a very good act indeed.

Most of my earnings went of necessity into household accounts, and I felt a more worthwhile person to be making my own contribution. I was no longer financially dependent. I took other temporary jobs over the years – an assortment of bits and pieces. These included driving a dry-cleaner's van, telephoning, supermarket-cleaning and shelf-stocking, baby-sitting and working behind the counter at the local post office. At Christmas time for several years I worked at the Central Mail Exchange, and each July at the Taxation Office as a clerical assistant. I was still easily intimidated, therefore a model lower-echelon worker, and I still felt pretty helpless and hopeless most of the time. I saw myself as unattractive, unfeminine, an 'unnatural' mother, and was convinced I was sexually 'frigid'. What I know now, but didn't know then, was that for years after my discharge from hospital, I was still in a state of chronic depression. At that time I saw my state as the result of my chronic laziness and incompetence. I made it difficult, if not impossible, for anyone to help me, because it seemed essential to my survival not to admit to there being anything wrong. This followed from my decision to 'ignore my emotions'. I had therefore to keep myself cut off from everyone. As I had done during childhood, I accepted the isolation imposed by this as a necessary condition of my continuing existence.

I still had to find answers, and began to take night classes in philosophy. The first of these was appropriately entitled 'Clear Thinking'. I didn't learn to think so clearly in a six-week course, but this was a beginning, and gave me something constructive to think about. My next class was 'An Introduction to Philosophy', and directed me back to many of my old friends from the local library, like Hegel and Sartre. I discovered that these, and other figures such as Tillich and Rilke, were all, in one way or another, preoccupied with a common theme: that of the unique individual imprisoned in other people's expectations. For me, this was the nature of a Pauline revelation. I suddenly saw what I'd been doing all my life. I'd sought my own identity by trying to live inside the roles provided for me by other people. Other people's ideas of what they thought I ought to be had directed my whole life. I knew now why I always felt like a misfit – I was. None of the roles fitted me because none of them was me. This realization gave me a great boost up out of the depression chasm. I knew immediately that having accepted it, I could never go backwards – for anybody, or whatever the cost. I wasn't immediately ready to discard my ill-fitting roles: they were the only ones I had. I knew though, that other people were going to have to get used to me, as I was, and as I chose to present myself.

My next evening class went off at a tangent. I learned to play the recorder, and a group of us used to meet together to play regularly. The group of women varied in its composition, but there were usually about six of us. At that time we were all in our mid 30s and had relatively young children. I was the only one who worked outside the home and, in general, we had little beyond the family which could give an alternative source of value or identity. We worked together to improve our playing, and in this way achieved something of significance to ourselves as individuals. As we came to know each other better, we began to talk more, breaking down barriers as we began to trust one another. Most of our individual problems were suddenly seen to be common to most of the group. In various ways we felt trapped and personally inadequate. We felt guilty about what we saw as our inadequacies, our shortcomings as housekeepers, wives, mothers. We could talk about the times we hated our children and resented our spouses, about feeling at breaking-point and screaming at the children when no one else was around. I talked about times I had walked out on my children, paced furiously down the street, for fear of doing real harm if I stayed.

The discovery of the commonality of problems was another revelation to me and lessened my guilt. I began to feel more comfortable and less of an outcast. The group laughed a lot too. This was partly to avoid seeing how awful the housewife thing was, and partly relief at the recognition of our common ground. We were so happy to find each other, to share our ideas and our tastes, as well as our problems. We had all felt like cultural oddities at times, and were delighted to share our oddnesses with each other – and we kept on playing music together. Within the group we all found understanding and support, and a realization of the value of women friends. There were times when we joked about being a therapy group. We know now that what we really were was a consciousness-raising group and what we learned about ourselves and our position was no joking matter.

In the meantime, my second son, then aged 12, developed all the problems that children of depressed mothers are supposed to manifest. He was depressed and withdrawn, and school problems increased. He was variously diagnosed – nobody quite recognized what was going on. This child was my 'victim'. In his withdrawal and learning problems I recognized aspects of myself that I hated and the tension between us increased. My son's behaviour worsened and we were referred to a child guidance clinic. Initially the child saw the psychiatrist, while I talked to the social worker, but this changed after a few weeks. I would see the psychiatrist while my son played chess with the social worker. For months I resented the psychiatrist, but kept going back. We argued interminably. Eventually, I stopped being angry with him, and he changed tactics, moving from analytical-type techniques to just trying to talk with me, to understand. I was back to reading psychology again, this time trying to keep one jump ahead of him. In time, he took on the 'good father' role.

We spent much of our time talking about books and music. The psychiatrist knew many of the books that had been important to me, and recommended others. He also encouraged me to broaden my choice in music. I imagined then that I was still avoiding recognition of emotional issues, and refused to listen to anything much later than the baroque period. In doing this I was ignoring the passion inherent in the music of such composers as Bach and Monteverdi. With encouragement I came to listen to the Romantics and the Impressionists. I found that even when they reduced me to tears, which happened often then, my world didn't collapse. Recognition of my sadness didn't plunge me back into the abyss, and suddenly I didn't feel like an outcast any more. My interests were acceptable to someone who had credibility for me, and I could accept the fact that my 'middle-class' interests were not made ludicrous by my 'working-class' pocket. I didn't have to see myself as belonging to any particular class – I was just a person. Our son also seemed happier. He had stopped going to see the social worker. We had been able to carry out a remedial reading programme at home, and in six months, the child's 'reading-age' had increased by something like three years. All the problems were by no means solved, but we'd survived the acute state.

My father died about this time; a slow, unattractive death. The GP offered me Valium, which I took, and found to be very comfortable. Thus began a minor dependency. I asked the psychiatrist for sedatives – and got them. I took them for the high they gave me, and came to believe I needed them. They undoubtedly blunted the edge of the anger and guilt I felt following my father's death, and I know now I could have dealt with those feelings more quickly and less destructively without the drugs. Around the second anniversary of the death, I again became very depressed and suicidal. The psychiatrist suggested hospital. I refused. In not committing me, he acknowledged that I had the right to control my own life, whatever I chose to do with it. His recognition of my right to choose forced me to take responsibility for myself. It made a profound impression on me. Until then I had been unaware of the possibility of choice.

This depression was different. Where I had been helpless before, this time I was angry, railing against what I saw as past injustices. Recognition of my anger allowed me to begin asserting myself as a person for almost the first time in my life. The next step towards putting myself back together again was to get things into perspective. I had to accept that things that had happened had happened yesterday – and this was today. I could choose to take responsibility for myself, rather than blaming other people and events of yesterday for my current state. ('What can you expect from someone who had such a rotten childhood?') I came to realize an extraordinary sense of freedom in this acceptance of responsibility. It meant I could have the personal autonomy that I had for so long handed over to others. I could now begin to act for myself. Whatever may have happened in the past, I now had choices I could make about my present and my future. I began to lose the passivity and dependence that had characterized me for so long. I was also angry enough at this stage to throw out religion altogether.

I was gradually becoming more aware of my own identity, was more sure of myself, and less vulnerable. And slowly, very slowly, I was coming to see that I was not stupid. I was interested enough to begin to find out what my potential was, without necessarily committing myself to doing anything about it. I picked up a copy of *Know Your Own IQ* from a secondhand book stall, and went home to find out. Not only could I do the brainteasers, but I enjoyed them, and for a time, took to doing one whenever I had a spare minute, instead of crosswords. Still not convinced ('They're probably easy tests'), I applied to do a Mensa test, and scored satisfyingly highly.

The psychiatrist had been suggesting for some time that I attempt some kind of study course. For a long time I had veered between ignoring these suggestions and being angered by them. Perhaps he was laughing at me. I was ready now to try some prematriculation subjects. I did well, and over the next three years, while still doing my odd jobs, went on to matriculate. I was accepted for an Arts course at the university of my choice, where I would major in psychology. I had obtained a student grant, and could afford to study full-time; full-time that is aside from the time involved in running a home. My two younger children were still only 10 and 12 respectively. Out of my grant I paid someone to come in and do the major cleaning jobs. In that way I could relieve myself of some of the actual work, if not the responsibility. I put a great deal of time into study, I was determined to succeed, and I did. I gained incredible satisfaction from intellectual wrestling with the course. It was still an extraordinary thing for me not to think of myself as stupid. That satisfaction kept me going through the four years of an honours degree. At the end of my first year at university, I stopped going to see the psychiatrist. I'd been seeing him for about six years, on a fairly constant weekly basis. I didn't find it easy to break the contact. Not surprisingly, I'd become dependent on my 'good father figure'. It is possible that other more direct methods may have produced comparable results in a shorter time, but I'm only grateful that someone saw fit to make any investment in me.

What else helped in the long run? Important external factors were the availability of night classes, going to work (and earning money), and acceptance by friends who showed me the commonality of problems. Given time, I could very likely have got myself back together again somehow, but long-term relating to the 'good father figure' encouraged me to start looking at who I really could be. More importantly, I was also encouraged to begin to do something about it. A crucial factor was the psychiatrist's belief in me as a person, and his ability to convey that belief. Another key factor was my growing ability to recognize, and use, salient points along the way. I had made an early discovery about my propensity to try to fit myself into prescribed roles, rather than risk being myself; it was only when I recognized the freedom of taking that responsibility for myself, however, that the implications became clear. I had abdicated control of my life to others, and had to learn that choices were indeed available to me. It took me some time to learn that passive acceptance itself had been a choice that I had made.

A crucial part of my being a person in my own right was to recognize and express my anger. This anger was initially directed against circumstances which had forced me as a small child into the passive protest position of depression. I remained locked into this for many years. Recognition and expression of anger released me from those defences, and allowed me to begin to act autonomously.

Having spent time researching causes of, and vulnerability to, depression, I know that I was a prime candidate for the disorder. The person typically diagnosed as depressed is likely to be a married woman who is also a mother, and beset with practical problems: children, interpersonal relationships, and spouse concerns. What I learned from my own depression and recovery and try to practise when working with clients is that people have the seeds of their own revival within them. I want to ask the right questions so that people can hear what they say, recognize what changes they want to make, and how they can choose to make them. Specific time limits are set, and I prefer to focus initially on people making changes in their behaviour, rather than mood. I explain that although the depressed mood colours their whole world, it has not been shown to be causally related to improvement, whereas behaviour has.

When clients know that there are specific and tangible things they can do, they often begin to experience an immediate upswing. A specific time limit is often motivating. People begin to see themselves making positive changes in their behaviour, and can begin to change attitudes about themselves. They begin to see themselves controlling aspects of their environment, and as this happens, helplessness and hopelessness begin to dissipate and self-esteem level rises proportionately. People see themselves to be improving as a result of their own efforts. Nothing can be more rewarding for a depressed person. This is what effects the metamorphosis.

Beginning to see myself as an effective person was what gave me the impetus and the reason to move out from my self-built fortress. The chief of my defences was depression. In a different analysis, depression can be seen as an intensification of some commonly ascribed 'feminine' characteristics. These include helplessness, passivity, dependence, indecisiveness, and so on. Depression becomes a protest position for those forced into it by social pressures, and we defend this position rigidly. Many defences are self-defeating, in that the more rigid and impenetrable they are, the more effectively they prevent growth and change. Psychotherapy enabled me to begin to trust the world enough to move out. Once I was out, the ensuing rewards have been so immediate, so apparent, and so great, there have been few temptations to return, and none to which I have succumbed.

Wounded Healers
Edited by V. Rippere and R. Williams
© 1985 John Wiley & Sons Ltd.

9   *Beginning to live*

By a Psychiatric Social Worker

I always vowed I wouldn't get married before I was 30. I judged that by that time I would have become established in my career, and done some of those exciting things which were incompatible with marriage. I never questioned the notion that I would marry and have children. Somehow there didn't appear to be any alternative: I accepted the opinion of my mother, the prevailing one of the time, that those who didn't marry were failures (they hadn't succeeded in attracting a spouse); those who didn't have children were either sad because they couldn't, or selfish because they didn't want them. I suppose my plan not to marry before I was 30 was my way of getting the best of both worlds.

When I met T, I changed my mind, thinking that here was someone whom I could marry, but still retain some of the advantages of being single. We had long discussions about other people's marriages, and the kind of lives we ourselves would like to lead as a married couple. Although we were very critical of other couple's relationships, we had been successfully indoctrinated into the romantic image propagated in our culture that ours would be a 'happy ever after' marriage. We knew of very few really happy marriages, but nevertheless, we felt absolutely certain that we could create one for ourselves. We somehow felt that because we both disliked the idea of the cosy domesticity and compromise we saw all around us, our marriage would be different.

In the early days of my social work career, working as a psychiatric social worker, I met many people who were depressed, many of them with marital problems. I always felt a great deal of sympathy for these clients, but I regarded their problems as something entirely personal to themselves, which could only be interpreted in terms of their individual functioning. It never occurred to me that any of them might be related to marriage as an institution. Consequently, I never imagined that I might have similar problems a few years later.

It was an enormous shock and disappointment to me when my marriage did not turn out to be as idyllic as I had expected. I just couldn't believe it, and for many months I avoided facing up to T's dissatisfactions. Without realizing it, I had reneged on many of my former ideals, and slipped into the kind of wifely domesticity upheld by all the powerful influences around me, which T and I had both abhorred in all our discussions and hopes. T was rightly very disappointed, and I just did not understand what was happening. I tended to blame myself for not being a good enough wife: I would try hard to do things to please him, but of course they didn't work.

Finally, after about two years, the full weight of it descended. Here I was involved in a relationship which was going badly wrong, and I didn't know what on earth to do about it. To make matters worse, we had moved to a new area, where we did not know anyone, and we became more dependent on each other. But neither of us could meet the other's needs. The more demanding T became, the less I felt I had to give. The more depressed I became, the more impatient T was. I felt helpless, desolate, empty, a complete failure as a woman, on the verge of tears much of the time, anguished inside, everything seemed bleak and pointless. I also felt trapped, because I could see no possible solution to our problems.

The image in my mind from those days is of greyness, bleakness, drabness. It was the only time I have ever written any poetry:

The day drags on,
Drab and dank.
Buses whizz by
Through empty streets,
And echo my feeling
That nobody cares.

In those days I used to wake late, stay in bed, not seeing the point of getting up, preferring to escape in sleep. I felt dominated by my hopeless situation, not able to concentrate on anything else. From time to time I considered the possibility of swallowing a bottle of aspirin in order to prolong the oblivion of sleep, but I did not even have the will to think about that constructively. I felt trapped, lifeless, helpless, hopeless, unable to appreciate the things that used to give me pleasure. One of these was sunshine and the open air. I have a vivid recollection in my mind of one beautiful sunny day, sitting on a cliff top overlooking a brilliant sea, birds circling around, the kind of scene which would normally be a high spot in the week. Rationally, I know it was beautiful, but emotionally I couldn't respond: there was a screen between me and my surroundings, preventing me from relating to them, blocking off my emotional response.

Going to work was something of an escape from an insoluble situation, because that was the one area in which I still felt reasonably competent and valued. However, I was unable to tackle anything resembling a marital problem, and I felt emotionally bankrupt, with nothing of myself to offer clients. I was unable to share my situation with my colleagues – I felt too ashamed, and no one seemed to notice I was not functioning very well. I've often thought since then that although we tend to be tolerant and understanding towards our clients, we put pressure on our colleagues to keep to the right side of the boundary between helper and client: we don't want to know about our colleagues' problems. We don't have any other way of dealing with the inevitable fact that we all at some time need to be allowed to be weak, to be supported by others, to opt out of our usual role of being the strong person on whom others lean, to give ourselves the help and understanding we offer to others, or just to have a rest from other people's problems for a while. Such needs are usually dealt with by leaving jobs, promotion into administrative positions, or going on training courses: there is a great need for legitimate and straightforward ways of catering for these human needs of helpers.

It was a long time before I was able to confide in anyone about my situation. I was living several hundred miles away from my family and friends, and apart from the odd outburst of crying, I did not express my feelings to anyone. I hadn't the energy to seek out new friends, and anyway I felt I had nothing to offer people. I was well aware of the need to find help, but I didn't know where to go. The area was very parochial. I knew all the social workers in the city professionally, and therefore did not feel able to approach the normal sources. Where do professional helpers go when they need help themselves? I decided to approach my GP. Perhaps he could refer me to someone. I shall never forget that brief interview. I told him something of my situation, and his only response was to advise me to get pregnant. Looking back, I would like to give that doctor a piece of my mind for giving such inappropriate and irresponsible advice, but at the time I felt devastated and misunderstood. I never went back to that doctor. Fortunately I realized that having a baby was the last thing I should be considering. Another woman I know who already had three children was given the same advice by her GP when she was depressed. Sadly for her, she followed it. Those doctors were amongst the many who believe that all women find fulfilment in having children. I shall have more to say later about the way in which 'helpers' so often have a stereotyped view of women's problems and therefore fail to offer any constructive help.

Finally, an old friend of mine, who realized the state I was in when she visited one weekend, gave me the name of a psychotherapist in a nearby city. It was such a relief to find help that I spent the first few interviews crying uncontrollably. I remember feeling extremely self-conscious when I came out of the clinic because of my tear-stained face. Oh for a recovery room and a cup of tea. But it was too professional and clinical for that. How different things are nowadays at some of the best centres of help with those comforting boxes of tissues, and accepting and informal atmosphere.

Apart from release of emotion, I can't say I got much immediate help from that psychotherapist. All I wanted at the time was help with my marriage, to enable it to work! I didn't understand the help that was being offered to change in a more fundamental way, to express my anger, to develop as a person, to discover my needs as an individual rather than in relation to my husband. I used to note down comments made by my therapist, because I thought they must be valid, but they didn't mean anything at the time. Things didn't improve while I was attending the clinic, but at least I had an outlet. At least there was some hope that my situation might improve in the future if I continued in treatment. The fact that T refused to participate except in the first information-giving session confirmed my feelings of inadequacy: I was clearly the sick partner.

There were two things I found much more helpful than formal treatment, although I'm sure the latter was the beginning of a long process of growth, the seeds of which took many years to germinate. The two more immediately helpful events were a new friendship and contact with the women's movement.

I've already said that I felt I had failed as a woman because my marriage was not working out, and that I had nothing to offer as a person either to my husband or to anyone else. I was completely dependent on T for validating myself as a worthwhile person, and it never occurred to me to look for emotional satisfaction from anyone else. I also took my situation in completely personal terms. I had no conception that it could be looked at in any other way apart for the attribution of blame to one of the partners; in this case, me. (Surely there must have been something in my social work course which would have led me to think otherwise?) The new friendship was extremely important because it helped me to begin to restore confidence in myself. Here was someone who actually found me attractive, and enjoyed being with me, someone who offered me affection and understanding. This came as a shock and revelation. It had never occurred to me since I married that I would ever be interested in any other man. For the first time for ages, I started looking forward to something – seeing S. Although my marital problems remained, there was suddenly a new dimension to my life which I could enjoy, and which neutralized some of the negative effects of a failing marriage. It convinced me that I wasn't a complete failure, and revitalized some of my deadened emotions. Fortunately I didn't see it as a replacement for or solution to my relationship with T, but it took the pressure off, and helped towards a gradual separation. The relationship with S was not only important in itself, but it started me thinking about the usual assumption that married people don't expect to have any other close relationships with people of the opposite sex. If they do, it is considered illicit and something to be conducted in secret. It led me to the view that it is arrogant and unrealistic to expect that two people can be expected to meet all each others' needs, and that it is better to promote close relationships with a number of people.

Contact with the women's movement was and has been since, a powerful force in my life. At that time, it provided a source of comfort for the present and hope for the future. Women were prepared to talk openly and frankly about their personal lives in a way which was entirely new to me, and to express anger at their situation, and from time to time even humour. Everyone was given a sympathetic hearing. There was an enormous strength to be found in those groups of women, sharing intimate details of our lives, which showed us that many of our personal problems were similar, leading us to the view that they were connected with our position as women. The women's movement also pointed to an alternative lifestyle, which we worked out in lively and exciting discussions – an independence and pride in ourselves as women we had never felt before. I felt close to those women in a way that was entirely new to me, having been brought up with the idea that women don't have anything very important to talk about, and that mixed company is always more enjoyable. We revelled in each others' support and companionship. Suddenly I began to have some sort of vision for a different future for me as a person of value in my own right. I also began to develop a new perspective on my marriage, seeing it in the context of the pressures and expectations of society, rather than as an individual failure.

The women's movement has been an important continuing influence in my life. It has given me a new respect for myself, a new confidence in my value and strength as an individual, a new realization that I don't have to define myself in relation to a man to gain satisfaction in life, that many so-called 'personal' problems are explicable in terms of our position in society.

Looking back on my period of depression, I feel it was a turning point in my life. It threw me back on my own resources, and although this was enormously painful at the time, it was the beginning of a long process during which I began to discover what I wanted for myself as an individual rather than as a wife. It saddens me that I had to go through a broken marriage to start along this path, but as long as women continue to be taught from infancy to define themselves in relation to men, instead of being brought up as independent individuals of equal value in their own right, then these situations will continue to happen. Despite the fast increasing rate of marriage breakdown, society's institutions continue to be geared to the assumption that marriage is the norm, and those who choose to be in other kinds of relationships are penalized both practically and socially. I get upset and angry sometimes when this happens, but most of the time I revel in my independence, I am delighted not to be married and not to have children because I now realize these things are not for me.

Professionally, after I had recovered from my depression, I immediately became more ambitious. Until then, I had regarded my career as subordinate to my husband's. I planned to give up work as soon as that elusive desire for children finally surfaced. I had never thought in terms of promotion or lifelong work. I slowly began to realize that I was capable of more than I was achieving, and that there was no reason why I shouldn't be thinking in terms of a more senior post.

As a social worker, my own experience provided a challenge to my work. What kind of service was I offering to women? Previously my aim would have been to help depressed women to 'identify with their role' as wives and mothers, to help them to find ways of adjusting to the expectations of their family and society. Just as my own doctor had suggested that the answer to my problems was to get pregnant, so my approach in helping a depressed mother would have been to enable her to become a 'better' wife and mother by improving her care of house and family. I was concerned with her role in the family rather than her needs as an individual person. Hence I was pushing her back into the very situation she had found depressing. I helped to run 'mothers' groups', in which cooking, sewing and discussions about caring for children figured prominently. This did little for the woman who felt guilty at not being a 'proper' mother.

More recently my approach has been to help the woman to work out a more satisfactory role according to what she wants for herself. I try to help her to recognize the conditions which have led to her depression, to understand that it is not individual inadequacy or failure which have made her depressed, but the situation in which she and most other mothers find themselves. I try to help her to see herself as an individual woman with needs and interests of her own, rather than as a wife and mother whose role it is to be looking after others' needs all the time. It is usually very helpful to link people up with others in a similar situation, but any group formed is a 'women's group', aimed at helping the members to understand their situation and take constructive action to improve it. At its best, this approach can lead to the woman overcoming her sense of isolation and achieving a stronger sense of her own identity as an individual and a woman. Women may join forces to improve their lives, for example, by organizing child care facilities for themselves, and thus giving each other greater independence as well as the satisfaction of organizing themselves and supporting each other.

Writing this has made me more aware of what an important time this period of my life was for me. I expected to 'live happily ever after' when I got married, but instead I experienced a time of profound unhappiness. My expectations, in common with many other people's, of what marriage would be like, were totally unrealistic. However, this first major challenge in my life enabled me to start formulating a set of values which I had thought out for myself through my own experiences, rather than inheriting from other people. For this I am profoundly grateful.

Section IV   Living with depression

The five chapters making up this section – the longest one in the book – all portray experiences of recurrent depression extending over many years. They are noteworthy both for the variety of the experiences depicted and for a certain commonality of themes, which they share with other essays in the collection. Both unipolar and bipolar illnesses are represented and the authors belong to four different professions: clinical psychology (two authors), occupational therapy, public health (though formerly general practice), and psychiatry. Both men and women are included and they all present their stories in unique and personal ways. Even were it not for their interest in relation to the question of depression in mental health workers, these essays would constitute a worthy contribution to the phenomenological literature of depression.

These chapters have some interesting lessons to teach. One is that a mood of profound sadness or melancholy is not necessarily the most salient feature of depressive experience in individuals with severe recurrent affective disorders, contrary to what textbook stereotypes of 'the depressed patient' might lead us to expect. Thus the author of the evocatively titled 'Wading through mud' (Chapter 10) notes that she was 'primarily conscious of a progressive cognitive impairment'. The writer of 'Life doesn't scare me any more' (Chapter 11) emphasizes her feelings of apprehension and anxiety, which were followed by feelings of unreality and terrifying delusions. The author of 'A doctor's depression' (Chapter 12) observes that 'Most noticeable of all was a feeling that people I saw about in the street were stupid', that 'everybody and everything they did was stupid and pointless'. The writer of 'Big D' (Chapter 13) stresses the salience of her sleep disturbance, and the author of 'A kind of termination' (Chapter 14) notes anxiety, fear, and self-doubt as his predominant feelings. The diversity of these subjective states suggests that the textbook stereotype of depression – as melancholia – may not be entirely representative of the subjective experiences of depressed people and may thus be misleading. Indeed, two of our authors note that they have had difficulty in recognizing the onsets of their depressions, apparently largely because their mental states, as they perceived them, did not conform to the stereotypical picture of overwhelming sadness and misery.

Another stereotype which these accounts call into question is the notion that in-patient treatment is mandatory for people with depressions that threaten their ability to cope. While three of the five authors received in-patient care, two were quite successfully managed on an out-patient basis and continued to work in their mental health jobs during their illnesses. The two authors who carried on working confirm the findings we have mentioned earlier that depressed women may be less impaired in the performance of their work roles than in other roles and that work may serve protective functions. The author of 'Wading through mud' notes that during treatment sessions, her 'feelings of alienation and of being judged (unfavourably) were less prominent and [her] role as therapist became an important part of [her] justification for getting up each day'. In a similar vein, the author of 'Big D' notes that 'Clinical work itself can be therapeutic. Often during a depressive phase I have felt a lessening in the intensity of my symptoms for a while after a session with a patient'. Rachman's (1978) concept of 'required helpfulness' is perhaps relevant to their observations.

In discussing psychological adaptation to repeated aerial bombing in Britain during World War II, Rachman observed that people who were given socially responsible tasks to carry out during air raids 'experienced a noticeable growth of courage' (Rachman, 1978, p. 240). He suggested that rising to the occasion when helpfulness is required in a crisis may be 'the opposite side of the coin that M. Seligman has labelled "learned helplnessness" ' (*ibid.*) In the case of depressed mental health professionals who go on working despite their illness, required helpfulness may be a function both of their role itself, with its implicit taboos on psychiatric patienthood, and of individual factors, such as the personal significance attached to the performance of this role – or to one's actual or anticipated inability to do so. The author of 'Wading through mud', who at the onset of her illness was already working in a psychiatric hospital, notes that, for her, 'becoming a psychiatric patient was a step taken not only with intellectual reservations, but also with a huge sense of failure and shame'. Her reluctance to assume this role led her to appreciate previously unsuspected condescension in her attitude to patients, seen as 'a race apart, incapable, helpless, and pitiful'. While she could readily make such attributions of herself, she notes that 'it was a different matter to have public recognition of my inadequacy'. It seems likely that if a mental health worker ascribes these kinds of meanings to becoming a patient, being able to continue working despite illness would assume considerable personal importance.

Although he is speaking of psychological deficits induced by cerebral dysfunctions, Lipowski's (1975) comments seem equally applicable to depressive deficits in mental health workers:

'Awareness of change in one's cognitive capacity and other psychological deficits caused by cerebral dysfunction is itself a form of information liable to be invested with personal meaning. It may be experienced by the patient as a threat to his integrity and identity as a person, or as actual loss. This appraisal as threat or loss gives rise to emotional responses such as anxiety, depression, shame, grief, and anger, and sets in motion defence mechanisms and coping strategies aimed at attenuation of suffering, regaining mastery, and compensating for the perceived deficits' (Lipowski, 1975, p. 111).

Carrying on in work could function as just such a coping strategy in depressed mental health workers.

Or others. The author of 'Big D' was not yet a mental health worker at the time of onset of her first depression. None the less she also had reservations about seeing a psychiatrist when her GP first suggested this course of action and she also carried on working throughout her series of recurrent depressions. In her case, since she was not yet working in the mental health field, her initial reluctance to assume the role of psychiatric patient cannot be attributed to the taboos of mental health professionalism, nor indeed need it be: there are certainly similar taboos still current in the rest of our society. It is probably significant that the author notes that her personal threshold for seeking pharmacological help with recurrences from her GP now occurs when her 'answer to the question "Can I cope with working tomorrow?" is an unequivocal "No" '. Her observation suggests that in some cases the ability to remain working while depressed results from deliberate strategic action undertaken with the aim of maintaining that ability. The coping behaviour and strategies of mental health workers who manage to remain working would be worthy of further study, perhaps following the 'antidepressive behaviour' model proposed by Rippere (1977 a,b).

That reluctance to become a psychiatric patient does not of itself suffice to keep a mental health worker working during a depression is suggested by the author of 'A doctor's depression', who described his initial efforts at self-medication, which ended in a deliberate overdose of barbiturates. In consequence of this action, he finally came under the care of a psychiatrist and over the years was seen by several, both on an in-patient and an out-patient basis. He cautions his afflicted fellow doctors to seek professional help 'even if it seems strange to adopt the role of patient', suggesting that he, too, found this role abhorrent at first. More information would be needed to specify the relationship, if any, between misgivings about becoming a patient and being able to continue working in a mental health job while depressed. But it is clear from these accounts that the matter would be worth pursuing.

Another by now familiar theme emerging from these chapters is the question of the effects of depression on the sufferer's mental health career. Although it might be expected on *a priori* grounds that severe recurrent affective disorders might be completely inimical to occupational survival in the mental health field, we find that in the case of our two clinical psychologists, at least, their illnesses do not appear to have been insurmountable occupational obstacles. In one case ('Big D'), the writer's experience may have been contributory to her career choice. This aspect of her experience is certainly shared with other authors in the collection. However, our occupational therapist describes having to drop out of a new post after only a few days in consequence of a relapse; our consultant psychiatrist took early retirement, and our former GP changed to a career in occupational health. Although the sample is, of course, too small to permit firm conclusions to be drawn, there does seem to be a range of possible occupational outcomes to severe recurrent depressions in mental health workers. In this respect, recurrent affective disorders may be more disruptive than isolated episodes or clusters of episodes that eventually resolve, but the difference is one in degree rather than in kind. Even a single depressive bout may profoundly alter a worker's career.

In addition to effects on work and careers, these accounts suggest that recurrent depressions may have important effects on sufferers' lives outside of work. Two of our authors mentioned that their spouses may have suffered more than they did as a result of their illnesses and all describe other effects on their daily lives. These chapters could provide hypotheses for further, and much needed, systematic study of the social and psychological consequences of susceptibility to severe recurrent depressions, not only in mental health workers but in others as well. At the present time, not very much is known about the effects of chronic illness generally upon the quality of life of sufferers (Strauss, 1975). Perhaps the time has come to extend research from consideration of life events which precede and presumably precipitate depression to investigation of life events and lifestyle changes which follow and presumably result from it. Because of the length of time required for the production of such effects and because the fact of being studied longitudinally might react with the phenomena under study, the psychosocial effects of recurrent depression might be more efficiently studied retrospectively than prospectively. Results of such enquiry would almost certainly improve our understanding of what it means to suffer from repeated episodes of affective disorder.

Moreover, in addition to lifestyle changes resulting from recurrent affective illness, these chapters suggest that personality changes proceeding from the same source would be worthwhile topics for further study. Several of our authors, both in this section and elsewhere in the book, mention personality alterations, for better or for worse, which they attribute to their experiences of depression and its treatment. Especially those who emphasize personality improvements in the direction of greater self-confidence, autonomy, and tolerance might compel a revision of traditional notions concerning 'the' personality of people who are liable to affective disorders and the personality status of recovered patients (i.e. Metcalfe, 1968, Altman and Wittenborn, 1980).

Finally, besides the general questions and themes raised by these accounts, there are also a number of individual issues that they touch upon. 'A kind of termination' raises the question of how depression interacts with an addictive tendency. Both this chapter and 'Life doesn't scare me any more' (as well as others elsewhere in the collection) introduce the issue of how lifelong traits such as anxiety or obsessiveness may predispose to depression. And, finally, 'Big D' brings in the question of childhood depression. All these are issues which have no satisfactory answers at present.

Wounded Healers
Edited by V. Rippere and R. Williams
© 1985 John Wiley & Sons Ltd.

10   Wading through mud

By a Clinical Psychologist

The first thing to be said about my experience of depression is that, despite five years' working as a clinical psychologist, I failed to recognize my own condition as 'depression'. I think this was because, rather than feeling profoundly miserable (although that was certainly the case), I was primarily conscious of a progressive cognitive impairment. I felt myself increasingly unable to concentrate (on reading, TV, etc.), to reason, or to think clearly at all. I constantly felt bewildered, as if I were struggling to find 'the answer' that would solve all my problems, if only I could remember what 'the question' was. There were physical concomitants: my head felt as if it were packed tight with cotton wool; there was a sense of pressure and a constant singing sensation, rather like white noise, in my head.

The first time I was forced to seek professional help was about 18 months after the sudden and unexpected breakdown of my marriage. My husband had abruptly upped and gone in pursuit of another relationship after two years of an admittedly unsatisfactory marriage in which I had, nonetheless, invested heavily. In retrospect, I think that the unhappy state of the marriage both undermined my self-confidence and caused me to work harder and harder to prop up the relationship, thereby reducing my basis of support outside the marriage and further increasing my sense of insecurity. When my husband left, I felt high and dry: I had no close friends of my own (most of my friends had been sacrificed to our marriage); I had become distanced from my family; and even my job had become, in my own mind, wholly secondary in importance to his career. Furthermore, since I had been so much taken by surprise by my husband's behaviour, I seriously questioned my ability as a psychologist to make judgements about people whom I knew scarcely at all. Most devastating of all was the thought that my husband's cruel behaviour was justified by my own past cruelty, that I had driven him to this extreme measure by my wickedness, that the collapse of the marriage was really my fault. The facts of what had happened meant that I had to reorient and restructure my life but, more importantly, the personal meaning that I ascribed to these events dealt a savage blow to my sense of identity and, I am sure, constituted the psychological basis to my later experience of depression.

In the first place, I lived through a relatively short period of acute anxiety and anguish, filled with a good deal of frenetic activity and endless emotional discussions with family and friends. During this time I assimilated the reality of what had happened and also discovered the amazing fund of warmth and human support that was immediately available to me. But this stage of activation gave way in a matter of weeks to a phase of depression when I felt low and miserable, lacking in energy and self-confidence. During this period I succeeded in getting a new and prestigious academic post which would involve teaching postgraduate clinical psychology students and research as well as clinical work. But although the change in job added to my loneliness and misery, I now consider that the 'lull' period between finishing one job and starting another protected me from awareness of the extent of my depression at this time. In any case, I never once considered going for medical or other professional help. As far as I was concerned, my present state of mind was appropriate to my 'bereavement', I also had a tangible goal in mind: self-sufficiency. I thought that one of the main reasons why I had persevered with an unsatisfactory relationship was my fear of being on my own. Therefore, I now had to learn to live alone to prevent this ever happening again.

By the time of the first anniversary of the separation, I was feeling pretty good (in retrospect, too good). I entered on my first full academic year with confidence and enthusiasm. I thought I had 'got over' the break-up and I was beginning to enjoy my independent way of life. My memory of the details of this period is meagre but I do recall having fits of uncontrollable giggles in the ward-rounds of a very serious and venerable, elderly consultant psychiatrist. I also remember having amorous intentions towards an agreeable young registrar and expressing these in fairly unambigious terms in the hospital canteen. But I received no adverse feedback.

The period of over-confidence was short-lived and gave way to increasing self-doubt and pessimism. This was unexpected. I could see no reason why I should feel this way. Other people were, as usual, reassuring and full of reasonable explanations. I was alone in a state of puzzlement which resisted all arguments. I seemed to be unable to grasp the very possibility of such a drastic change in mood ever happening. Well-meaning friends talked about the experience of loss, directed me to Freud and Jung and gently probed the nature of my early childhood relationships, but our conversations were at cross-purposes. I could not translate the processes invoked into the see-sawing reality of my subjective experience. I could think of no adequate recent experience to account for my condition. My divorce, it was true, was going through at the time and some people seized upon this event as an explanation. I was said to be mourning the loss of the marriage, at a subconcious level. At the very least, this interpretation was unhelpful (and quite untestable) because it did not relate to my experience: my thoughts were no longer preoccupied with the departure of my husband but with my failing powers of thinking and especially with my inability to do my job.

My difficulty in cognitive tasks increased insidiously. I became quite unable to hold more than one idea in my mind at the same time and, consequently, would lose the thread of an argument; worse still I had trouble understanding complex sentences in conversation and in a crowded place I had difficulty in following one person's voice. I vividly remember the panic induced by having to get together test materials before going to see a patient on the ward, something that would normally have been done virtually automatically, without conscious effort. I was unable to retain a list of some four or five items and would repeatedly have to rethink the list and recheck over and over again as my level of anxiety spiralled upwards. I had always possessed an excellent memory but now the making of lists became a necessity to cope with even simple tasks. Lists were useful in other situations too, such as the planning of time, where otherwise I could spend fruitless hours gazing into space, not being able to remember the things I had to do.

It is exceedingly difficult to give a description that does full justice to the scope of a global condition such as depression. One of the best metaphors for depression, as I experienced it, is 'wading through mud'. The expression captures the feeling of powerful resistance opposing and impeding any kind of action: thought, word, or deed. Introspection, as a means of analysing a psychological condition, is clearly of dubious value on its own and by referring to cognitive, motivational, and interpersonal aspects, for instance, I mean to suggest only that this is how I perceived my state of mind at the time and not that there were real, discrete areas of impairment. Nevertheless I think that my focus upon the cognitive aspect was a major reason why I did not recognize myself as depressed. I had been taught as a psychologist that depressed people only believed themselves deficient but actually functioned almost normally. I, on the other hand, knew beyond all doubt that I was not thinking properly.

Whereas I could begin to adjust to my cognitive difficulties when on my own, my problems became more acute and alarming in social situations. I was now involved at work in academic tutorials, the supervision of students' clinical work, as well as my own clinical practice, meetings with other staff and colleagues, etc. The ordeal of the weekly tutorial became overwhelmingly terrifying and I sometimes resorted to postponement and cancellation. But whereas my cognitive difficulties were particularly exposed in interactions as a teacher, social situations in general became difficult, causing such great anxiety and embarrassment that I began to think I was socially phobic. It seemed to me, though, that the fundamental problem was that I usually possessed not a thought in my head. Even if an idea did occur to me, I was unable to find the words to express it, or the energy or interest to try. Sometimes I would launch forth into making a statement only to find myself either running out of steam and winding down in futility or forgetting what I was going to say next. Contact with people, even with my long-suffering friends, became aversive. I was totally preoccupied with myself and my predicament, but my loss of fluency together with my friends' implacable reassurances left me frustrated, alienated, and miserable. In any case, conversation about myself was a predictable cue for tears, another effective impediment to self-expression. The repeatedly recurring thought and feeling was that I was different from other people, or worse, a nonentity that people ignored or were mildly embarrassed by. I watched whilst other people engaged in arguments and discussions with a fervour and commitment that baffles me and that, try as I did, I could not imitate. I frequently had a strange experience of being an observer watching my own behaviour, being surprised by my failures but unable to take corrective action. (The variation in my symptoms has always been such that, continually, I was taken by surprise by my shortcomings. Just when I noticed I was reacting more fluently and spontaneously, resistance would set in again and the system would seize up.)

For a long time my professional interaction with psychiatric patients caused me great worry. I felt acutely concerned about not carrying out my responsibilities adequately. It seemed to be a case of the blind leading the blind and I was behaving like a hypocrite by presuming to be a therapist. When I was receiving out-patient treatment myself, I found it particularly difficult to attend for my own consultation and then return to my hospital and straightaway resume seeing patients. The change in roles seemed to be too extreme. Later on I found that contact with patients became a relatively tolerable kind of social situation. Although the disfluency and blankness were omnipresent and must have interfered with my active therapy, the peculiar structure and function of treatment sessions had, to some extent, a disinhibitory effect. The feelings of alienation and of being judged (unfavourably) were less prominent and my role as therapist became an important part of my justification for getting up each day. I suppose, too, the clichéed realization that there were people worse off than myself was operative, although I am sure that on several occasions I, the therapist, was more severely 'ill' than my patients. The worst part was seeing a new patient and resisting the paralysing belief that I would not be able to help him. I would like to know how my patients saw me and whether I committed errors other than errors of omission in my treatment. My own opinion is that the assumptions underlying the sessions were so binding that most of my patients failed to recognize what was happening to me.

Meetings with members of the psychiatric team with whom I worked were high on my list of situations to be avoided if at all possible. Nightmare thoughts about what might happen if I attended a ward-round often prevented me from going at all. If I did manage to drag myself along, I usually sat with averted gaze, virtually immobile and hoping that no one would ask me anything. Still incredible to me, I received no direct adverse feedback apart from what I interpreted as puzzled or pitying looks and tactful avoidance of calling on me more than was absolutely necessary. It did become obvious to me, however, that I was a person to avoid in social situations at work. And this was not a paranoid perception. Nothing was further from my thoughts than the idea that people were against me. In fact, the reverse was the case: people were consistently kind and helpful. It seemed highly reasonable that people would sometimes be unable to stomach my company, because I seemed incapable of pulling myself together. The repetitive refrain to my thought: 'I'm no good. I can't do anything. I'm no use', was particularly painful in the context of my estimation of other people.

During the period of my increasing subjective incompetence I tried various means to pull myself out of it. These varied from weekends in the country, long country walks, and selective social contact with close friends to musical activities, physical exercise, comforting favourite foods, plenty of sleep, etc., etc. Nothing that I did made any substantial difference to my state of mind. Certainly some activities seemed to make me feel better for a short time (and it was definitely better to do something than nothing) but there was never any enduring change. Indeed I came to the conclusion that if I managed to improve my mood through some activity, I could expect to feel all the more the worse on the following morning. I seemed to be stuck in a homeostatic system in which an upward swing was inevitably followed by an equal and opposite downward swing.

My first attempt to seek help was via the staff clinic at the hospital where I worked. But the doctor seemed to operate under the assumption that two weeks off work and a virtually homeopathic dose of antidepressant will sort out most ills. Not mine. A discussion with my head of department (and my usual exhibition of tears) resulted in a telephone call to a trusted psychiatrist colleague at another hospital. Before I knew it, I had become a psychiatric case.

As a clinical psychologist who had had spirited disagreements with most of the psychiatrists she had encountered, I found that becoming a psychiatric patient was a step taken not only with intellectual reservations, but also with a huge sense of failure and shame. Before I took up the status of 'patient', I used to think that I had an egalitarian, humane attitude towards patients, but the meaning I ascribed to becoming a patient myself suggests that actually I had seen patients as a race apart, incapable, helpless, and pitiful. Whereas those epithets could have been taken straight out of my own self-portrait, it was a different matter to have public recognition of my inadequacy. I hasten to add that never did my psychiatrist betray that he shared my attitude. But little things rankled: like the apparent impossibility of communicating by telephone and being confident that a message would be passed on. There is also a sign on the door next to the waiting room which always strikes home whenever I see it. It says words to the effect that this is a staff toilet only – patients must use the toilets downstairs. It represents a kind of apartheid that is particularly distressing to someone who finds himself on the 'wrong' side of the fence.

The conclusions to my first consultation – the confirmation of the diagnosis of depression and the increase in the dose of antidepressant I had been prescribed by the hospital clinic – seemed at the time totally inadequate as an answer to my long-standing ordeal. That is not to criticize my treatment but to comment upon the pathetic predicament of a person who desperately seeks relief and comfort from another person, when the nature of the distress is unamenable to normal social influences. I had the covert expectation that, as a result of this appointment, something would be done immediately to put an end to my torment. As it was, I just had to go back to work: I was advised to continue working and to assume that I was functioning adequately at work until I was told otherwise. These were the first two bitter pills of patienthood that I had to swallow: first, the absence of miracles and, second, the obligation to follow the advice of the doctor whom you have consulted. As well as the disappointment, however, there was also great relief: now at least there was someone (who seemed decent enough) and who was prepared to share the responsibility for my condition.

Fortunately, on this occasion, I began to see a slight but definite improvement within a few weeks. But a facet that I had not appreciated from my professional experience of depression was the interminable duration of the episodes, most of which have lasted of the order of four to six months. It is easy to think, from the other side of the consulting room desk, that once a sign of improvement is observed, the battle is over. From the patient's point of view, much of the struggle remains ahead. Even relatively minor degrees of depression can be quite disabling. One aspect of my depression that persists well into recovery is the diurnal variation in mood. I experience a gradual improvement in the whole syndrome from morning until the evening so that in the morning I can have great difficulty in getting out of bed, be beset with pessimistic thoughts, and generally feel half dead whereas in the evening I can be sociable, jokey, and optimistic. It is extremely difficult to anticipate the morning feeling in the evening and vice versa. This means that in the evening I will punish myself for not having got up until noon and will make firm plans for the next day. In the morning I may be unable to emerge from the bedclothes or to make use of the highly reliable knowledge that in a few hours time I will feel quite different. For several years I have found it impossible to adjust my plans realistically to this variation. Another prominent feature is the global lack of interest in the environment, a state of mind that is, I think, difficult to understand without personal experience. I never appreciated how constantly one is engaged in purposive, motivated activity, which varies all the way from having an interest in historical drama to feeling uncomfortable and wanting to change from walking shoes into slippers. In my experience of depression all of this cognitive–affective content is removed, and as a result one feels as if suspended in a vacuum. There is no means by which to decide what to do. As a consequence, I have found my bank balance to profit enormously by periods of depression – sufficiently at least to finance my hypomanic excesses.

There was a great deal of work to be done in learning to cope with depression, even after having sought professional help. There were, after all, a good many hours of conscious experience to endure between the consumption of one dose of pills and another. That is not to belittle the usefulness of medication or of my treatment in general but to underline the necessity of having to find a way to live through the depression, an obvious but underemphasized aspect of surviving depression. In my own case, I turned down offers of more intensive treatment either by psychotherapy or hospital admission. I attended regularly as an out-patient but continued working, 'keeping a low profile' and leading a mainly solitary life. My contribution at work being nothing more than the bare essentials was tolerated largely without comment by my senior colleagues. I am grateful for their allowing me to work out my own solutions. The fact that I was surrounded by people whose principal professional concern was the understanding and amelioration of psychological disorders was an additional and bizarre twist to the experience. I felt rather like a goldfish in a glass bowl. But actually, although it is unfair to make such generalizations, I felt that their predominant reaction was embarrassment, resulting in avoidance or denial. A few individuals were truly marvellous and without their support I am sure I could not have continued working. Some had experienced depression themselves but all were able to accept my incoherent attempts to explain myself, without becoming over-anxious and without the way they viewed me as a person being affected.

When alone at home my principal goal was to blot out worrying thoughts that would otherwise interfere with my ability to do anything. I became quite good at just 'blanking out' and deliberately thinking nothing. I remember reading three volumes of Somerset Maugham short stories, with virtually no recall (and little comprehension). I also spent many hours attempting to learn how to do crossword puzzles. Both are strange tasks to attempt repeatedly with little actual success but they did succeed in obliterating the thoughts of dread.

My symptoms gradually remitted and my state of mind improved more and more until again I was aware of not being myself. Hypomania represented a virtually exact inverse of my depressed state. Where I was formerly lethargic, slow, withdrawn, and anxious I was now restlessly energetic, bright, sociable, and superbly confident; I slept rarely more than two or three hours per night; I had an enormous appetite and lost weight. Although I felt terrific in company, the feeling of not being able to stop doing things was aversive when alone. Treatment with haloperidol was effective in limiting the symptoms and allowing me some rest but it produced ghastly symptoms in its own right by way of Parkinsonian rigidity and restlessness.

During the next year I experienced another complete cycle of depression followed by hypomania. The appearance of the third depressive episode finally convinced me of the autonomous, biological nature of my illness and that I might be helped by taking lithium carbonate on a long-term basis. It is difficult in retrospect to understand my reluctance to take lithium. It meant that I had a major psychiatric illness with a presumptive organic basis. Even after three years of almost continuous incapacity I was not prepared to face this fact. Nevertheless, after another two years on lithium, I have now to admit that it has transformed my life and that I can think of no other explanation for the change. I have not since suffered any major mood swings and I feel that my normal state of mind is more stable than it was before I even became depressed. The change is very obvious in the marked increase in involvement at work and in spare-time activities. I did notice, however, in the first year that I was free from depression, that I tended to lead a withdrawn and solitary life almost as though I were still depressed. I think this was the legacy of a chronic illness that had resulted in changes in my expectations of myself, in the direction of increased caution. The 'low profile' habit was entrenched and I was unwilling to take risks. I also had to counter the expectations that other people around me had acquired during the illness. Since I had been working mostly throughout this period, this was a considerable obstacle at work, particularly with people who knew me only casually. I was conscious of a need to prove myself as a fully functioning individual in order to be taken seriously again. Having been aware of huge changes in my ideas and opinions during the illness, I am also conscious of a lack of confidence in my own judgement, particularly when it comes to major decisions like changing job, moving house, etc. I am still wary that my opinion might be affected by a transitory mood, I am also afraid of my presumed vulnerability: if I were to make a major change in my life, it might provoke another mood swing.

Throughout the five years since my first psychiatric consultation, I have seen the same consultant psychiatrist at three-, six-, or eight-weekly intervals as appropriate. My interviews have usually been quite brief (I suppose not more than 30 minutes at most) and I have been treated mainly on an organic, biochemical basis, but I am enormously thankful for my psychiatrist's manner of dealing with me which, I consider, made all the difference between my throwing in the towel and being prepared to struggle on. Certainly the value of my sessions with him was much greater than their overt content would suggest. At the risk of being interpreted, I think I can identify real facets of behaviour that account for my gratitude.

A great deal seems to stem from an attitude of respect towards the patient: I always felt that he was interested in what I had to say, took me and my complaints seriously, never being dismissive or telling me how I felt and always modulating his own behaviour to my state of mind. He was definitely an ally but not uncritically so. He tacitly acknowledged the struggle that I was living through and there was no claim of omnipotence for either himself or the pills. Sharing the responsibility for my illness and its implications was very important. He was there to be called on in an emergency (although I think I never did) and he gave me his home telephone number to facilitate this. But he never took advantage of his position of power by taking complete responsibility. Decisions about treatment were always made with reference to my opinion. For example, he accepted my decision not to take lithium, in the first place, without any attempt to pressurize me and without condemning me because I did not agree.

The implication of his respectful attitude seemed to be that I was a person who could be trusted to report truthfully, act sensibly, and make decisions wisely. I'm sure it was the resulting input to my self-esteem which made it possible to continue. I've certainly been conscious of a feeling that I could not let him down, that was supportive rather than threatening. He generally allowed me the room to fight my own battle and did not ply me with prescriptions about what to do, although he would give advice when he was asked.

Another attribute I value greatly is his level-headedness in the way in which he can weigh up the evidence, taking the temperature of my mental state, sensing any change or trend and making considered decisions. I have never known him to make a decision impulsively or to show frustration when my depressed episodes have been resistant to treatment. (How many times have I heard psychiatric colleagues accuse their unresponsive depressed patients of lacking the will to get better or impeding recovery in some other way? And how many times have I been thankful that I was not their patient?) The reactive effect of these assessment sessions was something I had never thought about in my professional role. While I was depressed, the process of, within a few minutes, scanning the state of my life with respect to its various aspects of domestic, social, and leisure activities, clinical and teaching performance, etc., had a devastating effect. Looking at all my failures together was something I never allowed myself to do. Having them mapped out before me left me feeling momentarily on the edge of an abyss. I have since noted a similar effect in some of my own patients.

The whole experience of increasing incapacity, becoming a patient, and receiving treatment has made an enduring impact upon my personality, attitudes, and behaviour. The personal experience of emotional upheaval has altered my sense of distance from other people. I used to have many trivial but inhibiting social worries that have been effectively exploded by the experience in depression of what amounted to the worst of my fears being realized and being survived. I now feel in much more direct contact with people, much less self-concious, and more responsive, I think, to the needs of others. This applies in all sorts of interactions but with regard to my clinical role in particularly, the behaviour of my psychiatrist has supplied a powerful model, aspects of which I now observe in the behaviour of colleagues whom I admire. As a psychologist in the experimental, behaviour therapy school, employing (and believing in) highly directive therapeutic methods, it has been a revelation to have been a patient who wanted help but not direction. I think I have learned a lot about what 'support' actually means and perhaps the conditons under which independent coping may be maximized. I am sure that my professional repertoire has been usefully extended to the advantage of all my future patients.

TWO POSTSCRIPTS

January 1983

After over four years on lithium, I remain convinced that it has had a major effect, in the absence of any obvious, alternative explanation. I have not suffered any major mood swing but I do still experience swings of a smaller scale occurring at roughly the same landmarks in the year: depressed in the autumn and winter; elated in the summer. When I am depressed now it feels like a pale imitation: I still oversleep and overeat, losing all interest and concentration, but my mood is more environmentally responsive and at times I would say labile. The word 'neurotic' has often passed through my mind in description of my behaviour. I am not so slowed up and dysfluent. I can perform quite well in social situations of limited duration. But at the same time I have episodes of feeling acutely desperate to a degree that seems new. In this 'poor relation' depression I have felt, for the only time, strongly suicidal impulses and acute depersonalization. I have seriously considered this new state to be 'worse' than the previous much more dysfunctional one.

As well as taking the peaks out of my mood swings, I also consider that lithium may also act to have the effect of lowering the mean around which the swings occur. In other words, when neither especially high nor low, I think my prevailing mood has shifted towards the more cautious, pessimistic, withdrawn pole. I am not sure whether I ever achieve in my own eyes or those of other people. I continue to see myself as 'sick'.

For the future: I think I am at the end of the road as far as present knowledge of biological intervention is concerned. What can I do to change a situation which I feel is not going to be viable for anything beyond the most immediate time scale? I speculate on the various options: make social changes, e.g. change my job, move house, look for a husband, take up new hobbies, etc; psychotherapy, e.g. explore the origins of my disorder in family and interpersonal relationships; could EST or transactional analysis hold the answers? There do not seem to be any clear indications. Like the pills, it is a case of 'suck it and see'. I continue to speculate, afraid of my vulnerability, lest any change I should make should trigger off another period of violent instability. I feel fairly sure that there are no further answers.

January 1984

1984 sees a brand new set of attitudes. I think that I may even have found an answer.

As a result of my professional interest in cognitive processes, I embarked this year upon learning about Beck's cognitive therapy. I became very impressed by the potential power of these techniques and offered myself for treatment at a time when I was between swings. As a result of almost three months' weekly therapy I was able to identify a family of rigid and powerful perfectionistic assumptions underlying my 'normal' emotional reactions. Subsequent to challenging these assumptions, I feel quite extraordinarily different: much more relaxed, confident, able to act without impedance. I find it hard to believe. And only time will tell. It is, however, interesting that I have come full circle. When I first sought psychiatric help some seven years ago my main complaint was that there was something wrong with my thinking. Perhaps I have learned to take myself seriously?

11   Life doesn't scare me any more

By an Occupational Therapist

INTRODUCTION

'I was dead and am alive again.' This describes how I felt when I emerged recently, safe and happy after a severe depression. For most of my adult life I have recognized that I am prone to depression, usually precipitated by life crisis situations, a bereavement or a change of environment, of which I have had many. Some of the later depressions have had a strong anxiety overlay and have been severe enough for me to require tranquillizers. These quickly relieved my fears that I was losing my sanity but revealed the depression beneath. For many years I had two fears even when well. One was of driving and the other of the necessity of returning to work as an occupational therapist. When the family returned to England after 10 years in Canada, I took a part-time position which necessitated driving to work and apart from the initial period of adjustment suffered no major problems.

My recent depression began about 18 months ago when my husband decided to return to Canada. Prior to his decision, I had sensed that he had really not settled in England. My anxieties over yet another move were so great I even considered divorce as the solution to the problem it posed. The children though seemed happy at the prospect of returning so I suppressed my fears rather than break up the family.

My husband was to precede us to a city in Canada 200 miles north of where we had lived previously. Initially I overcame my fear of the move by acting on the instructions left by my husband. I managed the packing, etc., and I coped well for the first six weeks until I went into high gear. Details such as quotations for removals, flight bookings, and sale of house, car, etc., created feelings of apprehension and anxiety.

By the eighth week after my husband's departure I was feeling that familiar tension across my shoulders and was having difficulties sleeping. I tried long walks and warm drinks before bed, but daily I became more tense and apprehensive. As my GP was unavailable I made an appointment with another doctor, who was very good at pointing out what I had accomplished, and that I had matters in hand. It seemed that I couldn't be convinced of this. That night, even with sleeping tablets and a mild tranquillizer, I tossed and turned all night, mentally packing and arranging my affairs.

Until this time I had been coping quite well at work, but now my feelings of distress were interfering with other areas of my life. At work I became increasingly unable to concentrate and organize myself. In fact I felt I had to leave work two days prior to my termination date, which caused me guilt feelings. At home I tried to pull myself together, but I couldn't accomplish anything or make decisions, and in a panic I phoned my father for help. I was by now experiencing strange feelings and I feared I was going mad. Even though I sought support, I was unable to explain my fears and began to feel that every decision I made was wicked. Despite my attempts to control my feelings it seems that other persons were expressing concern over my mental well-being. One evening, my brother insisted that I give him my husband's telephone number in Canada, in addition to the usual progress report. When he persisted I complied but I insisted that my husband couldn't help. By now I felt that no help was possible and I turned down practical offers of help from family, friends, and colleagues.

Next morning my husband phoned that he would arrive on the first available flight in two days, but I felt he was already too late. I spent the whole afternoon packing and unpacking and trying to list the contents of a single crate, feeling my mental faculties slipping away from me.

Additional depressive symptoms I experienced at that time included feelings of unreality – of somehow being able to stand outside myself. I was in a dream-like state and kept gazing off into space. I was terrified of going outside and perhaps meeting neighbours, of the doorbell or the telephone ringing, because these occurrences necessitated me making an appropriate decision or response.

That night I moved further into that world of unreality. I felt myself spiralling down an endlessly deep shaft which reminded me of a terrifying version of the opening of *Alice in Wonderland*. I plunged downward into madness despite frantic attempts to save myself. I questioned what I could have done differently in the past few days to have prevented this. The following day I felt that all was hopeless and I required external structure and directions from my father. Attempts at cooking seemed to become a travesty of a cooking assessment which only a few days before I had been giving to my patients.

It seems impossible now to realize that the thoughts – delusions – of the next night could have occurred. There again was the spiralling shaft. I felt I was now clearly mad – mad or was it bad? I tried in my imagination to find a tiny box to hide in, but try as I might I couldn't get inside it. I began to review my life, all of which I perceived as 'evil'. Obviously I was a 'Jonas', I questioned. I evaluated the evil effects I had on those with whom I came in contact – and considered that I deserved the crisis bestowed upon me – i.e. the death of the only natural child of our marriage shortly after her birth. I saw in my mind's eye my evil influence radiating out across the world. I remembered the patients whom I had treated during those past two years and especially those who had died. I felt responsible for their deaths and didn't reason that they had all been older than 65 years and many over 80.

I felt so guilty, so wicked. My life was in ruins, not only mine but I had destroyed my family's future. My evil influence would ruin the lives of all. There was no place for me in the world and everyone would manage better if I were dead. I lay in bed willing myself to die. I felt this feat was not impossible because I suffer from hypertension.

At long last morning dawned and I was apparently still alive. My husband was due to arrive later that day but that occurrence seemed remote and unlikely. My father no longer knew how to cope with me. I was retarded in behaviour and response, only eating when coaxed and sleeping little in spite of the sleeping tablets. My verbal responses were very slow and my speech slurred. My father insisted that he phone my doctor. Reluctantly I gave him my GP's name and admitted that I already had an appointment for that morning made weeks previously. I was ambivalent in my feelings towards the visit, at one minute wishing to seek the help of a doctor whom I trusted and then terrified at the prospect. I was uncommunicative with my doctor partly because I had difficulty understanding his questions. He mentioned Dr F, a psychiatrist renowned locally, who might be able to help me. I was becoming increasingly paranoid. During the return drive and even in the comparative safety of the house I believed there were people in the street, invisible to me, who were aware of my wickedness.

That afternoon I greeted my husband coldly, apparently only distantly aware of him. Again that night my sleep was broken and troubled. Terrifying thoughts and fears endlessly filled my mind. Suddenly I was aware of the sun shining. How long had I lain there I mused: days, weeks, or months? I believed it must have been a long time. The room looked neglected and packing cases and materials were strewn about. Possibly the sale of the house had fallen through, I thought.

Much later, a bearded man, whom my husband introduced as Dr F, arrived. After a few questions I was asked to get up and leave with the doctor for the hospital. I did this without even a backward glance at my family. The psychiatrist began his initial assessment on the journey but I wasn't deceived by his pleasantness. I had the delusion that a gossipy tongue was partly to blame for my predicament. I wanted to help rectify this by divulging the least possible amount of information. My husband told me later that this secretive attitude had really baffled the doctors in the hospital. The doctor seemed to be driving recklessly. I wondered if he hoped to kill us both; an impossible feat, as I now believed myself to be doomed to live forever.

FIRST HOSPITALIZATION

Upon entering the hospital I felt I was leaving the old familiar world forever. Staff and visitors might be able to move in and out freely but it would be impossible for me. I hoped it would prove to be a safe refuge. Very little of those first few days makes sense. I heard someone in the corridor telling my husband that he could not visit me because I was to sleep for two days. I was unable to distinguish reality and I tried to rationalize conversations and countless terrifying noises I heard beyond the curtains of the bed.

When I was eventually allowed up I was subject to even more confusion. Ward staff resembled nurses from the hospital where I had worked but they didn't recognize me. I got lost so frequently that I thought the rooms must be somehow changed or moved. I tried following other patients but they kept disappearing from sight. There was no consistency in my reactions and once I even denied knowing my own name. I was now sleeping better but I was very apprehensive about the safety of my clothes. I was very careful, too, of my watch and rings, articles which I believed might preserve my identity. Each morning I discovered at least one item of clothing missing and I would helplessly go through my case to find things to wear. I later found out that one disturbed patient did collect clothing. Fortunately the terror of this phase has been forgotten now, but during a later stage of my illness I relived it all and wrote down much of what I experienced. I had the delusion that each day more of my clothes would disappear until I would be quite naked and when doctors, nurses, and friends came looking for me they would find *nothing*. Thoughts of God and the Devil were constantly with me. The Devil, whom I felt I must be serving, seemed very real. God seemed remote yet I was terrified of being discovered by him. I was still disorientated with respect to time, believing that I was somehow not subject to the same laws of time as others outside the hospital. I thought that I kept reliving each day in some sort of purgatory and each day would be worse than the previous one. This tied in with my fear of losing all my clothes. When they all disappeared it would be the end for me, a longed for and yet feared oblivion. At other times I had the delusion that I was reliving an earlier hospital experience which was without doubt brought about when I heard a baby crying.

TURNING POINT

When a friend, a nursing sister came to visit, I couldn't speak until she told me of a minor accident she had encountered on the journey. I then started apologizing for letting her down and all the other staff. No doubt she thought I was alluding to my precipitous departure from work, but I was referring to all the evil I believed I had brought on her and to the hospital. She told me of all my friends who were praying for my recovery. This visit proved to be the turning point. I checked the date with my friend and realized my family must have moved from our house the previous day. That evening, I allowed a nun, a fellow patient, to take me for a walk in the beautiful, park-like grounds. She was elderly and I helped her down the steps. I was surprised that no one stopped me. The next day I went for several walks with her and that night I couldn't sleep at all. The contents of my mind seemed to go around and around until suddenly my thoughts became lucid and I felt I now 'knew all'. I had to share the realization that I was sane, so I crept quietly down the stairs and found my way unhesitatingly to the nurses' office. The night staff didn't know my family's whereabouts but they said they were glad to see me better. I was given warm milk and Valium and sent back to bed but I was too exhilarated to sleep.

My husband was surprised to receive my phone call next morning. On his last visit I had said that I didn't want to see any of my family ever again. When the doctors returned to work after the long weekend they met with my husband and asked him to postpone his return flight and to book flights for the whole family. I was interviewed by the psychiatrist and a roomful of others and was asked for my reaction regarding discharge. I admitted to some apprehension but was reassured that I would cope and adjust. Two days later I was discharged, having spent only nine days in hospital. The next day we flew to Canada after bidding farewell to my family.

INTERLUDE

In Canada I felt like a convalescent for the first few weeks in that I tired easily and was emotionally labile. I forced myself into activity in the house and garden and took long country walks with my daughter. When I visited my new GP for more antidepressants I told him I believed I had been diagnosed as having suffered from anxiety neurosis, the same diagnosis as given to my mother.

During the remissions I was nearly my normal self, except that I lacked a sense of humour and had no memory of the fears and apprehensions of my previous episode. During one remission I made enquiries about courses I could audit at the university before applying for another job. During the depressions though I felt that a very secluded life seemed the only possible future for me. As the depressions grew more intense I lost all my self-confidence, not even trusting my five senses, my memory, or my judgement. I had no sense of direction either and on necessary shopping trips with my daughter I relied on her to guide me across roads and around stores and to choose suitable clothes for herself. I didn't seem to have an opinion and was unable to help the children with their homework.

I dreaded winter's approach but felt I might somehow escape it. In spite of a beautiful home and a loving family I felt desolate and bereft of feeling towards them. Occasionally I had the illusion that time stood still for a few moments and I had difficulties with appliances, e.g. the washing machine and vacuum cleaner. Because of this and accompanying apprehension and lack of concentration the housework deteriorated, shopping lists were inaccurate, and meals were seldom cooked satisfactorily or on time. My family all tried to bolster my self-confidence and morale but I was disgusted with myself and my inadequacies.

I daydreamed of finding some sort of escape or even death. I considered running away to a strange town, or walking under a car, but no doubt I would fail at this too, I reasoned. A crisis must have been reached on the day when I accompanied my husband to town to do some necessary shopping prior to a weekend visit to friends. Although I should have been excited I was dreading the trip because I was unable to behave naturally. My behaviour must have been more odd than usual that day because my husband insisted upon driving me back home from town.

As so often happened at that time I awakened that night in an acute panic attack. I tried to pray, but if I was as wicked as I believed myself to be, there could be no God to help me. In the morning when the family left for school and work I determined to finish it all. As if in a daze I collected the few Valium, the barbiturates I had hidden away, my husband's whisky and the aspirins. I started to swallow the tablets and there my memory ends.

SECOND HOSPITALIZATION

The next thing I remember is waking in a hospital bed, surrounded by a maze of tubes. I felt disgusted with myself for still being alive. I later learned that only my daughter's quick response when she found me, my husband's skillful resuscitation and the resourcefulness of the ambulance men had saved my life. My husband visited me briefly to say that he and the children would go away for the Thanksgiving weekend as planned. Doctors and nurses came and went. There was the usual medical business. Blood pressure was taken every few hours and lab girls forever wanted blood until both arms had black bruises. To doctors' and nurses' enquiries regarding my health I responded, 'Fine thanks'. 'Did their words have a deeper meaning?' I wondered. No part of me was fine; not my unrecognizable thin body, not my mind and not my spirit. I felt calmer but rather numb now, possibly the effect of the drugs. I was concerned about the result of my attempted suicide and kept wondering how I could defend myself in court. This fear kept returning to haunt me during this hospitalization. I believe that it is an offence, but charges are not brought if the person is under psychiatric care. It was probably for this reason that I agreed to see the psychiatrist. Sometimes I felt that I might be ill, and at others that I was incredibly wicked.

The psychiatrist paid his third visit before I recognized him. I begged to be transferred to a ward under his care, because he was the first person who seemed to be sympathetic and understanding towards me. The nurses were only concerned about my body, blood pressure, and bowels, while the doctors examined my eyes, my swollen face, and a suspected skull fracture. I noticed at the time that my skin didn't register sensation, i.e. the prick of the syringe needle or the cold of the ice packs.

Five days later I was transferred from the medical ward to the small psychiatric ward. This led to my grudging respect and trust of the psychiatrist. The ward was almost self-contained: bedrooms, laundry and kitchen facilities, dining, recreation, and conference rooms for the treatment of 20 male and female patients. The move posed new confusions and anxieties. I wanted so much to conform but I didn't understand the rules and regulations. Once again I kept getting lost. I was ill at ease because I couldn't distinguish some of the patients from the nurses because no one wore uniforms. I think I had less bizarre delusions than during the first hospitalization. However, I still thought I was capable of doing great harm and should be locked away somewhere. At no time during my illness did I mention these thoughts or fears to anyone. Although I thought I couldn't distinguish that which was real from the products of my imagination, I must have been able to do so. Patients on this ward had very busy schedules: group therapy of many types, physiotherapy, and occupational therapy both group and individual. There were recreational activities inside and outside the hospital. Patients were responsible for their own laundry, and for much of the day to day running of the ward.

I particularly hated the first formal interview. There were so many others present and my psychiatrist asked so many questions that I accused him of prying. He patiently explained that I would expect to give a history for a physical illness so he must take one too. I then reluctantly attempted to co-operate until he asked what training I had, and how my mother had died. The previous day a nurse had asked if I would go to occupational therapy and I had of course refused – 'Anywhere but there', I thought. At the next interview I was no more communicative, so my husband was asked to come in. My husband later told me to hold nothing back for the psychiatrist, as he had told him that my mother had been diagnosed as suffering from anxiety neurosis before she had died of an overdose of barbiturates. The doctor now knew too that I was an occupational therapist and of the fiasco of my last job. He was unaware though that my application was still on file at the hospital where I had been admitted and daily I expected someone to confront me with this fact. At every interview my psychiatrist suggested ways in which I could organize myself. I wanted to please both him and my husband but I felt powerless. For two weeks I sat about on the ward showing no initiative and doing nothing constructive towards my cure; my mind either a blank or buzzing with thoughts which generally revolved around madness and badness. I would sit rigid in a chair for hours, my hands gripping the arms, much to the discomfort of the other patients. I was very distressed by my poor eyesight and my inability to tell time, especially in the early part of the day. These disabilities I later discovered were caused by the medications and not by my condition.

My first brief visits home during those early weeks were not successful. Everything had a feeling of unreality and I didn't seem to belong there anymore. My husband visited every day and was incredibly patient but I suspected he must have had some ulterior motive. The only time I was truly glad to see him was after the day when I thought I had sent him away for good. I had the conviction that I was hovering between two worlds, not knowing which was the safer one to choose.

During this time none of the nurses managed to make contact with me, although one after another they tried. One afternoon a French-Canadian nurse tried to comfort me and I began to feel that I could trust her. She then asked me to accompany her and a group of patients when they went out that evening to play basketball. I consented, but later the nurse said I couldn't go because I was still under close supervision so she couldn't both play and watch me. I felt so hurt and humiliated that I later told my husband that she had treated me like a two-year-old. I was very conscious of how far I had regressed and wondered how much further I would go. Each day when I saw my psychiatrist I had to confess that I had achieved nothing. His questions were probably very simple and straightforward but I found them so difficult. I would try to answer yes and no alternatively rather than admit that I didn't understand. My doctor must have decided that I had had ample time to acclimatize to the ward routine but that, as I seemed incapable of self-direction, I needed help to establish a treatment programme. All through my hospitalization, and especially after my doctor found out that I was an occupational therapist, I felt that he expected more of me than I was capable of at that time. At last the occupational therapist came to visit me on the ward to arrange for my first appointment. Now that what I dreaded had happened, I felt relieved. All the medication I had been having must have had some effect because I have in front of me a piece of paper on which I had tried to do some constructive thinking after talking to my doctor the previous day about my future. It reads as follows:

'Possibilities

Return to work via university?

1. Not at present able to concentrate or understand printed matter.
2. Unreliable.'

I think 'unreliable' must have referred to my having had to leave work in both England and Canada. I remember putting my note book away thinking it was all hopeless, but at least these fears were realistic ones.

WORKING TOWARDS MY CURE

On my first individual session in occupational therapy I was encouraged to draw out a geometric design for a hooked cushion top. I had some problems with this because squares often appeared to be distorted. I chose wool to suit the colour scheme at home and although before its completion I changed colours and altered the design several times, I continued on it until it was finished.

I found my occupational therapist much more approachable than the other staff. She seemed to have time for me and to understand how I felt. I think I became a little more open and related to my husband and family better. I was very critical of my craftwork but I enjoyed the feeling of achievement and working on articles that others admired. Another treatment medium used in occupational therapy was tooled leatherwork and my therapist had many talks with me in which she was very encouraging and supportive as regards the present and my future. She gave me practical encouragement too, i.e. taking me over the faculty of rehabilitation to get information concerning courses I wished to audit after discharge.

THE JOURNEY BACK

Having been locked down into a deep and unremitting depression since admission, my upswing into an approximation of normality seemed to happen quite suddenly. I had two successful trial weekends at home before being discharged, having spent five weeks in hospital. It was arranged that I attend as an out-patient for two full days a week. My programme was to include occupational therapy, both group and individual, recreational activities, an encounter group, and calisthenics, a group which I had previously found helpful in relieving my tension and anxiety.

About a week after my discharge my mood swung up into a 'high'. At first I enjoyed the delightful feeling of euphoria but later became scared when I experienced feelings of unreality, coupled with the belief that I was someone very special, which I knew could not be true. I was exhausted by constant compulsive activity, housework, etc., but unable to sleep at night. To obtain relief from my racing thoughts I took to writing them down. I relived past episodes of my life and as I wrote I experienced emotions not experienced during the actual event, i.e. anger and hatred. I re-experienced, too, the delusions and paranoid thoughts of my earlier illness and I felt compelled to commit as much as possible to paper to give to my psychiatrist.

My treatment schedule was now reorganized and I dropped group therapy; probably because I was a disruptive influence. My reactions were very fast and I tended to answer questions before the question had been asked. In occupational therapy I was given clay wedging to relieve my aggression, which I found very amusing. My family now found me almost impossible to deal with because I was assertive, argumentative, and convinced of my infallibility. My drugs were now changed again and in conjunction with others I was to take lithium. I did not realize the significance of this because lithium is new since I worked in psychiatry. I responded quickly to the drug and soon the amount was found to keep me stable and I was discharged as an out-patient before Christmas, seven and a half months since I was first admitted in England.

The refresher courses which I took at the university, kinesiology and psychiatry, and the volunteer work at an auxiliary hospital, were part of my rehabilitation programme and were carefully followed by my psychiatrist and my occupational therapist. Now a year after discharge I feel that I am again leading a useful and fulfilling life. I have held a part-time position for several months now and I am happily re-united with my husband and family.

CONCLUSION

I would like to be able to say that since my recovery I have conquered all my character deficits but unhappily this isn't so. I do, though, now have a much greater understanding of myself and my character flaws. I have a greater self-respect, too, because of the knowledge of what I experienced and survived.

In the past I never worked with the acutely sick in psychiatry because I felt I lacked the necessary strength, but perhaps in the future I will do so. My experience will have given me empathy for these patients. It was my occupational therapist who told me, after my discharge, that I suffered from manic depression. My earlier depressions I had labelled as reactive depressions, so I was surprised that I had suffered from a psychotic illness; perhaps many lack insight into their own condition. This explained, I suppose, why I had relapsed so quickly after my first hospitalization. My occupational therapist told me of a colleague who had suffered the same condition and how she had experienced no prejudice among staff with whom she worked. This knowledge helped me to accept my condition and adjust to it.

Surprisingly enough, I have never for an instant felt bitter about it and I am often filled with an overwhelming joy and thankfulness that I am alive and feel so well. I too have been unaware of prejudice among those who know of my condition, except possibly a coldness I have felt when I have met nurses on the ward where I was treated. Of course I was not warm and friendly towards them when they knew me.

I have a very high regard for my Canadian psychiatrist, not only because he correctly diagnosed and treated my illness, but because he always treated me with thoughtfulness and respect despite my behaviour. My self-confidence and self-respect were completely shattered for a while by the depression and the delusions it engendered. My psychiatrist, and later my occupational therapist, helped me to return to the real world, by having confidence in my abilities and by setting new goals for me to strive for.

Probably the most painful part of my illness was the loss of my faith in God, especially as I had already lost my love and trust for my husband. I felt completely desolate because I believed there was nowhere I could turn to for help and I was unable to voice this fear. After discharge, during the manic phase, my faith in God and my love for my husband returned in a blinding flash. My marriage is now on a firmer footing than before. I am no longer haunted by the fear of yet another depression, which of course I used to try to hide from my husband and family for as long as possible. My husband says I am less straitlaced now and because I am better balanced emotionally I am easier to live with. I will probably always be an anxious person, but I hope this trait is less pronounced now. The illness was a terrible experience, which may well have been harder on my husband than on me. However, now I am no longer subject to devastating mood swings and I feel more in control of my future than I did in the past.

Lydia Scotting

12   A doctor's depression*

By a Doctor Patient

'Where nothing ever pleases,
And everything is vile'.

It is difficult for someone who has never had the experience to imagine what it feels like to suffer from depression. The above misquotation from Bishop Heber's well known hymn will perhaps give some idea.

In this personal account of some 18 years of depressive illness, I will try and give some idea of what it feels like, together with some comments about treatment and its effects, and some effects on work, leisure and family life.

CLASSIFICATION

Depression is usually divided into endogenous – where there is no obvious cause – and exogenous or reactive depression, which follows some precipitating cause, such as bereavement, marital troubles, and so on. This seems a useful classification on the whole. In my case it was endogenous depression, coming on out of the blue, with no precipitating cause at all.

ONSET AND SYMPTOMS

I noticed apathy, insomnia, irritability, and increasing difficulty in getting up in the morning; I had never been a good getter-up at the best of times. Most noticeable of all was a feeling that people I saw about in the street were stupid. I would see some lame old lady walking slowly along and think, 'Why on Earth doesn't she get a move on?' or some young man walking briskly and think, 'What on Earth is the hurry?' In other words, everybody and everything they did was stupid and pointless, as indeed was everything I did myself. There was no point in doing anything, as it wouldn't do any good and nobody would be any the better for it.

---

* Reprinted with permission from *The Practitioner*, **225**, 1692–1693 (1981).

TREATMENT

To begin with, I treated myself with short courses of different antidepressant drugs, which seemed to help for a time. However, I cannot stress too strongly that this is a great mistake. Any doctor with an illness of any severity, particularly a mental illness, should see a colleague, even if it seems strange to adopt the role of patient. This continued for some months in a cyclical pattern, but getting gradually worse. I finally came under professional care after taking an overdose of barbiturates, of which I had plenty in my surgery. I was admitted to a hospital and after recovering from the immediate effects of the drugs, I saw a psychiatrist. He put me on a tricyclic antidepressant, which gives its side effects for some days before any benefit is felt. He also gave me a hypnotic to help me sleep. Apart from some initial drowsiness, the main side effects were a dry mouth, which felt like blotting paper, and difficulty in micturition, amounting at times almost to retention. However, the benefit was considerable: I felt a lift in mood and life was worth living again.

After a while, I saw another psychiatrist, who was a parson as well; he put me on a monoamine oxidase inhibitor, together with a sedative to counteract the stimulant effects. His theme was to use the time when you were feeling better to sort out the underlying problems. However, apart from some marital dysharmony, probably secondary to my depression, I didn't really have any problems. But I was stable on this regime and so continued it for some years. Later I got worse and saw another psychiatrist, who put me on ECT, which was very effective. The effect of pentothal is most pleasing; I can understand anyone getting hooked on that. At this time I had left the practice I had been building up and gone to a partnership in the country. That broke down after only six months and I was doing locums and casualty work; the psychiatrist told me it was important to get some settled employment, so I moved and went into public health – now called community medicine – and have been there ever since.

After this move, I had a rather rough passage, involving in-patient treatment with more ECT. I improved again and actually went seven years without medication, except at night. This was not to last, however; I had to be admitted and start antidepressants again. After a few trials and errors, I found one that suited me – another monamine oxidose inhibitor – and am still stable on it now. There are the inevitable dietary restrictions; liver and cheese are the only ones that affect me, apart from alcohol, which I am allowed in the forms of lager and white wine, which suits me very well. At one stage I felt so tired and exhausted I thought I must have some physical disorder. However, it turned out to be merely the effects of chronic depression and cleared up in a few weeks.

EFFECTS ON WORK

When depression is really severe, work becomes impossible, particularly medical work, as it is so emotionally demanding. After all, depression is a disorder of the emotions, as opposed to the intellect. However, during less severe phases work is still possible, though very tiring. I have to make a conscious effort with each individual seen (there are no patients in community health work) though it is surprising how much the circulating adrenaline can do. It is as though the body realizes that extra demands are about to be made on it and reacts accordingly. I still notice a marked diurnal variation, feeling worst in the morning and improving as the day goes on. When I come home after work and the tension relaxes, I feel so exhausted that no one can believe I have done all I have. This, of course, only applies during 'down' phases; most of the time I can work quite normally.

EFFECTS ON LEISURE

Depression has its effects on hobbies and leisure activities as well as on work. The lack of drive and total feeling of pessimism have their effects here too. My main hobby is choral singing; apart from the mood described above, the voice itself seems to be affected too. Far from being elating, the whole experience is irritating and tiring; I just can't be bothered. The same sort of thing applies to other relaxations, such as photography.

EFFECTS ON FAMILY LIFE

The main person to suffer as a result of my depression was my wife. It must be very difficult to cope with an irritable, weepy husband who won't get up in the morning. She it was who had to bear the brunt of this and at times to deal with the patients as well. Fortunately, I had a very helpful colleague who lived nearby and would see my patients for me when I couldn't deal with them myself. Shortly after my illness started we adopted a baby boy. We had been planning this for a long time and my psychiatrist assured us it was all right to go ahead. He was a source of great pleasure to us both, but during his early years showed signs of mental retardation, associated with hyperactivity. These features have become more marked over the years, as he has grown physically but not mentally. Since leaving his residential ESN school, he has lived at home and attended the local training centre. He gets very stubborn and difficult at times, which makes me very irritable. Most of the time, however, he is as cheerful and affectionate as ever.

DEPRESSION IN DOCTORS

There seems to be a high incidence of depression among doctors and of its most serious complication – suicide. Over 100 years ago Sir James Paget followed up 1000 of his pupils and found that 120 of them developed melancholia, as it was then known. Several studies have shown a high incidence of suicide as a cause of death among doctors; the incidence in one study was one in 50, or about one a month. In a large American study the incidence of suicide was 33 per 100,000 of the population, compared to 11 per 100,000 for the population as a whole. There seems to be little doubt that we are a very inadequately treated group, especially in the field of mental illness. This surely bears out what I said earlier about the importance of consulting a colleague if you are unwell, especially if the symptoms are mental ones. So, if you or a colleague feel ill, for Heaven's sake see that you get proper treatment. It might, quite literally, save a life.

LESSONS TO BE LEARNT

Firstly, like other illnesses, both physical and mental, depression tends to exaggerate one's own characteristics, e.g. the irritable become more irritable, the sleepless become more sleepless, the withdrawn become even more withdrawn. Simiarly, those liable to mood swing tend to have more marked swings of mood and become the manic depressives of this world.

Secondly, the classification of depression into endogenous and reactive, though useful, is by no means absolute. Thus my own depression was of the endogenous type, there being no obvious precipitating factor. However, things that happen to me along life's way, e.g. periods of tiredness or overwork, arguments and upsets at home, worry about relations, do have an adverse effect.

Thirdly, during marked 'down' periods, no amount of talk and logical discussion have any effect at all; life is just as hopeless and pointless whatever anyone says. This is equally true about religious faith, at any rate in my experience. This probably explains attempts, successful or not, at suicide. The effects on other people who love and care for you just do not penetrate the barrier of utter pessimism which envelops the depressive during extreme 'down' periods.

As regards the effect on work, I have no patients now, working as I do in the community health field, so I am unable to use my experience in dealing with other depressives.

13 'Big D'

By a Clinical Psychologist

It started one night with a clear, sudden onset. There had been no prior warning of what was to happen, or would continue to happen over the years. That was how it seemed at the time. But now? I am uncertain: with hindsight and after the experience of training in clinical psychology, perhaps there had been some earlier warning signs. If so, I was unaware of them at the time and if others had noticed they did not comment. Very simply: I went to bed one night and was still awake when it was time to get up the next morning. Except for that one, single event, nothing else was distinguishable about that night. Nothing like that had ever happened before and I can remember feeling only some degree of surprise and dismissing it as 'one of those things'. The following night the same thing happened and by now I was feeling tired and bewildered. The third night I slept and hoped that that was the end of whatever 'it' had been. As the weeks passed, a consistent pattern of disturbed sleep emerged: some nights I could not sleep at all, others I fell asleep only after several hours of wakefulness. In other words, sleep onset became the problem.

Very soon I felt tired most of the time and noticed a disturbing loss of concentration and decreased interest in things. I also started feeling 'down' with periods of crying without apparent cause, which were very bewildering. These latter, affective components of my depression appeared late in the sequence. I now wonder if other people notice a similar chain of events and if so, whether this sequence could account for the fact that many people fail to recognize the onset of depressive episodes. I also wonder about the nature of the relationship between depression and sleep. Even now, lack of sleep can result in my feeling temporarily 'down', even when I am not experiencing depression in a clinical sense. It is also normal for me to experience diurnal variation in mood every day, feeling worse on waking with gradual improvement throughout the day and evening.

In attempting to overcome the insomnia, I used a variety of self-help measures to promote sleep, including milky drinks at night, reading, long walks, warm baths, etc. In general, these methods failed to help. It felt then, and still feels when it happens now, as if a switch sending me to sleep failed to click off, as a light switch might be turned off. At some point during this period, I began to feel more anxious about going to bed and about trying to sleep, which probably counteracted the usefulness of the sleep-inducing measures. By this time, I knew that I could no longer cope alone with whatever was happening to me and I sought help for the symptom which, to me, appeared to have started a sequence of experiences and which, therefore, was the symptom which worried me the most, namely insomnia. I can only recall one question from that initial session with my GP: 'Will you see a psychiatrist?' My main feelings were of shock and bewilderment: a psychiatrist for problems in getting to sleep? I refused and was given sleeping pills instead, but only for a short time and, in retrospect, I think that the doctor knew that I would be back. His insight was greater than mine at this stage.

The first sleeping pill was fantastic. Even now, many years later, I can remember the wonderful feeling the next morning of waking up refreshed, wide awake, and alive in a way that was quite alien to me. Did people usually feel so good? Even though I had not had insomnia before, I had never felt so good, especially in the morning. My experience with the sleeping pills further reinforced my view that lack of sleep was the causal factor for subsequent symptoms and it was the sleeplessness that needed to be treated. Too soon I habituated to the sleeping pills; too soon I ran out and too soon I re-experienced the other symptoms. At a crucial time, I caught 'flu and was under pressure at work. This time I knew that whatever was wrong with me, I could not cope with it and had to have help of whatever sort. I went back to my GP, accompanied by a very caring flat-mate, and again met with the same question: 'Will you see a psychiatrist?'. I was not aware of when the shift in my thinking occurred, from viewing my problem as simple insomnia to depression. I was, however, aware that something seemed to be beyond my control and that, however embarrassed I might be, I had to accept help from outside. In retrospect this feeling of necessity was important and it still remains a crucial criterion by which I decide to seek external help, the feeling of *having* to accept some other person's help because my problem has gone beyond me. As a working clinical psychologist, I think some people are referred for treatment before that point has been reached and, as a consequence, they are unable and/or unwilling to let go and accept help.

Out-patient psychiatric help came quickly from one of the London teaching hospitals and with it came relief, after the 'experience' of being interviewed in the presence of the inevitable group of medical students. I do not recommend this public exposure and I think we are not fully aware of the impact of such interviews on patients undergoing their first encounter with the hospital, even as an out-patient. During this interview I remember feeling sympathy for one medical student whose tentative suggestions were criticized by the consultant in charge. My out-patient treatment consisted of the prescription of tricyclic antidepressants plus weekly psychotherapy with a psychiatric social worker for three years, followed by weekly group therapy for one year. Four long years in all, which even then was only the start of a life-long process of learning to cope and manage the recurrent depression. During these years many things were discussed, tears were shed, and my loneliness, despite my having very caring friends, revealed. It is all too true that a feeling of being lonely can occur in crowded rooms, in the midst of friends, etc; it is quite distinct from being alone. Much of what we discussed is still a private affair, the sessions having something of the quality of a confession: a sanctuary in one room for one hour a week without the danger of meeting the other person in any other setting in one's daily life. After treatment ended and while at university reading for a psychology degree, I was asked by that same social worker what the experience had been like and had it helped. Even now I am uncertain: I needed it and persevered when it would have been more comfortable to give up. All I can say is that I know myself better now, but the process of acquiring this knowledge in therapy is confounded with the effects of other life events. My own training in particular has also given me a more objective view of myself and of depression. The psychotherapy happened concurrently with drug treatment and it is tricyclic antidepressants which then and always seem to me to have given the most immediate relief from depression. In retrospect I can say I am grateful for the opportunity that psychotherapy gave me and if Miss F is reading this: thank you. How much influence I can attribute to her personality and how much to therapeutic methods I shall never know: the theoretical model used still eludes me! I strongly suspect that without the tricyclics, psychotherapy would not have been sufficient but perhaps it was necessary. It also did very little for the original problem of insomnia.

The thought of group therapy was initially frightening and again I refused at the first time of asking but realized that I was avoiding a problem area. If I were to gain as much from treatment as possible, I could not continue to avoid problems. In retrospect, I was glad that the group lasted for as long as one year: many members became my close friends and remained so for years after the group ended. I am no longer in contact with any of them now but I realize that life is made up of a series of phases with perhaps different needs in each. The people around us maybe reflect that. We should not feel sad over loss. The group experience was good at the time and I hope we all satisfied needs for each other. Can we ask for more?

All I have described so far was really just the beginning, the seemingly minor problem which started in my early twenties. Other attacks of depression were to follow over the years, each lasting for a few months and each controlled and treated with tricyclics prescribed by local GPs. I have always considered myself lucky in the knowledge that if all else fails, medication works and that GPs have always allowed me to play a major part in deciding when to start and stop medication and the level of therapeutic dose needed.

Subsequent attacks of depression followed a similar pattern to the first (with periods of increasing difficulty in falling asleep followed by the subjective feelings of depression, loss of concentration, loss of appetite, etc.) although there were some variations: once or twice, my depressed episodes were preceded by a short period (two to three weeks) of intense anxiety for no apparent cause. But control of the anxiety with anxiolytics did not prevent subsequent depression. On each occasion, I seemed to reach a point where all self-help measures failed to prevent the development of a deeper depression. My subjective feeling of having reached 'a point of no return' has always indicated to me the need for another course of antidepressants, although earlier and later in the sequence relief of symptoms has sometimes been possible by other means. It always felt as though something were happening inside my body over which I had no control. Each attack always lasted at least a few months (six to nine months) and the last, one of the most severe, just over a year. If medication was reduced or stopped during these periods, all my symptoms returned in a very short space of time. This suggests to me that the antidepressants served to mask my depression rather than to cure it until remission occurred. My decision to stop antidepressants is determined by the return of their initial side effects, which presumably indicates that the current dosage is now excessive and a reduction is required.

The problem of how to recognize the onset of depressive attacks is still a difficult area for me: at least two attacks were completely unrecognized because the symptoms were milder than previous attacks; another occurred after what seemed a period of elated mood or at least a feeling of well-being. This elation almost immediately followed finals at university and the gaining of my first degree so perhaps it was not totally unexpected under these circumstances. For most attacks the reasons for their occurrence have not been clear to me. It is all too easy to point to one's last recent life events and claim these as the causal factor. In my case, however, these life events, if present, have always been different and several of my depressive attacks have occurred without such 'precipitants'. Perhaps an absence of life events could just as easily be important in triggering a depression as their presence?

My last attack was one of the most severe, lasting over a year, and was unusually preceded by a lengthy period of recognizable symptoms. I suspected that again I was heading for another bout of depression and tried self-help measures in a systematic way thinking that, for once, I could forestall a full attack. I think I made a mistake in varying each seemingly important factor in turn, in a scientific manner. As a result, I ran out of time and reached my point of no return. I had no choice then but to resort to medication, this time for longer and less effectively. Despite their moderate effectiveness, the drugs still enabled me to function again at a reasonable level. For me the point of no return is reached when my answer to the question 'Can I cope with working tomorrow?' is an unequivocal 'No'. Then, I have always sought medication to prevent the necessity of a period off work which would entail a secondary set of problems.

What now? I have recognized that I am someone with a predisposition to depression, that I can have long periods – lasting even several years – free from symptoms, but that I can never comfort myself with the thought that it will never happen again. I am getting better at recognizing the onset of an attack but I am still no further on in predicting which potentially stressful situations precipitate an attack, if stress is indeed a precipitant. I have been wrong many times: many periods of stress have not been followed by depression. I fear further attacks, especially after the severity of the last episode which followed several milder ones, but I try to forget about depression in the meantime. I know they last only a limited period but the interval between attacks is beoming longer and, in general, each attack is milder. But I must admit that the knowledge of the last episode still worries me. My fears about sleeplessness are still present but less intense. I have been greatly helped by my husband influencing me towards an alteration in my thinking about depressive bouts and my worries about the effects of lack of sleep. This change is perhaps what was missing in psychotherapy but has been achieved in my marriage. My husband has always helped greatly in many other ways, not least in his reassurance that variations in daily mood do not necessarily herald a return of 'Big D' (hence the title of this essay). 'Big D' is his label for my state of clinical depression. To be told: 'Don't worry, it's not "Big D" ' is immeasurably reassuring. Unfortunately, such reassurance is not readily available on the NHS at the precise moment it is needed. This, plus Tender Loving Care, go a long way to help me both within and between attacks of depression.

After all these years, I am still left with the question of whether or not my apparently first depressive attack was my first experience of depression or whether I had had it before without full recognition. The first episode I have described was certainly the first time I had clearly failed to cope in an obvious way, needing external help and failing to keep my difficulties to myself. But I can remember from very early childhood being puzzled about myself, sometimes being very withdrawn and shy, not wanting to play with other children, etc., and yet at other times being outward going, cheerful, and happy. I am not aware of having felt depression in the adult sense but mainly of the alteration of these two states and of being rather bewildered by them. With maturity I have a feeling that the withdrawn, shy state came to dominate and influence the majority of my life by adolescence. I can certainly remember in my mid to late teens people telling me to 'cheer up'. I must have looked miserable but did not particularly feel that way. At about this time I started working and remember feeling isolated in the sense that I did not want for myself the sort of styles of life that I observed around me. I wanted more, or something else, but could not specify what it was I did want, only that I did not share the desires of other people. I did not seem to be satisfied by the same things. This feeling of isolation persisted until I went to university as a mature student and indeed found there what I needed and wanted. Only there did I feel satisfied. University did not, however, prevent further attacks of depression. It is obvious to me now that I should have gone to university earlier in my life and that my feelings of being apart and unsatisfied had, partly at least, to do with lack of intellectual stimulation.

In my career as a clinical psychologist, I have seen depressed patients who have also expressed similar feelings of not quite fitting in and yet not really wanting to belong, because they did not hold the same values implicit in the lifestyle of their social groups. At the same time, they had no clear idea of what alternative they did want. Having experienced these feelings myself, I understand how they feel both from a personal point of view and a professional one but I am still unclear as to the relationship between such feelings and depression. If there is a causal relationship, in which direction does it go? All that I can say is that circumstances, feelings, and observations of myself before my first attack of clinical depression suggest there probably was a lengthy period of at least sub-clinical or precursor signs of depression in both my childhood and my adolescence. Whether one calls this condition childhood depression or a precursive state needing other factors to trigger it into clinical depression is unclear. My own uncertainty is consistent with the conclusions of some current writers who still debate whether or not childhood depression exists. My guess is that it does but that is myself as a person who is proposing it and not necessarily myself as a psychologist.

That has been my experience of clinical depression and will, I suspect, continue to be so. The main problems remain those of learning to cope and live with this experience and learning to cope with living 'normally' in between episodes, without being beset by fears of anticipation in between attacks. These fears exist but they are controlled. I refuse to allow myself to dwell on depression when I am not depressed and get reassurance from my husband that normal, daily fluctuations in mood do not herald the return of 'Big D'. Otherwise, talk of and about depression is minimal. In my clinical role, I neither avoid nor seek work with depressed patients. I help those who come my way and manage to do so without feeling threatened or too personally involved myself. The only deliberate avoidance decision I have made in my work as a clinical psychologist is not to do research on depression. Previously I have felt tempted: as a psychologist who has experienced depression I feel I would have a good starting point but I think it would be detrimental to me as a person to work in this area. It would serve to remind me about depression even when I am not depressed and that is something I would find too hard to live with. (Between attacks I try to forget about depression. That is my way of coping with it.) This single constraint is not too severe. I have the rest of the full spectrum of psychological topics to play with. I have never been totally convinced that being a 'sufferer' necessarily makes for a better researcher in that particular field, even if it may help in the clinical role of being a therapist. Writing this essay has re-affirmed my belief that I do not want daily reminders of the clincial state to which I am prone.

So what things were and/or are most helpful in dealing with my depression? Once an attack is established, I think that tricyclic medication is the single most important treatment. I have been prescribed several different ones within that group and all seem to work similarly and give relief. All start producing a therapeutic effect within a few days to two weeks. In the meantime, some of the initial side effects of the drug (especially sleep-inducement and drowsiness) are, in fact, welcome because they partly relieve the symptoms of insomnia and fatigue. The drowsiness puts me into a lovely oblivious state of mind in which I do not notice that the antidepressant effect has yet to work. The other initial side effects: a feeling of falling, dry mouth, blurred vision are less welcome but most of these usually retreat after the first few weeks, leaving only a permanently dry mouth which usually persists throughout the treatment. But I find that when I am very depressed even this is acceptable. As the antidepressive effects increase and the side effects decrease, I am usually left feeling 'normal', as if nothing were wrong: my mood is unremarkable and I do not feel as if I am taking drugs.

If medication is stopped, however, all the original symptoms of depression return. I always know when to reduce or stop medication by a return of the initial side effects of the drug, particularly drowsiness. Medication has always been withdrawn gradually and sometimes a low maintenance dose kept for a while, depending on the initial severity of the depression and the duration. Some studies have shown that low maintenance doses can prevent further occurrences of depression. In my case I cannot be sure that the medication acts to prevent relapse but it makes sense to me to stop taking the drug gradually rather than abruptly. On one occasion I did try, on medical advice, to avoid a depressive episode. I was prescribed medication not when I became depressed but some months before an event which my doctor at university felt might precipitate a depression, namely my finals. The Student Health Centre doctor thought that, given my history, I was quite likely to become depressed as the exams approached. If this were to have happened, treatment would have been inadvisable because the initial side effects of antidepressants would have interfered with revision and performance during the examination. Following this argument, the doctors suggested taking a low maintenance dose of tri-cyclics for a few months before finals. Obviously, I cannot know whether this medication was even needed or not but I did observe that immediately before and during finals, other people reading psychology with me suffered more than I did from sleep disturbance, changes in mood, and impaired concentration.

For me tricyclics have worked well and have offered relatively quick relief when other measures have failed, but I have the impression that their success is partly because I have allowed them to help and persevered with their use. In my dealings with patients, I have met many who have been prescribed tricyclics, used them at most for a few days, then given up. The overwhelming reason has been the initial side effects – for which they are unprepared. This raises the whole area of doctor–patient communication and specifically the need to communicate the reasons why particular drugs are given, their side effects, the long-term effects, how they work, etc. Given a better rationale, I suspect many more patients would comply with prescription instructions and gain long-term benefits. Simple advice as to how to live with the medication, especially during the first few days would, I am sure, be of benefit and prevent cessation of medication because of alarming sensations and the frightening feeling of not knowing what will happen next. For example: I have learnt never to start taking antidepressants until a Friday evening, having stocked up on food beforehand and prepared for a 'lost weekend' during which the main activity is sleep, and not to plan social events for at least two weeks afterwards. That way I avoid the embarrassment of appearing lethargic and drowsy in the presence of others and of attempting to work, shop, etc., while feeling incapacitated. Plan for a 'lost' weekend and by Monday I might just be able to face the work situation again without having to cope with a host of strange new bodily sensations at the same time. How many doctors or psychiatrists explain these practicalities to their patients? Yet without information like this, patients are likely to discontinue medication and run the risk of missing out on the real, long-term benefits these drugs can offer.

Patients also need the opportunity of a choice: how much do they want to be rid of their depression if it means the continuation of some of the side effects? In my case, 'the point of no return' determines my acceptance of drugs with their attendant difficulties; others may decide that even these drawbacks are unacceptable. After the initial impact of adverse drug effects, there may be a few such side effects that persist. These may vary between individuals. Mine are always a dry mouth and an increase in weight with, I suspect, an alteration in body metabolism. The weight increase and accompanying craving for food are the most distressing side effects. I find that if I omit meals, try to cut down on food intake, I experience dizziness, extreme hunger, feeling hot, blurred vision, and irritability. These feelings decrease after discontinuation of medication but can persist for up to six months after that. Cravings for food and weight gain follow a similar time course. I suspect the antidepressants exaggerate my normal bodily state in that normally I need regular meals and experience small-scale versions of these symptoms if a meal is missed or delayed. Although these features have been described, their effects and the subsequent distress to patients should not be underestimated. Again, I have accepted these side effects because I have felt bound to take help from outside.

What about other things that are helpful in coping with my depression? At the point of no return itself, one further factor helps and this is a cognitive one, an *acceptance* of the fact that it has happened again and that for a time, probably a few months, life will be different, medication will be needed, as well as a feeling of giving in. Acceptance is, however, not a negative state but a positive one for me. At that point, I recognize that I need to be kinder to myself in the sense of not attempting to push myself as hard as usual, not taking on too many things for me to cope with, not attempting more than my limited capabilities permit at that period. I do not know how this period seems to people around me. It may appear that I am not doing the things that I usually do and that I am less active in general. In other words: I may present the typical picture of a depressed person. But for me it is a time of protecting myself from more demands than I can cope with. Do others feel the same? An important aspect of this acceptance is that I know the period of withdrawal, although indefinite, is limited. I do not know how long it will go on for *this* time nor how intensely I shall feel depressed, but I do know it will end. This knowledge has arisen from my past personal experience of recurrent depression and was not, could not be available to me during my first episode. I think this knowledge that the experience will have an end is important in helping people during their first episode when they cannot have the knowledge and are frightened of the unknown possibilities. Knowledge that episodes are time-limited might certainly help later in subsequent attacks to offset the often overwhelming disappointment at realizing that yet another episode has started.

Before and during medication, I have found other self-help measures invaluable, not necessarily to stop or prevent the depressive attack but to offer transient relief from its intensity for a while. If things can be helpful even for a limited time during an on-going depression, they are welcome. These may include visiting friends, reading, watching films, etc.: gentle things that are not too demanding but are practicable. Even clinical work itself can be therapeutic. Often during a depressive phase I have felt a lessening in the intensity of my symptoms for a while after a session with a patient. Help can indeed be two-way but I hope that my need for help has not been to the detriment of the patient.

One of the features of depression I find hardest to deal with is the diurnal variations in mood. Again, this is something I experience normally but it is much exaggerated in depression. Mornings are the worst and my mood improves throughout the day to reach a peak at evening. During the evenings I am often lulled into a false sense of security, thinking that the depression is gone, only to be plunged into deep disappointment and despair the following morning. If I can survive until lunch-time on any day (whether depressed or not!), I know I can make it through the day. If there are other ways to manage diurnal variation in mood I have not discovered them yet.

To sum up: I am someone who has had several episodes of clinical depression lasting from six to 12 months but, luckily, I appear to respond readily to tricyclic medication. The interval between attacks is quite long and that means that I can get on with my life the rest of the time without continually being reminded that I still remain someone liable to depression. Between episodes, I am afraid of it and of when the next one will happen, but the intervals are long enough to enable me to push the thought to the back of my mind most of the time. The only daily reminder that I do get is the experience of diurnal variation in mood. However, I cannot be sure that this normal-to-me phenomenon has any connection with the problems that I get during depression. So, in general, I ignore the association and deal with the daily problem by means of self-help measures which in general work and with the cognitive strategy of telling myself that by lunch-time I should start feeling better.

For me, the best thing about depression is that it does not last forever. In my view, the problems are mainly to cope with it at the time and to deal with anticipatory fears of recurrence in between attacks. Learning plays a major role: learning to handle oneself during the depression, irrespective of the theoretical view to which one subscribes to its causation. I think I am getting better at this and although it may not prevent depression, it may make the attacks (or myself) more manageable. From my last episode, however, I have learnt that there is a danger in being too intellectual about it and seeking to outwit the problem.

I hope that in this article I have conveyed an attitude of hope. It is possible to experience recurrent depression and cope most of the time. Its impact on my working life, has, I think, not been very disruptive, and in my clinical work with patients the experience has helped. I do not, however, intend to confuse patients with myself: their problems are unique to them and need individually tailored treatment approaches. I try hard not to fall into the trap of supposing that similarities between us must necessarily mean that whatever helps me will help them and that their reasons for depression are the same as mine. My main message and self-consolation is that, however bad depression is at the time, it does not last forever. What I have done over the years is to learn to recognize and live with it. I hope that some of what I have learnt and discussed here will be of help to others.

14   A kind of termination

By a Retired Consultant Psychiatrist

I am a retired psychiatrist and what follows is a case presentation of myself. Although I have written technical papers, autobiographical experience has been limited to one essay and that was within a professional context. I have little of a direct solution to offer others but perhaps the act of sharing will benefit both them and me. I wish to conceal my identity behind a pseudonym because of consideration for my family: for myself I should be interested in the mystification, obloquy, or empathy which some of my acquaintances might feel.

Saul Bellow's description in *Herzog* is relevant: '. . . how I rose from humble origins to complete disaster'. In both respects it would exaggerate my story but it is certainly more felicitous than my clinical summary of my problem as 'fluctuating anxiety–depression with addictive complications in a vulnerable personality which maintained adequate compensation until middle life'.

THE BACKGROUND

I was born nearly 60 years ago in a terraced house in a city side street. I am the only son but have one sister some years my senior. Family history suggestive of frank psychiatric disorder comprises the admission of a paternal uncle to a mental hospital but I have no clinical details. I think of my father as an intelligent radical. He had, I understand, mood changes (but within a normal range) and he had a variety of then rather esoterical interests, for example Esperanto, caravanning, and dynamic psychology. He left school at the age of 13 but achieved professional status as an accountant. He was dogged by physical ill health and died, when I was 11, from heart failure secondary to asthma. My mother was an affectionate, anxious perfectionist who resumed secretarial work after my father's death. She was phobic in some matters and sadly more so in her later years: she died from cancer when I was almost 28. My sister was employed in the Civil Service but after her marriage took an external degree and started a new career as a schoolteacher.

My own education was mostly at a nearby private school succeeded by grammar school and despite precarious family finances I was able to train in a London hospital. Medical qualification was followed by two hospital jobs, two

133

years' military service, and then entry into psychiatry. After junior appointments, including one in a general teaching hospital, I became a consultant in a large, backward, provincial mental hospital where the efforts of many resulted eventually in a much more humane institution. At the age of 55, when the option could be exercised, I retired and since then I have only undertaken part-time medical – but non-psychiatric – work for about a year.

Sexuality developed painfully, with excitement but self-denigration. An active fantasy life persisted in the background of overt adjustment but has latterly lost much of its vigour. Two relationships of importance preceded a third which resulted in marriage at the age of 28. My wife and I share much but necessarily not all and I regard myself as in some ways the more dependent partner although in others I bear the responsibility. Despite a harsh upbringing she has an equable temperament which has, however, been punctuated by a number of distressing but essentially self-remitting episodes of depression. She has also suffered severe attacks of migraine which are often physically and psychologically disabling. Our three children are academically successful but two had moderate to severe anxiety about school attendance and about physical health. I am comforted by their basically sound inter-relationships – after all, siblings are not *obliged* to like each other! We have always lived within our means and were fortunate in acquiring a pleasant house in the country some years ago.

Religious belief was important in my earlier youth but at about 18 I became agnostic and I continue so although my uncertainty has perhaps become less certain and less acceptable to me.

Many of my personality traits show a familiar bipolar distribution – anxiety proneness yet adequate professional confidence; pessimism yet a capacity for humour; a liability to view people in black or white rather than a realistic grey; a tendency to take the introvert's backward step in some situations but to be moderately adventurous in others; a difficulty in expressing aggression and an uneasiness over attracting others' anger unless an impromptu occasion suddenly releases it; a defensiveness against feeling, for example in failing adequately to mourn my parents' deaths, yet a readiness to be moved by music or literature. I have generally been a striving person, often concerned by fear of failure but capable of real enthusiasm. A frequent and disturbing theme has been the feeling that life is somehow happening elsewhere, producing a frustrating sense of loss. Alcohol lacked importance until my forties but an addictive hazard was demonstrated by the grip which tobacco rapidly acquired when I was 26: this lasted for 13 years and I then seized the opportunity for abstinence offered by an attack of pneumonia.

THE MORBID EXPERIENCE

It all began so long ago I – he – was a cautious, physically timid, quite bright child. He had for a time the weird notion that his mother stood outside his junior school during the whole of each morning session. Fear of bullying lessened with an increase in size and strength and finally disappeared, although scholastic success remained associated with lack of confidence in sports. Obsessive–compulsive symptoms were often a distressing intrusion and were typically linked with gas taps, door locks, and so on.

The first few terms at university commenced with intense nostalgia for home and even strangers who had travelled with him in the train were missed, with a spasm of anxiety, when the journey ended. Subsequently independence became a stimulating and enjoyable experience. His first love affair was a delightful but distracting surprise and may have delayed qualification for a few months, although no examinations were failed. In the Services there was one informal discussion with a psychiatrist, prominence being given to obsessional symptoms but the basic problem being impotent rage with a commanding officer.

Entry into psychiatry was followed within a few months by the development of a duodenal ulcer which did not finally heal until he attained the freedom which consultant status gives. In retrospect it seems extraordinary that no attention was given to the possible psychological implications of this dyspeptic state which could in fact be related to suppressed anger with a senior doctor and to the ease with which many patients, especially the more manipulative, could deposit unreasonable burdens of responsibility on him.

Anxiety over public speaking was considerable but probably within normal limits. Finally, however, his delivery was so impeded by palpitations and difficulty in breathing that all planned occasions were avoided, the threat seeming to lie in the *expectation* of the audience. Impromptu situations, for example in the committee work in which he was quite widely involved, were only mildly disturbing, although once again the isolation of chairmanship could be direly problematic. This problem led to about 20 sessions with a psychotherapist in London (over 150 miles away) but these he discontinued because they were both unpromising and expensive. That this was not the whole story is indicated by his failure to pursue his suspicion that behaviour therapy might be more efficacious than an insight-giving approach.

He arrived in the early 1970s, an established and seemingly respected consultant. He had taken part in upgrading his base hospital, had a busy out-patient department in a general hospital, was a careful clinician, and had enjoyed technical writing, modest research projects, and the triumphs of publication. Whence then his decline?

The beginning of each week and generally of each day had long been tense. In retrospect this anxiety should have been more firmly and acceptingly followed through as an experience, as a discomfort of everyday life, and thus disarmed and deprived of some of its evil capacity to undermine resolution. Instead he fought with it with increasing fear and self-doubt and with the feeling that 'it' – this personalized inner threat – would ultimately triumph. Anxiety about work came from a variety of sources. Realistically it is inseparable from the complexity of some clinical problems and from the ethical recognition that all patients should be justified in expecting a serious and committed approach. Such anxiety was augmented to some extent by the unrealistic assumptions of others and by the spate of official enquiries into other hospitals although nothing of this kind came his way. A deeper anxiety – which partly illuminates the foregoing and to which further reference will be made – concerned the discrepancy between outer adult adjustment and the profound disquiet of the inner child. A similar theme entered into helping with family anxieties – he felt that as a psychiatrist he imperatively *should* have the answers. The merciless recurrence of the need to exert himself became disheartening and the recognition that all challenges in life (ranging from the intricacies of friendship to simple practical requirements in the home) carry the polar possibilities of success or failure, of satisfaction or self-criticism, sometimes led him to feel the happy rebellion of defeat – 'If that is inseparable from all existence then I want none of it!'

After about a year he entered his first long period of sick leave and in the five and a quarter years until his retirement he worked only about half the time. In the employed intervals he was able to cope adequately but he would wish to pay tribute to both his employing authorities and to the immediate consultant colleague who bore responsibility for the extra workload during his absences.

For some time alcohol had become increasingly and insidiously important, although only during non-working hours. Consumption eventually reached the approximate equivalent of three and a half bottles of spirits per week and at a later stage this quantity was doubled. Alcohol relieved distress and was, as Wilfred Trotter so eloquently put it, ' . . . a sinister but effective peacemaker, a means of securing for however short a time some way out of the prisonhouse of reality back to the Golden Age'.

Over much of this time he experienced fear and despair, often difficult to communicate to his advisers when a kind of social gloss could become an obscuring screen. Nor do these words now convey the sense of desolation in which the past pressed for apparently fruitless analysis, the present was destructive by the sheer persistence of inner insecurity and dilapidation, and the future was comfortless and indeed threatening. At intervals his whole interest in life was dreadfully eroded and on other occasions alcohol released outbursts of anger. There were affective remissions, some as brief and sudden as the transitory and mysterious cessation of toothache, and some more prolonged and allowing, as just mentioned, effective return to work. Alcohol consumption sometimes produced a kind of chronic intoxication insulating him from anxiety and gloom but experienced by his family as very isolating. The latter remained concerned and supporting with a desperate stoicism (although he feels sure there was admixed anger over his self-willed behaviour) and the loyalty of his wife was of inestimable value. Maybe he could claim to have contributed in the past to the strength of the relationships. Maybe too the contemporary persistence, between crises, of an obsessional drive to deal promptly with the practical transactions of domestic life was reassuring – thus, it could be felt, the world he inhabited was not *entirely* falling apart.

Tolerance for alcohol was high during much of the time but he recalls two particular occasions of great physical distress, the first commencing with the vomiting of an early morning drink of whisky while the second was consequent on abstinence following admission to hospital. They involved a sense of disolution with restlessness, tremor, nausea, and a pounding heart, and were extraordinarily unpleasant – perhaps especially so as they were self-induced. He was agitated but not confused or hallucinated and the episodes remitted in about two days. At one point liver function tests showed a small but potentially sinister abnormality. This was related to alcohol abuse as possibly also was some enlargement of his heart, while a degree of hypertension at about the same time has since been suggested as due to stress. Follow-up by a physician has continued to confirm that all these abnormal signs have resolved.

Some weeks after retirement he made an impulsive suicide attempt which was both released and rendered ineffectual by alcohol. It involved two savage incisions aimed at femoral and radial arteries and was accompanied by relative insensitivity to pain and a vaguely recalled sense of peace.

He must try to explain why all this started when it did and why it followed the pattern described. Constitutional factors (of genetic origin or acquired from early environmental experience) must be given due place, and could be regarded as laying the foundations for breakdown. Certainly there is the phobic similarity in three generations – him, his mother and his children – and perhaps the most persuasive postulate is inheritance of autonomic over-reactivity together with the effect of unwitting example. Contemporary psychological–physiological influences may be given a role. In the middle of middle-age, striving for the future might become inappropriate when reasonable achievements have been made in professional and domestic fields and where, then, can energy be directed and fresh satisfactions gained?

The stage is thus prepared for decompensation and, for him, the most psychodynamically convincing precipitant is the notion that once he reached the age at which his father died he too began to behave like – and indeed could well have become – a dead man. The discovery of his father's death was certainly traumatic. It began with an anxious discussion between mother and sister at breakfast-time and suspicion strengthened on returning home from school for lunch. He stealthily climbed the stairs, black toe-capped shoes left in the hall, and quietly opened his parents' bedroom door. On the bed was the sheet-covered outline of his father's body, on a window-sill a pot of snowdrops. His first recalled question afterwards was as to whom his mother would now marry – the gap, it would seem, had to be filled somehow. For about three days he joined in the family grief but he then used religious belief to inhibit its further experience. Later on in life he was aware of his ambivalence, feeling that his personal development had somehow been more free in the absence of a father. Maybe this links with the privacy of part of his inner domain – although he can confide much in others an area of reserve remains as perhaps it does in the lonely recesses of all humanity. The bereavement helped to set the pattern of response to future losses and must, he feels, be expected to make a major contribution to his general attitude to death. It also reminds him of Alfred

Torrie's comment that when childhood mourning is not completed a person may be 'haunted throughout his life with a sadness for which he can never find an appropriate explanation'.

THE TREATMENT EXPERIENCE

He had an in-built concern that his problems should become intelligible, and the approach to them potentially under his own control, rather than endogenous and based in the chemistry of his nervous system. Thus he favoured psychotherapy. A reservation in this attitude lay in the apprehension that greater mental flexibility might lead to loss of the obsessional rigidity of purpose which seemed to have been important in past endeavours. Perhaps, too, Hermann Hesse's dramatic words in *Steppenwolf* were relevant: ' . . . a suspicion that he may meet himself face to face; and he is aware of the existence of that mirror in which he has such bitter need to look and from which he shrinks in such deathly fear'.

Apart from the occasion mentioned previously, psychotherapy commenced, under the direction of another therapist, on a private group basis in London. The group met weekly for one and a half hours and over the next two years, with return to work about half way through, he attended 73 times. Space does not permit a full description of the experience but some profitable internal changes occurred, many of which were valuable in a professional context rather than in a trend towards personal recovery. Acceptance by the group – although the depth of general empathy was uncertain – encouraged the basic belief, not merely the intellectual assumption, that we all inhabit one world and this made his inner life one of less harsh contrasts, while a useful discovery was the frequent need to repeat, to rehearse, fresh insights as if their initial impact were sometimes only temporary. Of the time he left the group he has an obscure memory of its general disintegration and there had also seemed to be a change in the therapist's orientation to it.

During group membership there was an initial period of abstinence from alcohol and in retrospect he sees how this drug could blunt the edge of a search for insight by giving easy, if short-lived, symptom relief: in addition, however, a high level of motivation could be the common factor underlying both control of addiction and energetic pursuit of the psychodynamic trail. Contact with the psychotherapist ended with three individual interviews in the early morning (necessitating leaving home at 3.30 a.m.) and the agreement that further treatment, especially of the alcohol problem, should be arranged nearer home. There ensued a little over one and a half years' contact with two general psychiatrists (the change-over being due to the departure of one of them overseas) and this included three short admissions to the private wing of a small general hospital for drying out or for more intensive assessment of his affective state or for both. With these he was able to give full co-operation, slipping with comparative ease into the role of in-patient. It was during this time that he joined Alcoholics Anonymous but he became disenchanted, especially with an aggressively patronizing organizer, and left. Trial with a group of alcoholics run by professionals survived only one meeting when it was clear that psychiatrists were viewed with distaste, but he foolishly did not seek clarification of the insensitivity he encountered. These two events may suggest that he was too ready to be offended, but this particular vulnerability does not of course preclude real offence being given.

The warmth of a social occasion, attended by many friends from considerable distances, was a major factor in his resolution largely to abandon the role of patient. In this he was successful for many months but his retirement from work the following year was preceded by a further few weeks sick-leave. A satisfactory holiday abroad was quickly followed by the impulsive suicide attempt already recorded and this led to emergency admission to a local general hospital. Referral to a general psychiatrist was followed by out-patient attendance and eventually a further essay at psychotherapy was agreed. Altogether 53 sessions were held locally but it is doubtful if much was gained from this experience other than the possibility – and this must not be undervalued – of enhancement of self-discipline by the need to report to a colleague. Some affective improvement occurred and the year of part-time work was commenced, but it remained difficult for him to relate these developments directly to psychotherapy in the absence of any clear causal relationship.

He was throughout fortunate with his medical advisers (with one gross exception where admission was peremptorily suggested without initial assessment), although it is interesting that of the three psychotherapists only one 'scored' positively in all the critical issues of empathy, genuineness, and nonpossessive warmth. He learned the value of emotional responsiveness in others and three particular episodes are quite vividly recalled. One involved a light, encouraging touch on the arm by a psychiatrist, another was the preparedness of a night nurse to sit and talk and listen for a while, and the last was the gentle tearfulness of a young nurse after his suicide attempt. Probably, it is true, these occasions would have been less remarkable if he had been admitted – as was once suggested – to a specialized psychiatric unit where support of the kind implied could have fortified him in a perhaps more frank confrontation of the meaning of his symptoms and behaviour for himself and others.

Various drugs were employed at different times. Tricyclic antidepressants were mostly noteworthy for their side effects with the exception of amitriptyline, in which case a nightly dose of 50 milligrams of Tryptizol has been helpful. Of the monoamine oxidase inihibitor group, tranylcypromine (Parnate) was effective but the only alternative tried may not have been prescribed in adequate dosage and the dietary limitations needed with these compounds can be more tiresome than, as doctors, we may (always) appreciate. With regard to sedative and tranquillizing drugs, chlormethiazole (Heminevrin) holds subjective pride of place: it was initially provided to cover alcohol withdrawal symptoms and at that time he thinks its capacity for inducing dependence was not appreciated. Finally, disulfiram (Antabuse) must be mentioned and certainly proved helpful during periods of abstinence from alcohol in reinforcing the necessary resolution and providing a sense of increased safety in this respect.

Electroconvulsive therapy was not recommended and would probably have been ineffective at best and aggravating, via the effect of memory impairment (in such a personality), at worst. Prefrontal leucotomy was once tentatively mentioned by a general practitioner and certainly some features would favour it: he has felt, however, that his level of distress would not generally justify this procedure and the hazard of reduced control of alcohol indulgence would need careful consideration. In addition he would fear the loss of some subtle aspect of individuality which may make his past referral of other patients for psychosurgery seem hypocritical. Reflection, however, does not alter his conviction that these people were in extreme need of relief and that this relief was very often most impressive.

THE OUTCOME

It would be artificial to distinguish too sharply between personal outcome and implication for my former work. I recall Solzhenitzyn in *Cancer Ward* – 'It's the truest of all tests for a doctor to suffer from the disease he specializes in'. This may be an extreme viewpoint but certainly one can learn professionally from personal adversity. I think I had generally been able to feel with my patients but only discovered in myself how suddenly anxiety can overwhelm one in blinkered panic with all the options closed except that of flight. I encountered the phenomenon of almost gleeful surrender to patterns of evasion but also realized the crucial importance of working through rather than acting out certain problems. Another experience was the relief of tension which self-injury can bring, so that – with retrospective astonishment – I recall my subsequent calm and my failure to recognize the meaning of the episode for my family or for the hospital staff. Personal symptomatology is of course not always interpreted constructively at first – for example the persistence of my phobia about public speaking could sometimes be felt as painful evidence of *professional* unworthiness.

My own experience of psychotherapy led, regrettably late in my career, to some improvement in skill with others, but I feel that the need to *show* empathy in some simple but explicit way should have been more obvious to me in my final years at work. It became clearer to me that my own rights, as well as those of my patients, should be recognized and that this recognition could give them and myself a greater sense of security. It was similarly clear that limits should be set to one's inner demands, giving more internal freedom of decision and challenging such destructive notions as that of therapeutic omnipotence. The need to be kinder towards – more tolerantly aware of – the inner child seemed highly important and indeed became a sort of article of faith which gave me more confidence in interpersonal relationships. Nevertheless, despair in others, the recurrence of some psychotic illnesses, the irremediable nature of some combinations of personality inadequacy and problematic social circumstances, and of course suicide, are felt by the would-be therapist as very, very stressful. The desperation one's own advisers might equally feel can only be accepted with difficulty, which perhaps indicates how readily they can sometimes become invested with unrealistic powers of understanding and resilience. Since my retirement I have often felt that my morale could, and my finances would, have benefited greatly from continuation to work: on the other hand, it is not too fanciful to suspect that some complication of sustained anxiety might have been fatal.

I recall a patient who would reply, when enquiry was made as to his welfare, 'Well, I'm still here'. This seemed possibly evasive, possibly a veiled suicide threat, but it could also be regarded as a statement of simple survival which I have since had occasion to echo. I am still depressed and tense at times and fear of these sometimes seems as important as their actual experience. My consumption of alcohol is above the level currently regarded as physically safe but it does not significantly interfere with my pattern of life. I continue to take Heminevrin (in controlled and carefully recorded dosage) and it could be argued that this and alcohol are factors perpetuating depression. Alternatively the emphasis could be reversed and these drugs could be viewed as reducing distress to a tolerable level so that a moderately acceptable compromise is achieved. Nevertheless, their continued symptomatic use can only be regarded as unsatisfactory and the assumption that they must in some ways distort the validity of experience is disturbing. I generally feel little faith in my ability to cope with fresh crises, but I was relieved to find that I could give my wife reliable support when she recently underwent hysterectomy.

Retirement was partly connected with an obsessional desire for completeness, for the safe conclusion of that part of my life. Well, despite intellectual preparedness, it left a gap, a gloomy supposition that my time as an effective combatant in the clinical field had permanently ended. Medicine has been a dominating interest in my life and I have never regretted it as a career. Nor do I regret spending 28 years in psychiatry, although I think it is an extremely difficult speciality and there were two occasions when the physical technology and, by comparison, impersonal nature of anaesthesiology strongly beckoned me. Further exploration of part-time possibilities would still be highly anxiety provoking but I admire and sometimes envy those who work in medically deprived countries where, whatever their motivation, the benefits for their patients can be enormous.

Unfortunately comparative medical isolation has extended into the social sphere and there my own intolerance is a factor. As previously suggested, this does not preclude the contribution of difficulties by others but I do not think it reasonable, behind the cloak of concealed identity, to expand on this theme now. A further personal factor is the role of patienthood, a role which has its self-indulgent advantages but which is very damaging to morale. I have of course been frank with some of my friends (and needless to say with my medical adviser) but I do not know how far rumour may have spread so that there is an area of obscurity in some of my social relationships. An unattractive face of

neuroticism is its egocentricity, but I do not think this has been a significant
obstacle, at least outside my long-suffering family. I am more inclined to
suspect – and I do not think this paranoid – that psychiatric illness, especially
perhaps in a psychiatrist, makes one something of a renegade: certainly, and
with a certain justice, it marks one off from those who – maybe despite
considerable intra-psychic distortions – continue overtly to adjust with
reasonable adequacy. At the same time I am glad to recognize that many
relationships prove on renewal to have a refreshing warmth.

I think a lot about the past and tie in much of my future with that, in its
various aspects, of my children, although I try not to manoeuvre them towards
the vicarious satisfaction of my own ambitions. In this context I am aware that
my variable ambivalence towards them reflects, among more general factors,
the mixture of subterranean feelings in me towards my own father because of
his 'desertion' through death. Despite my maturity in years, my professional
activities in the past, and my personal experience of psychotherapy, I have not
really come to terms with the polarities of love and hate. Nor I suspect has
mankind in general, but how many, one wonders, have in fact recognized this
inner dilemma and how far is insight an immediate blessing or a curse?
Nevertheless, it is true if trite that only in enhanced understanding of human
destructive potential – ranging from the personal to the global – can any hope
for the future lie. Questions of 'Why'? rather than 'How'?, or purpose rather
than mechanism, have sometimes seemed more pressing and I have wondered
how far my remaining problem was more philosophical than clinical, although
too clear a distinction would for me be fruitless. Discussion of some of the
issues in this story with my local vicar was helpful to some extent, especially
because of his benign pragmatism. Of course I think of death, but the frequent
difficulty in keeping it in focus indicates that I have so far failed to approach
acceptable terms with it.

My mood is labile and it is difficult to make a clear statement of the present
situation. The personal experience of breakdown can severely damage confidence – often perhaps, as in my case, misplaced confidence – in one's
psychological integrity, and it would seem unrealistic not to fear deterioration.
When more optimistic I can see positive prospects in my changed role and find
new – or rather reinforce old – foundations for a sense of identity. Thus before
retirement *I* was a psychiatrist: now *I* am the husband of my wife, the father of
three children, the friend of my friends and of two dogs, a person interested in
reading, writing, music, and so on. At such times I recognize the good fortune
which has so far attended my physical health and I feel able to give more
prominence to my relationships with others and to my various interests. When
pessimistic, however, memories can be an important source of reassurance
(and sometimes of course of regret, recrimination, or self-recrimination).
But perhaps my prolonged emotional convulsion *is* to be followed by an
opportunity for re-orientation and not entirely by paralysis on the cliff-face of
anxiety. Or perhaps the possibility of comparative equanimity is related to
instinctual fires burning lower and inspiring a less determined search for

further truth about my life and times. I feel more often hopeful than when I wrote the first draft of this chapter and the *active* acceptance of life seems precariously a little nearer.

Phoenix

POSTSCRIPT (1983)

The modest note of optimism in part of the last section was unjustified and could be misleading to others. I have since had various affective and addictive crises, one of which was associated with an impulsive overdose of drugs and consequent admission to a general hospital. I recognize that I have sought and found a life of variable sedation and I have confirmed a limitation of my commitment to change – although I travelled with hope to my therapeutic encounters, my degree of resolution was inadequate. I have also recognized that, whatever vicarious satisfactions there may be, one still needs an inner personal basis (to which one's occupational role may well contribute significantly) for a sense of identity and purpose, and this I now lack and seem largely unable to regain. It can be difficult – for some of us it may be impossible – to escape the harsher confines of our temperaments. But I would urge those who suffer from problems similar to mine to make early and sincere, strenuous and realistic, efforts towards improved adjustment. And needless to say I wish them well.

Wounded Healers
Edited by V. Rippere and R. Williams
© 1985 John Wiley & Sons Ltd.

Section V Depression in retrospect

The three accounts comprising this section portray experiences of depression that contrast sharply with those which were depicted in the previous one. Our three authors, all male, had relatively brief, self-limited episodes of depression in early adult life but since then have not been troubled by recurrences. Accordingly, they are able to look back with a certain distance on these earlier sufferings from the vantage point of their years of professional work in nursing, psychotherapy, and general practice, respectively.

Despite the relative brevity of their depression, the authors of the two more elaborated accounts, 'Thro' a glass darkly' and 'Looking back' (Chapters 15 and 16) strike themes which we have encountered in other chapters, in particular the disappointing nature of much routine treatment for depression, the stigma attached to those who have received it, the frequent lack of understanding which mental health workers may show depressed people, and the usefulness of experiential knowledge of depression for would-be therapists. Both authors comment on the way their episode of depression improved their understanding of patients they subsequently encountered professionally.

In the course of their reflection, both authors refer to the related notions of 'snapping out of it' and 'pulling oneself together', which require a brief comment. These two injunctions both appear to be based on an elderly faculty psychology in which 'will' is a principal component of the 'psyche'. They appear to be part of the contemporary popular folklore of depression, in particular part of a socially shared stock of 'things to say to a depressed person', a conditioned reflex-like response to learning that someone is feeling depressed. Underlying these stereotypical exhortations is the supposition that a depressed person can, and should, upon verbal command, eject himself promptly from his depressed state by a sheer act of will. Comments by the author of 'Thro' a glass darkly' suggest that this lay belief system may survive more or less unscathed through professional training in psychiatric nursing, despite the acquisition of a parallel professional frame of reference regarding depression. In the case of our author, at least, the lay belief system seems to have been internalized to the extent of being brought to bear upon his own depressed state. He notes that his expectation was that he would 'snap out of it'. Having found the hard way that this expectation was not borne out by his experience, he revised his view of the injunction and resolved to expunge it from his repertoire. In a similar vein, the author of 'Looking back' noted that when he was on the receiving end of advice to 'pull himself together', he felt that it was simplistic and that people who gave it revealed their lack of understanding of what was happening to him. This experience led him to reject such expedient approaches to 'advice' in his subsequent professional work.

These different people's similar experiences suggest that the facile faculty psychology concept of depression as a conative disorder is both widely held and generally unhelpful. We know very little of it, its origins, distribution, variants of the advice derived from it, and how this body of lay belief is organized. Nor do we know how this popular belief system coexists and/or interacts with the organized knowledge which mental health workers acquire in the course of their professional socialization, with or without benefit of a depressive experience along the way.

A start to answering these sorts of questions is to be found in earlier research on the development and change of popular mental illness stereotypes (Nunnally, 1961). But what seems to be needed is less a description of the affective dimensions of popular semantics of mental illness – interesting and relevant though this may be – than a codification of the substantive content of implicit and probably poorly articulated beliefs in society concerning the nature of depression and the related conventions of exhortations to depressed people. The work of Rippere (1977a,b, 1980a,b,c, 1981a,b) on the Western social stock of knowledge concerning depression comes closer to what is needed, but the emphasis in this work has been upon classically-derived advice to follow when feeling depressed rather than on 'things to say to depressed people'. It may be that there will turn out to be two (or more) bodies of popular knowledge about depression, each deriving from different historical origins and each leading to widely differing conclusions about 'the thing to do'. If so, it would improve our understanding of the experience of depression in general and in mental health workers in particular to discover more about the way in which their experiential learning interacts with lay – and professional – belief systems.

The author of the third account (Chapter 17), a retired GP, at the time of writing in his late eighties, has, by contrast, little to say about other people's reactions to his two early episodes of depression. His friends, he reports, did not seem to notice his distress. In this respect, his experience is certainly not unique, for we have heard from other of our authors that little apparent notice was taken of the state they were in. Neither does he mention having received any treatment for the first episode. The second, he reports, cleared up spontaneously when he developed diphtheria. Both these experiences of spontaneous recovery appear to be unusual amongst our authors' experiences. Both probably reflect historical differences as much as if not more than uniquely personal ones. In the early years of this century, depression was not the household word it has become today and diphtheria, like fever hospitals, was a relatively common phenomenon, which, fortunately, it no longer is.

The difference between our retired GP's experience and those of the other authors, whose depressions have occurred more recently, draws attention to the importance of a factor which we have hitherto not had occasion to mention, namely the particular historical and cultural milieu in which affective disorders take place. Until we came to this chapter, all the authors whose affective episodes were described, experienced them in the 'modern' era of conceptualization and treatment: the contemporary social and historical milieu was a constant in all these accounts and for this reason receded into the background of what writers in the tradition of the sociology of knowledge term the 'reality-taken-for-granted' (Schutz, 1972). The contrast between the reality-taken-for-granted in our retired GP's brief account and the other chapters brings home the fact that at any given time contemporary conventions of shared belief, both professional and lay, concerning health and illness generally, and individual illnesses in particular, and the collection of accepted practices associated with these illnesses, must exert profound effects on the quality and meaning of an individual's experience of illness. As Herzlich (1973) has noted, the meanings of health and illness for the members of our society

> 'emerge partly through individual experience and partly from the views current in society which reflect its values. To be ill or well could appear at first sight to be essentially an individual rather than a shared experience. And yet this kind of uncommunicability involves some relation to others; a person is ill or well not only in himself, but also for society and as a function of society' (Herzlich, 1973, p. 1).

Thus we would expect to find that the social and medical arrangements for dealing with a particular kind of illness, in this case depression, contributed substantially, if perhaps subtly, to determining the nature of the sufferer's experience.

Three obvious differences between the contemporary and the early 20th century *Zeitgeist* concerning depression spring obviously to mind. First is that contemporary treatment for affective disorders is much more specific than it was in the first few decades of the century. Then, as Laqueur (1962) has noted:

> '. . . most hospital care for the sufferer from psychosis and disabling psychoneurosis was strictly custodial. Shelter, food, clothing, and moderately kind supervision contributed the major part of the treatment; barbiturates, chloral hydrate, hyoscine and hydrotherapy were used as adjuvants in cases of dangerous and excited states' (Laqueur, 1962, p. 157).

Nowadays antidepressants, lithium, antipsychotic drugs, minor tranquillizers, and electroconvulsive therapy (not to mention behavioural and cognitive treatment) are more specifically applied to affective disorders. The availability of relatively specific treatments must surely shape the experience of those who undergo them. Second, in the early years of the century, psychiatry had only just begun to assimilate Kraepelin's new concept of manic-depressive psychosis, first introduced in 1899 (Zilboorg, 1941). Today the concept of bipolar affective disorder (and unipolar affective disorder) is commonplace and specific diagnoses lead to the application of specific treatments. Contemporary psychiatric nosology must in its own way contribute to the quality of depressive experience. And finally, many facilities for treatment of depression that are commonplace today were not available in our retired GP's early days: neither voluntary treatment nor psychiatric out-patient clinics were provided for in Britain until the *Mental Treatment Act 1930* (Jones, 1960). Imagine what it would be like to be depressed today if the only treatment available were on a compulsory, in-patient basis. Voluntary treatment and out-patient facilities undoubtedly have a major effect on the experience of depression in the 1980s.

Without our retired GP's account, we would not be led to imagine the absence of the many features of contemporary conceptualization and treatment for depression which we so readily take for granted and the historical relativity of depressive experience would have remained unnoticed. By the same token as secular trends affect depressive experience generally, so they must also willy nilly do the same for the depressive experience of mental health workers.

15 Thro' a glass darkly

By a Psychiatric Nurse

Families and friends know a great deal more about caring for the depressed individual than any health professional. That's the conclusion I came to when, for a short while only, I suffered from depression.

Anyone who has experienced this illness (and it *is* an illness) will know what I mean when I say others have no idea how devastating it really is. Everyone suffers from some form of 'depression' at one time or another, but to endure this lingering state for weeks or months on end is totally indescribable. Minutes literally drag by and one feels totally apathetic.

As a recently qualified psychiatric nurse, I had some knowledge of the present theories and trends in the psychopathology and management of this illness. I regularly came into contact with many individuals (patients, friends, and colleagues) suffering from some form of depression. However, in retrospect, I realize that I was totally oblivious to and ignorant of what these people, deep down, were actually experiencing. I remember during my general nurse training one of the tutors demonstrating how to insert a nasogastric tube. She stated that in her view nurses should have a smiliar tube passed on themselves, so that they would have some idea of the discomfort they were inflicting on their patients. At the time I thought she was just an 'old timer' intent on seeing the young nurses suffer, as she herself had probably done in her younger days. Yet, much later, it dawned upon me that maybe she did have something there.

My own experience of this illness occurred when I had returned to this country after a short spell of working abroad. I was convinced that it was a reactive depression precipitated by returning to a strange yet familiar environment. Yet even with my own insight, I didn't feel able to cope with the problem, I felt I couldn't be bothered to talk to anyone. I just wanted to be left alone. I just wanted to stay in my room uninterrupted. The first few days were hell, but I thought I would 'snap out of it'. It's so easy for people (and especially the so-called caring professions) to say this; I know I have done so frequently. But for the person concerned, actually to *do* as he is told is virtually impossible. I know I will never resort to repeating those words again.

To get out of bed at midday was an ordeal. I felt that I had nothing to look forward to, no interest in anything – in short, I felt totally apathetic. I couldn't even be bothered to talk to my girlfriend or father, the two people who were closest to me. I just wanted to be left alone. I had no interests at all. I wouldn't listen to the radio or stereo, or watch TV, never mind go out. I never even felt the desire to drink beer! I think it was because of this that both my girlfriend and father realized that something was wrong with me. I would just lie on my bed, staring at the ceiling, or walk aimlessly in the garden. Often I would burst into tears for no apparent reason. Both my girlfriend and father would spend hours trying to communicate with me and encouraging me to socialize.

Eventually, for their sake, I decided to visit my GP. Although I have the greatest respect for my doctor, in the context of my illness he was as much use to me as the milkman. I realize he is a busy man, but although he tried to appear attentive I suspected he felt that I was a neurotic nurse just wasting his time. He stated perfunctorily that I was just a bit 'run down' and would soon get over it. He prescribed me a tonic and told me to 'take things easy'. The tonic was useless. I did not want any form of medication because I have never felt the desire or need to take medication in any form. I suspect that what I really wanted was a sympathetic ear – and a push in some direction, any direction, just something to get me motivated. The sheer frustration of the illness was that I knew deep down I was severely depressed but could not do anything about it. My frustration and boredom turned to anger and despair. If people spoke to me I would rebuke them severely for no reason at all. As far as work was concerned, I should have taken a new post in nursing on my return to England, but I couldn't even be bothered to turn up. I think what I really wanted was help and moral support.

My sleep patterns were totally changed. I would lie awake at night with feelings of despair and unworthiness. My appetite diminished, and accompanying the anorexia was weight loss. Attention to personal hygiene diminished, as did my patience with others. I was generally bad-tempered, ill-mannered, and cantankerous, with my girlfriend unfortunately taking most of the brunt. Despite all this, my girlfriend, much to her credit, would come to see me daily and try to motivate me to start back at work, to socialize again, and in general to take more pride in myself. I feel sure that it was because of her positive and understanding manner that I regained my former self. My father, by helping me to help myself, also played an important role in assisting me to regain my normal lifestyle.

My depressed state continued for about one month. It took me about a week to come to terms with trying to resume my pre-depressive state. I started to socialize more and to frequent various places of interest. My girlfriend encouraged me to watch TV comedy programmes and to read short stories. We started to go to the cinema and night clubs. I gradually resumed writing letters to friends both at home and abroad. By doing these things, I forced myself to become more motivated. I applied for a new job not too far removed from home and much to my surprise I was successful in obtaining the new position. Whilst relearning my lapsed skills, I was continually discussing my problem with both my father and my girlfriend. Other friends who were also aware of my depression were very helpful in motivating me.

Retrospectively I feel I have learned a lot in experiencing and coping with some degree of mental illness. If I had this illness before becoming a psychiatric nurse, I would have had a totally different attitude towards my patients. I would have appreciated better that these people need a great deal of understanding and patience. When I was depressed I felt that I was neither of use nor ornament to anyone. Although I never felt suicidal, I often thought about it and I can now understand severely depressed individuals carrying out a suicide attempt. I appreciate that it is difficult for many to conceive that a mentally ill person is experiencing pain, yet, having experienced some of this pain myself, I know that it can be very real to the individual concerned. I find it harder than I would otherwise have done to believe the dismissive views sometimes aired in psychiatric settings, i.e. that patients are depressed because they are 'feeling sorry for themselves' or because they are 'just seeking attention'. But I also am fed up with hearing time and again that 'no one cared'; many people *do* care, but it is often difficult for them to know what to do for the best. And they are helpless to help someone who will not help himself.

My experience has also helped to make me aware of the extent to which nurses and doctors often fail to understand the ordeal of a person suffering from mental illness. They often do not seem to appreciate how difficult it is for the sufferer to explain what is wrong, or that it takes not only trust but also courage as well. I have found that people in general seem to have only a vague understanding of what is wrong and this seems to be even less if the sufferer is a man. No one really expects men to become depressed. With women it is somewhat more socially acceptable, but in general it remains true that mental illness has never really achieved the same acceptance as physical illness. People also expect a depressed nurse or doctor (especially if they are men) somehow to recover of their own accord; they seem to assume that people with some knowledge of the disease should somehow know how to extricate themselves from it unaided. This may work for some, but I found that it was other people that made the difference for me. With their help, I recovered quickly and did not require psychiatric treatment, which I feel is fortunate.

Even in this day and age it is somewhat frowned upon for nurses to suffer from mental illness. Everyone knows of instances where this disapproval has meant that a nurse is refused a job because of having a medical history of mental illness. This stigma creates an additional difficulty for nurses, who, because of the widespread expectation that they can somehow do without help, find it difficult to cope with their illness. Moreover, as I have suggested earlier, there is much ignorance of the condition within the profession. Many of my colleagues who are trained nurses have virtually no knowledge of mental illness nor of how to deal with people suffering from it. They often seem to have no idea of how to approach a depressed individual or how to talk to him or her and they often react to such a person by ignoring the problem or by dismissing it with some vague comment. Yet whilst working in a psychiatric setting I found, much to my surprise, that it was not uncommon for some of my colleagues to be themselves attending psychiatric out-patient clinics. Most often their attendance was surrounded by a great deal of secrecy. The need for secrecy makes it more difficult for depressed professionals to use their own experience of suffering in their work with others. The nursing curriculum is also sadly lacking in attention to the general problems associated with mental illness. The problem of the depressed nurse is never mentioned. My own experience suggests that much unnecessary suffering might be avoided if both problems could be brought out in the open. Meanwhile, family and friends can do much to alleviate suffering that trained professionals would prefer not to know about.

16   *Looking back*

By a Psychotherapist

My first reaction to the city where I had come to escape from my problem was a despairing loneliness that crept over me as I stepped outside the station and was greeted by the roar of traffic making its way along a dual carriageway. In the taxi which took me to my digs I realized that I was on my own for the first time in my life and it was not a feeling that I liked.

Looking back it was fairly predictable that I would experience problems on leaving home to go to a university. During my years at school I had suffered from a series of psychosomatic illnesses, the most debilitating of which had been the headaches that prevented me from studying for my 'A' levels except in a very sporadic manner. During that period various drugs were prescribed for me and I was seen by a psychiatrist, but none of this seemed to help.

By this time I had become involved in a Christian young people's group and following a conversion experience the headaches disappeared and I was able to study intensively for a few weeks before taking my exams. Inevitably my performance was not very good, though, and I decided to spend a year at the local college of further education.

Generally this was an enjoyable year, but during the second term my feelings for one of the girls I was with at college became more and more of a problem. I realized fairly early on that she did not feel the same way about me and only wanted a close friendship. It was equally evident that I could not carry on this kind of relationship and that I needed to break off contact at least for a while. Going away to university provided the way of doing this and before leaving I told her how I felt and she agreed not to write to me during the first term.

Consequently I left my home town very much with a desire to escape from the situation I was in and with little thought about what life would be like in the place to which I had committed myself. I naively imagined that I could become immersed in academic work and forget about the rest of life.

After a few days in the city to which I had gone it was clear that I had to take one of two paths – to go home or to seek some help with the way I was feeling. Over the first weekend my panic and anxiety had risen to the point where I had no hope of being able to concentrate on lectures or study. Something within me found the option of giving up and going home unacceptable so I went and talked to one of the doctors at the Student Health Service about the depression, anxiety, and loneliness that I felt. In particular my fears centred on not being able to sleep and that this would lead to tiredness which would result in failure at my course.

Antidepressants were prescribed for me and helped by numbing my feelings and making me sleepy at night. As time passed, though, I was concerned because gradually the dosage I was taking had been increasing, and it seemed that an ever greater quantity of drugs was going to be needed to produce the same effect. Somehow I managed to struggle through to the next summer and was able to pass the exams at the end of the first year. A move from digs into a hall of residence had helped bringing me into contact with more people. Also I was pleased that my feelings towards the girl at home had changed and this was no longer a serious problem.

That summer I thought that I had every reason to feel optimistic about the future and this was reinforced by the fact that I started going out with a girl during the vacation and there was a good chance that the relationship would last. It was therefore with some confidence that I returned in October to begin my second academic year.

However, what happened was rather different from what I expected. Instead of feeling more secure, I felt less, and I was particularly afraid that I would lose my girlfriend and that this would add one more to a list of relationships with girls where I had ended up being hurt. By the third week of term I had deteriorated to the point where I would go out and wander aimlessly in a daze and had thoughts of taking flight and of suicide.

On telling my GP of the way things were going I was told that he felt the situation could not be allowed to carry on, and he asked me whether I would be willing to go and stay at a place where students who were finding things difficult could go to rest for a few days. I too realized that something had to be done, and the idea of a short break away from the university campus seemed to make sense, so I consented. It was left for me to work out from the appearance of the building, the uniforms, and a chat with the other people there, that the place to which I had come for my 'rest' was in fact a psychiatric hospital, where I was now an in-patient. The idea that I would be there for a few days also proved to be less than accurate as it was over seven weeks until I was discharged.

During my first days there I was angry that I had been tricked into becoming a psychiatric patient, and wanted to run away. I then entered a period when the hospital represented security for me, and I did not want anything to do with the outside world. Part of this was not wanting to face anyone I had known before; in particular I could not tell my parents what had happened and a friend 'phoned them at my request. Also I discouraged people from visiting me, and I am not sure to this day whether they understood how I was feeling or took it personally as a rejection by me.

Amongst my fellow patients I found much acceptance, companionship, and humour, and they greatly contributed towards my recovery. If I received from the other patients more than I expected, I received from my psychiatrist less. I thought that I would be given time and help in looking at the reasons for the way I was feeling, but our meetings were short and I was never quite sure when they would happen. My biggest fear concerning the hospital was that I would be given ECT, which I saw as an unspoken threat hanging over me if I did not 'get well'.

Towards the end of the last week of term I was discharged from hospital and survived a few days in hall before going home for Christmas. Returning four weeks later I was reduced to a state of desperate depression within a few days and decided that the only sensible course was to give up the university and return home. There then followed several months of uncertainty about my future.

Many people assumed that the reason for my depression was that the academic work had been too much for me. I found this lack of understanding difficult to take as in fact this had never been a major problem. Other attitudes were equally difficult to cope with, especially the 'don't call us – we'll call you' that followed job applications about which I then heard nothing further. I was grateful for the clerical post I eventually obtained and the attitudes of the people at the firm towards me were a great encouragement.

During this time I also tried to find some help other than drugs which might be of benefit. My girlfriend's work as a nurse in London brought me into contact with a doctor who was willing to offer some counselling to me. The sessions went well whilst I was sharing my feelings of inadequacy, and this encouraged me to venture talking about some of my grievances against other people. He responded by telling me firmly that I was in the wrong, and took what I felt to be a very unsympathetic approach. I was hurt that someone whom I had come to expect would understand had treated me in this way, and angry that I had allowed myself to reach a position where I was so vulnerable.

Following this a local minister felt that he and his church should pray that I would be healed, and I went along with this. After the service I stopped taking my tablets and was bitterly disapppointed over the next few days as nothing seemed to have changed, and I was forced to resume taking drugs through not being able to sleep. However, I felt that this did mark the beginning of a period of change for the better.

This meant that by the early summer I had recovered enough to be finding my job boring and to be thinking positively about taking up again the place at university that had been kept open for me. Although I did not feel that things would go any differently than before, it seemed to me that I had little to lose by trying. Over the next year or so life was far from easy and I frequently reached points where I wondered whether I would be able to complete my course. Slowly, though, I began to be able to enjoy life again, and to tolerate pressures without undue anxiety.

In going over these events of a decade or so ago I have been surprised at how difficult it has been to get in touch with the feelings I went through. Undoubtedly it would be painful to enter again into many aspects of what life was like then, but I do not feel that this entirely accounts for my difficulty. The contrast between what life is like now and what it was then is so great that this also contributes towards a feeling of remoteness about that time.

During most of the period I was depressed life seemed hopeless and futile. Whilst I never again felt seriously suicidal following my admission to hospital, most of the time I was very tired and weary and felt that it would be a great relief if life came to an end. I frequently sought escape in sleep and would stay in bed until mid-day as often as possible. At times panic and anxiety would come upon me powerfully for no apparent reason, often resulting in irrational fears as the feelings attached themselves to whatever circumstances I was in at the time. Also I found myself in an insoluble dilemma in my relationships with family and friends. Part of me very much needed people, but another part wanted to avoid them, and this produced a painful conflict.

Despite the intensity of my feelings, and my preoccupation with them, I found it hard to share them with anyone. Much I was able to tell to my girlfriend, but I hesitated at confiding my more desperate and despairing states of mind for fear that she would not be able to cope, and would end up breaking off the relationship. I volunteered very little to my parents and they asked few questions. Any comments produced a strong defensive reaction in me which surprised me by its intensity. I could not make much sense of my relationship with them at that time. The impression I had from my mother was that I ought to be able to do more to change my state of mind and that I was being bad, or at least lazy and rebellious, by remaining as I was.

At that time I had little understanding of why it had all happened. Obviously leaving home had triggered it off – and yet something inside convinced me that the only way I would sort out the problems was to be away from home. It was only as years passed by that I could see clearly some of the reasons for my depression. I came to see how the picture of the world that had been presented to me in childhood was of a threatening and dangerous place where I needed to be always on my guard. This defensive posture was reinforced by a congenital foot condition which prevented my full involvement in PE and games at primary school.

On leaving primary school another pressure came on me as I was faced with the contrast between a very middle-class grammar school and my own working-class family. This forced me into a choice between these two very different ways of looking at life. Choosing the latter ensured academic success but cut me off from the world of my parents. I no longer identified with their goals in life and they could not understand the subjects I spent all my time studying.

The help that was offered to me whilst I was depressed often proved as much of a problem as a benefit. Antidepressants, tranquillizers and sedatives of various kinds were prescribed for me over a period of about three years, and at times were valuable in keeping the symptoms within some bounds. However, this was gained at a price. I was fortunate enough to experience no severe side effects, but drowsiness and a dry mouth were unpleasant and inconvenient, and the dizziness produced by one drug in particular was distressing.

More seriously, I developed a dependence on drugs which made it difficult for me to be weaned off them once they were no longer necessary. I suspect that this dependence was more than psychological, especially in the case of the Mogadon tablets which I found the most difficult to give up. A reduction in dosage of these brought about several nights of semi-sleep with vivid, and sometimes disturbing, dreams.

My thoughts surrounding hospitalization were similarly mixed. Whilst the deception involved in my being admitted was, I feel, inexcusable, at the time I needed a place of refuge where I could feel secure, and the hospital certainly provided that. A serious drawback was the label I was left with and that was certainly a great handicap in the months following. Even now I am concerned that people's conceptions of me could be changed in situations, such as job applications, where it is likely to emerge.

Within the hospital system I found much that disappointed me. The occupational therapy staff seemed to operate on the principle that 'the Devil makes work for idle hands' and the coercive tactics they employed earned them the name of 'the Gestapo' amongst the patients. One of the most irritating aspects of life there was the lack of privacy. I used to read to one of the older patients and it was impossible to find anywhere quiet enough for this. We finally discovered what we thought was a suitable room, only to be told that we could not use it because there were gas taps in it. It would be wrong, though, to paint a totally negative picture as there were many kind people there – it was often the structure in which they were working which was the problem.

During the course of my depression I saw a number of psychiatrists, none of whom helped me in the way that I had hoped and expected. Whilst I was at school I had read Freud and Jung and, whilst I realized that very few psychiatrists were ardent disciples of either, I did expect to be offered some psychotherapy where I would have the opportunity to talk through my problems. Consequently the short appointments and the failure to explore my difficulties in depth puzzled me. Except when I was in hospital the appointments were rarely more frequent than every six weeks, a length of time that seemed an eternity when I could not see how I was going to get through the next few days.

In the light of this it is not surprising, perhaps, that I jumped at the offer of counselling help I received in London. The effects of that experience, which I have already described, were exaggerated by the fact I had invested so much hope in it. After I broke off that arrangement I had no substitute except a resolution to try to work things out by myself because this was safer than asking others for help. Within my church people were generally accepting and supportive, but I felt were rather at a loss in relating the Christian faith to the experience I was going through. Throughout the time I was depressed I felt God's presence in a more direct way than I have done since, and this was a great comfort, especially at times when I thought I could not go on.

The immediate lessons I learned from being depressed were hard ones. I realized that a person could feel much more depressed and anxious than I ever imagined and yet still manage to carry on some kind of superficial functioning. Somehow I imagined that someone or other would step in or that life would stop long before such a point of suffering was reached.

Also I came to see that those who seemed to be in a position to help me, or who offered some kind of assistance, were not necessarily going to help in a way that I saw as relevant. Much worse, they could not be relied on not to let me down.

These experiences have all had their effect on the way I approach my work as a psychotherapist and marital therapist. I feel that it helps me to empathize with those who come to me for help. Even having been through similar feelings does not completely prevent the tendency to devalue others' suffering, and I continually need to remind myself what it is like to feel that way. I try to get from the person as clear an idea as possible of the help he or she thinks would be best. As far as possible I try to go along with what they want, in so far as it seems a reasonable approach and is within my area of expertise. Also I try hard not to let people down, although inevitably sometimes people feel that I have.

The fact that my situation did change so much for the better, and that I have been able to achieve what at one point seemed totally beyond me, gives me great hope and optimism that the same can be true for other people. Whilst I was depressed I was unsure whether I would ever feel much better, and certainly dismissed the possibility of any academic success. I was half resigned to life going on in a similar vein indefinitely. To hope for more seemed to be hoping for too much, and would open myself to the possibility of a disappointment that I might not be able to take. Discovery that life could be different, and that my horizons need not be as limited by my past as I had come to accept, was an exciting one and something that I enjoy helping people I see to discover for themselves. I have also learned that offering quick 'solutions' to problems also relates more to the need of the person offering, who feels something must be done, rather than the situation of the person with problems. When I was given these kinds of answers I just felt that people were not understanding what was happening to me, or else they would not have such a simplistic view of things and be giving such inappropriate advice. The answers that I was given were that I should give up university because academic work was too much for me, or that I should have a determined effort to pull myself together and not be ruled by my feelings.

What I really needed was someone who I could feel was on my side in trying to sort out my problems; someone who did not need to prove his or her own competence by coming up with a neat solution, or hide behind a professional role that cut me off from the person; someone who did not have to put my parents' viewpoint or that of society or have to protect someone else's interests. Such a person could, I feel, have given me the security within which to look at why I had become depressed, and I am sure that I would have come out of it a lot sooner as a result. This has obviously had its effect on the way I approach trying to help others, and the kind of relationship in the therapy which I try to offer.

One of the ways in which the depression clouded my perception of reality was that it tended to make me see all the problems I experienced as being internal ones. This persisted for a long while after I stopped being depressed.

By this I mean that I usually felt that any difficulties I experienced were a result of my own weakness and that if I overcame my 'neurotic' traits such problems would disappear.

Over the last few years it has been something of a shock to realize that this hope of a problem-free life is a fantasy – that life is inevitably often a stressful experience, producing anxieties and disappointments alongside pleasures and joys. This realization has enabled me to dismantle my fantasies of the 'easy life' and to challenge similar utopian views which I often find in people whom I have for therapy.

In many ways I am conscious that what I went through whilst I was depressed has had a profound effect on the course of my life. Not only has it had a great effect on the way I approach people with problems, but it has been a major factor in my ending up doing this kind of work. In the light of this it is surprising, perhaps, that I do not think often about that period of my life in a specific way, and certainly it does not seem relevant to share it with the people who come to me with their problems. Sometimes, though, I am very tempted when someone says something like 'It's alright for you – you've never had this sort of problem' or 'You can't understand because it has never happened to you'!

Whilst in some ways I have lost contact with the feelings I had whilst depressed I can only think that this is a healthy sign, especially for the people I am trying to help. A preoccupation with my past problems would cloud my perception of other people's, and make me less, rather than more, able to be of use to them. It was not at all easy when I found myself confronted with someone going through similar problems as I had at a similar point in life.

Although there is much to be learned on the journey of life, the relevant point is where we are now. To try to distil the past and extract some essence which meets the need of the present is an exercise doomed to failure. The main relevance of the past is that it has brought us to where we are now and made us what we are now.

Wounded Healers
Edited by V. Rippere and R. Williams
© 1985 John Wiley & Sons Ltd.

17   Depression 1919

By a Retired General Practitioner

I can remember two bouts of depression when I was in my late twenties. The first was in 1919 shortly before I qualified in medicine and the second a year later when I failed to get a house job at my teaching hospital. Both attacks came on rather quickly but I was not aware of the recovery – I only noticed they were gone. I did not consult anyone about them and was perfectly well physically. I remember that there seemed to be a background of gloom about me. There seemed to be no joy in anything. But this was not noticed by my friends. An almost exact description of my symptoms is to be found in *Hamlet* (Act II, Scene 2, 300):

> 'I have of late, but wherefore I know not, lost all my mirth . . . and indeed it goes so heavily with my disposition that . . . this most excellent canopy the air, look you . . . this majestical roof fretted with golden fire . . . appears . . . to me . . . a foul and pestilent congregation of vapours.'

Intellectually Hamlet knew that the sky is a most excellent canopy, but emotionally it seems a foul and pestilent congregation of vapours.

The next year, 1921, I felt the same thing coming on again. I was working at a fever hospital at the time and I caught diphtheria. The symptoms of depression vanished. I wondered at the time whether this was because diphtheria is a danger to life.

During that illness I read the whole of Shakespeare and I have been an addict to his works ever since. They have been a lifelong solace to me.

Depression is not a new disease. As we have seen, Shakespeare described it very accurately 400 years ago. Before that it occurred in the monasteries and was called accidie – a feeling of utter failure, of utter futility and despair. It is found in the Psalms (notably Psalm 38 and Psalm 77, vv. 6–8), which takes us back more than 2000 years.

I have thought a lot about the causes of depression. There is no doubt that some people are more susceptible than others. I have classified the causes under four headings:

1. Increase of self-awareness, possibly due to education.
2. Absence of danger: after the Irish troubles re-started in 1969, it was noticed (as reported in the *British Medical Journal*) that psychoneurotic illnesses diminished in Belfast.

161

3. Modern luxuries: spring beds, electric blankets, central heating, and mod cons generally.

4. Suppression of tears, turning acute grief into a chronic 'aching of the soul' In Old Testament times people were not ashamed to weep aloud in public. My daughter, who spent a few weeks studying the Amer-Indians in Surinam, described how the tribe spent the whole night wailing after the death of one of their children. It is probably necessary to give physical expression to grief.

I myself was suddenly seized with a paroxysm of sobbing and weeping in 1916, when I was 23. My two best friends had been killed in the Somme battle and I had been slightly wounded and was in hospital at Rouen, suffering chiefly from fatigue and exhaustion. Luckily I was alone at the time and that was more than 60 years ago, so I can confess it without shame. Another officer told me that the same thing had happened to him, and even Wellington, the Iron Duke, is reported to have shed tears after the Battle of Waterloo. I did not suffer from depression at that time.

Wounded Healers
Edited by V. Rippere and R. Williams
© 1985 John Wiley & Sons Ltd.

Section VI Depression – no way out?

Earlier we emphasized the possibility that some depressions, if used constructively, may lead sufferers to make beneficial improvements in their way of living. The two chapters in this final section of the book present the opposite face of depression, which is also the mental disorder with the highest rate of suicide (Stengel, 1964).

Some of our other authors briefly describe unsuccessful suicide attempts or mention suicidal feelings which they refrained from acting upon. The authors of these two chapters, a senior nursing tutor ('There won't be a next time') and a general practitioner ('From the brink') consider suicide more extensively. The author of 'There won't be a next time' (Chapter 18) anticipates suicide as 'a proper and desirable way out' of a subsequent episode of depression. The author of 'From the brink' (Chapter 19) notes that she is 'not at all grateful for having been rescued from attempts in the past'. In their deliberations, both writers seem to be speaking from behind an impenetrable barrier. The tone of their words seems to confirm Alvarez's (1974) observation: 'Once a man decides to take his own life, he enters a shut-off, impregnable, but wholly convincing world where every detail fits and each incident reinforces his decision' (Alvarez, 1974, p. 144). This state of isolation from the everyday frame of reference in which 'the very thought of suicide is abhorrent' (as the author of 'From the brink' puts it) it would appear to represent an intensification of the characteristic cut-offness of depression as formulated by Dorothy Rowe (1978). She notes that:

> 'the person who experiences depression has in his language structure a group of propositions each of which concerns a way in which he seperates himself from other people . . . . Depression is that experience which accompanies the selection from the set of possible states of a person's language structure that particular state or system of propositions whereby the person sees himself as being cut off from and as choosing to be cut off from interaction with others . . . ' (Rowe, 1978, p. 30).

Each of our authors refers to this sort of cut-offness in the context of discussing her suicidal wishes and these references require our attention.

The ability to contemplate suicide without flinching appears to be a criterion which irrevocably divides people. The author of 'There won't be a next time' notes that her isolation was intensified by other people's responses to her suicidal ideas: 'I did not expect anyone to help me to achieve my wish to be dead, but I found that the way many people laughed about it or tried to change the subject or avoid it altogether merely confirmed my general feeling of isolation'. Her experience of becoming more isolated as a by-product of her suicidal state contrasts with that of the author of 'From the brink', whose isolation appears to be desired as instrumental to achieving her goal. She closes her essay with the chilling statement:

> 'I am fortunate now in having the means and the opportunity to kill myself without fear of failure should the need once more arise. My strongest wish is that if the present depression deepens, then it will progress too rapidly to allow anyone to detain me compulsorily before I have time to reach the point at which suicide becomes mandatory.'

In both cases the separation of the suicidal person from non-suicidal others seems to depend in large measure upon the difference in their respective evaluations of suicide as something desirable and desired on the one hand and something abhorrent, to be either denied or prevented, on the other hand. The 'closed world with its own irresistible logic' (Alvarez, 1974, p. 143) of the intending suicide excludes those who hold the latter view. The writer of 'From the brink' succeeded in getting her wish; shortly after completing her account, she took her own life.

Shocking as the suicide of a young doctor may be, it is not a statistically uncommon event. A leading article on 'Suicide among doctors' in the *British Medical Journal* 20 years ago observed that 'this month and every month a doctor in Great Britain, on the average, will kill himself'. The article noted, further, that the suicide rate in male doctors is two and a quarter times higher than in all males and one and a half times that for males in social class I (BMJ, 1964, p. 789). Roughly comparable figures have been reported by Rose and Rosow (1973) for California in the years 1959–61. Based on death certificates for the entire state, their findings showed suicide rates of 74 per 100 000 per year for male health care workers (doctors, nurses, dentists, pharmacists, but not psychologists) as compared to 32 per 100 000 per year for other professional and technical males. For females, the absolute rates were lower, but the differential between health care workers (33 per 100 000 per year) and other professionals (19 per 100 000 per year) was maintained. Other investigators (Craig and Pitts, 1968; Steppacher and Mausner, 1974; Pitts *et al.* 1979) have reported excessive suicide rates in American women doctors. British data for suicide rates in female doctors do not come readily to hand – the latest government statistics do not give a breakdown of the figures by sex (Office of Population Censuses and Surveys, 1978) – but they are unlikely to be negligible. It is a commonplace in this literature that one factor which contributes heavily to the high rate of suicide in doctors and allied professionals is their ready access to potentially lethal drugs, coupled with their expert knowledge of pharmacology (BMJ. 1964; a'Brook, Hailstone, and McLauchlan, 1967; Murray, 1974, 1977; Franklin, 1977; Office of Population Censuses and Surveys, 1978). There is no reason to suppose that access to dangerous drugs and knowledge about how to use them to destroy oneself are less salient for female than for male doctors.

Behind the statistics are people in great mental pain and distress. Both of our authors highlight the extreme suffering they experienced when contemplating suicide. '. . . given the cumulative difficulties as I perceived them at the time', notes the author of 'There won't be a next time', 'it would have been better to be dead'. The author of 'From the brink' stressed mental pain rather than insurmountable difficulties:

> ' . . . I cannot see why one should not have the right to end a life of intolerable mental pain. Promises that the pain will vanish, one's suicidal wishes evaporate, and the rest of one's life be perfect euphoria, are irrelevant. It would still not be enough to compensate for the agony of the present.'

This quality of intolerable mental anguish which may occur in depression (though it does not invariably do so) seems to be poorly represented in textbook descriptions and in standard self-rating instruments used to 'measure' it. This pain goes beyond feeling 'sad' or even 'miserable'. It may be that there are no words in the language to describe it adequately. It is our impression that such pain must be experienced to be understood and that this experience can make the suicide of some depressed people perfectly intelligible. No doubt there are many other reasons for killing oneself when one is depressed, but as far as this mental anguish is concerned, killing oneself is the only sure way to put a stop to it and to be absolutely certain that it never happens again. Under conditions of recurrent episodes of intolerable mental agony with no prospect in sight of being able to abort further episodes or mitigate their severity, suicide could readily be seen as 'a proper and desirable way out'.

18   There won't be a next time

By a Senior Nursing Tutor

My intention is to write about my experiences of being treated during my depressive illness, now at least two years in the past, but this cannot be separated from the experience of the illness itself, so I should like to start with a few random comments on this. I have nursed patients suffering from all types of depressive illness. I have, I think, genuinely listened and have talked to many patients. I have written about depression and talked to student nurses about it. Yet, it is frightening to me even now to have to admit it – I did not recognize my own depressive illness. I did not have any insight into what was happening while I slipped into depression, nor did I recognize any of the florid symptoms I had at the depth of it as being those of a depressive illness. Even now I don't know when it first started, but I do know very well when it began to come to an end. All the words I had heard from so many patients to describe the end applied to me – 'coming out of a dark tunnel', 'seeing a glimpse of light', 'feeling a weight being lifted off my head and shoulders', 'coming out of fog' . . . I could try to find more poetic or descriptive language but it is no use. Coming out of depression is something one must experience to understand. It is difficult to describe to others, even to remind myself at this stage what it was like to enjoy music again for the first time, realizing only in retrospect that for years I had gone through the motions of enjoying music without the sensuous pleasure of the real thing. The ecstasy of the beauty of spring in the Scottish landscape is another landmark in my recovery which it is difficult to convey to others.

It is the positive experience of *not* being depressed which make me believe that I had been depressed for much longer than other people are willing to acknowledge. In 1975 I sustained a complicated compound fracture of the leg which in spite of repeated heroic interventions by orthopaedic surgeons refused to heal for the best part of two years and has left me with permanent slight disability.

I know all about the importance of significant life events in the aetiology of depression, but I can not accept other people's explanation of my depression in terms of my orthopaedic history. I found it helpful to have sympathy for my accident, but infuriating to be told time and time again that I had ample reason to be depressed. Perhaps there are patients who find it more acceptable to be depressed because of a physical ailment. For me this kind of attempted reassurance merely confirmed me in my view that people had a total lack of understanding of how much worse it was to be depressed than to have a broken leg. I found it devastating to be forced to have a physical reason for the way I felt and a belittling of my very real and overwhelming personal and emotional problems. I think I tried to explain this on a few occasions but very soon learned to give up trying. The resulting distancing from many people who, until then, had been good and valued friends, is one effect of illness which has not been remedied since. I now know which ones among the people who thought they understood me never got anywhere close to hearing me, never for a moment felt prepared to shift from their stance, never considered anything other than their own preconceived explanations, never doubted the appropriateness of their attempts to solve my problems. I now know that I could never confide in these people even problems of less importance and I am the poorer for having lost friends and companions.

I don't blame any of my friends for not understanding about my depression – I did not do so myself, as I have already indicated. It could not have been much fun for any of them to keep visiting in spite of my bad mood, incessant tearfulness, and long string of complaints about what in normal times would have been trivialities but what at that time were deadly serious difficulties.

What kinds of difficulties did I find to complain of or cry about? Well, of course, the incompetence of the orthopaedic staff, grossly exaggerated I am sure, but the one bit of reality others were willing to grasp at. What went with this was my firm conviction, not only that I would never get any better, but also that life was not worth living. It seemed quite obvious to me that I ought to have committed suicide, but I was too incompetent, indolent, and helpless to do it.

My preoccupation with ending life was very pressing for a long time and has certainly not left me entirely. At the moment life is good, but given the cumulative difficulties as I perceived them at the time, it would have been better to be dead. Should a similar combination of circumstances ever occur again, I hope to be better prepared than I was the last time to take my life. I am certain that there is nothing psychotic about wanting to commit suicide – it is the delusional beliefs which lead to the wish to commit suicide which were of a psychotic nature in my case. I did not expect anyone to help me to achieve my wish to be dead, but I found that the way many people laughed about it or tried to change the subject or avoid it altogether merely confirmed my general feeling of isolation.

It is frightening to realize how difficult it was to distinguish between real and delusional causes for despondency and despair. Any tactless or even faintly critical remark about my work was instantly picked upon as proof of my incompetence and uselessness. The fact that a student's dissertation was rejected by the examiners seemed proof that I was no good as a supervisor; the invitation to a colleague to join a committee was proof that I could not possibly have any contribution to make. I could go on for a long time listing all the areas of my activities in which I suddenly seemed to have lost competence, but then quite a bit of my loss of confidence was brought about by the real deterioration in my abilities and competence. At my age, a realistic reappraisal of strength and weakness was justifiably called for. How could I, or for that matter anyone else, help me to do this? How in the future will I be able to recognize when to withdraw from activities which make demands beyond my abilities? The answer of course is not to try this reappraisal while in the depth of depression – but how can one recognize that state of affairs?

Two people stand out in my memory as having helped me in this, both nurses but neither a psychiatric nurse. It is no fault of the first of these, a colleague and very good friend, that her efforts did not have any success. She was the first person to realize that I was in no position to make any decision. She simply took charge and insisted that I went to see my GP. Unfortunately he was away and his assistant, believing with so many others that my chief problem was orthopaedic, gave me sympathy and a tranquillizer. A couple of weeks later my then boss took matters into her own hands and phoned the Professor of Psychiatry. She felt guilty and apologetic about her action, but within hours I was admitted to hospital. The relief I experienced the moment that responsibility for decision making was taken over by someone else is now impossible to convey. It was made very clear to me that any objections would be overridden but I had no intention of objecting. Of my four or five weeks in-patient stay, I have only good things to say, though many details have now slipped into oblivion. The X Hospital has a nursing home. It was there that I was given a comfortable, spacious, single room and provided with peace and quiet, allowed to refuse visitors, given the opportunity to talk and to weep. I was, of course, appropriately medicated. There are three aspects of my in-patient period which I would like to discuss briefly.

First, the fact that I was given a private room. I don't really approve of special treatment for people who are either rich or important, but the fact probably is that hospitals try to give such people the best they can offer. I would never have believed that it was best for patients suffering from depression to be given a private room and allowed to stay there. My belief was, until I was the patient, that it was better to be in public places with the opportunity and indeed the expectation of being sociable. Yet for me privacy and solitude were what I desperately needed and fully appreciated. If this is the best environment in which to treat the influential, then should we not re-examine the more usual approach to treatment?

The second comment I wish to make concerns the skilled way in which the nursing staff managed to combine observation with respect for my and other patients' privacy. Breakfast was served in people's own rooms, lunch and supper as one wished, in one's own room or in the dining room. It was made clear that coffee and tea were available downstairs – a very diplomatic way of enticing people out of their rooms. If a patient did not appear for coffee, nurses would bring it along, having a perfect excuse for checking up on everybody's actions and mental states. In spite of my general lack of interest or responsiveness at the time, I could not help admiring the way in which the nurses succeeded in getting me to sit in the garden, to go out on accompanied walks, to play an occasional game of Scrabble, even to help one or two of the other patients. The psychiatrist seemed concerned that I might get bored and that I might find it difficult to be cared for by staff who had known me professionally. Neither fear seemed in the least grounded. Boredom was ruled out, partly by my preoccupation with morbid thoughts, but also by the opportunity I was given either to read or work if I was able to talk to the staff and patients. Any problems of possible embarrassment about being in the hospital were prevented by the respect and tact which every member of staff showed, not only to me, but to all the patients at all times.

My third point is one which I have frequently discussed with my students and to which I have not found an answer. Many depressed patients want to be left alone. Should nurses respect their wish or should they attempt, against the patient's wishes, to establish communication and relationships? I can only say that I think I needed both. To be allowed to escape from company at that particular point in my life was precious indeed, but so was the knowledge that I was not really alone. I felt safe in a place where the nurses knew what I was doing, where people seemed to care about my safety, and where someone could always be found for a quiet chat or just for sitting beside. I did not feel any need to discuss my past life with anyone. The psychiatrist seemed satisfied with a brief history. Whether I would have benefitted if either he or any of the nurses had got me to look more closely at my personality shortcomings, I don't know. Talking about current problems was compulsive on my part but, since most of these problems were at least partly delusional, such discussion was non-productive. I did not seek or find scintillating intellectual conversation. But I appreciated small talk and social conversation which was natural, unforced, never condescending, and which never seemed critical or derogatory. I know the nurses reported to each other what had been said, because often one nurse picked up a conversation where another one had left off. Conversation appeared spontaneous. Whether it was actually planned and purposive from the nurses' point of view, I don't know. The nurses were instantly alert to any hint of suicidal thought and without fail the psychiatrist was informed. Neither the nurses nor the psychiatrist ever avoided the subject, but no one made this particular manifestation of my illness seem any more important than the others.

I left the hospital improved but not well, when the psychiatrist left. With antidepressants prescribed by the GP, I coped until I was readmitted to the orthopaedic ward for a bone graft. From then on things went from bad to worse. The surgeon, the anaesthetist and the nursing staff knew of my depression, they knew I had stopped taking antidepressants specifically before the operation, yet no one was able to cope with even the mildest show of moodiness or irritability on my part. After a sleepless, somewhat tearful night, no one spoke to me in the morning, but a staff nurse I had never set eyes on before reported to the surgeon, in my hearing, that I had 'played up all night'. The surgeon ordered a tranquilliser without talking to me about it. After another brief spell of weeping, an injection of Largactil arrived, without a word from nurse or doctor. At that point I phoned an SOS to the Department of Psychiatry. It brought immediate response but no comment from the staff in the orthopaedic ward. Even now, so many years later, I find it difficult to think about that period of my illness without bitterness.

I must have been a difficult patient to care for. Surgeons don't like to be confronted with their failures. Nurses don't like people whose ailments don't fit the appropriate diagnostic label for the ward; they don't like people who don't get well fast enough; they don't like nursing professional colleagues, let alone those in more senior positions, and I certainly did nothing to make things easier for them since I was morose and critical and extremely irritable.

There is no point listing all the things I found to complain about. What I found exasperating beyond all else was the incessant change of staff. None of the nurses who descended on me ever introduced herself, ever seemed to have taken the trouble to inform herself about my condition, my treatment, my nursing needs or my personal idiosyncrasies, such as food preferences or positioning of pillows. None seemed interested even in problems of loco-motion, let alone in problems of emotional equilibrium.

Medical care was no better. An endless procession of housemen and medical students inspected me from the knee downwards without appearing to be aware that I was attached to my tibia. Even on subsequent out-patient appointments, there rarely seemed the same doctor present. Only the sister and the plaster-room technician appeared to register any signs of recognition when I turned up yet again for confirmation that no progress was taking place.

There were several ups and downs in the state of my depression, so much so that lithium seemed indicated. A double-blind lithium–amitriptyline trial was at the time in progress and I was asked if I would be willing to enter into the trial population. Participation in the trial meant continuing with follow-up appointments not only with the psychiatrists but also with the teams of re-searchers who wanted to take blood specimens and fill in questionnaires, beyond the time when I had probably recovered and might otherwise have been discharged.

Two points may seem worth making. One is that I can't help having doubts about the outcome of part of the research in view of the incompetence, as an interviewer, of the young man who tried to find out about relevant life events. At a time when I was particularly intolerant of all kinds of people, he managed to get me close to screaming point by not listening to my answers, asking questions I had just answered, and insisting on asking me how my life in the last week had differed from normal.

The other is the extent to which I came to appreciate the value of having each follow-up appointment fixed at the time of the previous appointment. It would have been terrible for me if the decision to contact the psychiatrist had been left to me. There were days when I felt so much better that I was longing to say that I no longer needed help, and days when everything seemed so wrong that I felt it was no use going on with drug treatment or with seeing the psychiatrist. If I had not had an appointment anyway, I would have spent a lot more of my time observing myself, trying to decide whether I was too well, too rotten, or just ill enough to phone for an appointment.

In retrospect, how can I summarize what I have learned?

First, that I was lucky in my encounter with the psychiatric services and in my choice of colleagues and friends.

Second, that there is an urgent need to convey to nurses and doctors at least in the orthopaedic service, but perhaps in the medical and surgical service generally, that depression and physical illness are not mutually exclusive and that, of the two, depression can be the worse affliction.

Third, that I hope I shall recognize depression if it should happen to me again and that I shall have the sense and the opportunity to look for help. I fear, however, that just like before, the sense of hopelessness will prevent me from diagnosing what is realistic and what is delusional. If this happens, what I think I shall have learned is that suicide is a proper and desirable way out.

Annie Altschul

Wounded Healers
Edited by V. Rippere and R. Williams
© 1985 John Wiley & Sons Ltd.

19 *From the brink*

By a General Practitioner

When I was 21 I was a fourth-year medical student and my ambition was to be a psychiatrist. Four months later I was a patient in a psychiatric ward, suffering my first attack of endogenous depression. I never did get to be a psychiatrist, but I now work full-time as a principal in general practice.

In the intervening 16 years I have had a total of 17 admissions, sometimes for months at a time, to four different mental hospitals. I have had 71 ECTs, dozens of different antidepressant and tranquillizing drugs by mouth and injection, even insulin to make me hungry, not to speak of innumerable contacts with psychiatric doctors and nurses, occupational and recreational therapists, psychologists, and social workers.

My curriculum vitae, written down as for job applications, looks distinctly patchy and disorganized. I took five years longer to qualify than the rest of my undergraduate class, yet never failed an examination. On the positive side, if asked at an interview, I could claim to have filled up that gap by gaining experience in other fields of the health service: notably eight months' auxiliary nursing in a homeopathic hospital, one year as a junior technician in a clinical biochemistry laboratory, plus all that time spent seeing medicine from the consumer point of view.

After qualification, the random pattern of my career became even more erratic. Each job was in a different speciality, always in the most junior post, occasionally part-time, and often terminated prematurely – and in between, those ominous gaps, demanding explanation.

Knowing the probability of relapse in depressive illness, I have never shirked this explanation, since I believe that anyone willing to employ me should be aware of the risks. I am sure that I have been turned down for jobs for this reason, although this reason has never been stated directly. I am grateful that so many people *have* been willing to employ me, despite the risk, and that all have shown sympathy, if not great understanding, if I have had to let them down.

You may wonder why I persist in trying to pursue a career for which I seem unfit. My contention is that my depression is neither caused nor exacerbated by my choice of profession, but is due to some innate abnormality in my physical and/or mental constitution which would be present regardless of what I worked at.

I have wanted to be a doctor since the age of 10, and this determination has never altered since then during sickness or health. I gain enormous personal satisfaction from the practice of my profession: I cannot imagine enjoying any other work quite so much. I am certain that it is more fulfilling to work at a job one likes, and that a repugnant, though less demanding, job would be more likely to precipitate than prevent mental illness.

This argument sounds selfish, but I consider myself (at least when well) to be a reasonably competent GP. I would not claim any special benefit from having known mental despair; indeed, I think it possible that it may produce as much unhelpful bias as empathy. However, all doctors draw on their individual experience when trying to understand and sympathize with their patients. For example, those who have suffered physical illness, bereavement, divorce, racial prejudice, sexual discrimination, religious doubts, use the insight gained to supplement the theoretical knowledge gained by formal medical education. I trust I use my particular experience in as constructive a way as possible.

When I am well, I have never been loathe to admit to a past history of depression. In fact, I rather enjoy doing so in order to provoke a response revealing attitudes to the mentally ill. All my friends and colleagues know I have been depressed. I have on occasion told a patient if I thought it might be helpful to him or her, but on the whole patients consult doctors to obtain relief from their own suffering, not to be burdened by the doctor easing her own soul in confession.

Contrariwise, when I am ill, I become withdrawn and secretive, at the same time vehemently denying that anything is wrong, such is the shame I feel at having let myself down again. Yet I know this attitude only makes it more difficult for those who wish to help. Eventually, I will come to realize that I need professional help again. One of the perks of my job is almost instant access to psychiatric consultation, for which I am very grateful, though saddened that it is not available to all NHS patients. I am blessed in having an excellent psychiatrist, a very present help in time of trouble. This man has known me now for several years and it is a comfort to me not to have to recount my entire history to a strange doctor with each new episode of illness.

At the time of writing this account I am on the brink of another breakdown. At work I am saying little, doing less, and panicking inside at the effect this behaviour is having on my patients and colleagues. In consultations, I am tense, irritable, and rejecting, and I deal with problems at their most superficial level. At best, my patients must feel I have lost interest in them; at worst, my conduct may seriously affect their health.

My worry now is whether I ought to take sick leave. My mind is confused by conflicting emotions: guilt at letting my partners down; doubt that it may be a delusion that my clinical judgement is impaired; anger that self-pity suggests the coward's way out; fear of the damage I may do to my patients, my colleagues, and hence my career. The whole is complicated by the pervasive indecisiveness that goes with depression. I pray to abolish mistrust and allow others to guide me through this dark spell.

Even in my happiest periods, when I look forward to a long and fruitful life, and the very thought of suicide is abhorrent, I am still not at all grateful for being rescued from attempts in the past. Despite doubts, I do follow the ethics of my profession in actively resuscitating all those who make attempts upon their lives. I presume the justification for this is that all such people should be considered as suffering from some form of remediable mental disturbance. Even if this is true, I cannot see why one should not have the right to end a life of intolerable mental pain. Promises that the pain will vanish, one's suicidal wishes evaporate, and the rest of one's life be perfect euphoria, are irrelevant. It still would not be enough to compensate for the agony of the present.

I am fortunate now in having the means and opportunity to kill myself without fear of failure should the need once more arise. My strongest wish is that if the present depression deepens, then it will progress too rapidly to allow anyone to detain me compulsorily before I have time to reach the point at which suicide becomes mandatory.

Conclusion

Having heard from our 19 contributors, we may now reconsider the five questions to which they were asked to address themselves in their accounts of their experiences of depression.

1. WHAT SORT OF EXPERIENCE OF DEPRESSION HAD THEY HAD?

No ready generalizations leap forward in answer to this question. Our authors' experiences span a tremendous range. At one extreme are the brief, self-limiting episodes, described in Chapters 15 and 17, from which the writers recovered without either professional help or apparent sequelae. At the opposite extreme are the severely disabling, chronic, or recurrent illnesses, described in Chapters 14 and 19, from which sufferers either do not ever fully recover or which they do not even survive. Between these two extremes are depressive experiences which vary in nature along most conceivable dimensions. Some appear to be reactions to events, while others appear to lack obvious precipitation. Some are unipolar, others bipolar. In some, the sufferers retain insight, while in others they hold delusional beliefs. Some sufferers are agitated, others retarded. Some sufferers have and others lack suicidal ideation and/or behaviour. Some are relatively containable, allowing the sufferers to continue working throughout; others require hospitalization; while in still other cases the sufferer has to take time off but not go into hospital. Our authors' depressive experiences also vary in chronicity, as mentioned previously, and in degree of consequent disability; some of our authors recovered to a higher level of functioning than they had achieved before their depression, while others were left with apparently permanent deficits in personal functioning.

Considering this extensive range of possibilities, we are struck by the absence of a typical pattern in our authors' experiences of depression. We conclude that mental health workers experiences of depression appear to be pretty much like those of other people.

2. UNDER WHAT CIRCUMSTANCES DID THEY BECOME DEPRESSED?

Like our authors' experiences themselves, the circumstances in which their depressions occurred are extremely varied, especially since many reported more than one episode occurring under different circumstances. In the majority of cases, the author's work as a mental health professional was not an obvious precipitating factor. Five started their depressions before they became mental health workers (see Chapters 3, 8, 13, 16 and 19); two others were on courses of postgraduate training (see Chapters 2 and 5); another was between jobs (see Chapter 15). Two were on maternity leave (see Chapters 4 and 6). Thus over half our contributors were not actively engaged in day to day clinical work when their depressions started. In only one case (see Chapter 1) is the writer's mental health work implicated as a factor. In view of our material, we are inclined to agree with Pond (1969) that conditions of work do not seem to play an important role in the depressions of mental health workers.

Of course, our 19 self-selected authors' accounts in no way prove that *other* mental health professionals do not succumb to the wear and tear of their jobs. We have no way of sampling the entire universe of depressed mental health workers in order to determine how representative our contributors are. But it seems to us worth pointing out that more of our authors who remarked at all on the role of their work in their depressions commented on its protective, supportive functions than on its contribution to precipitating their illness.

Where obvious precipitating factors were involved, they were chiefly events in the individual's private life, events such as the birth of a baby, the death or loss of a loved one, changes of country, or adjustment to personally unsatisfying feminine stereotypes – all of which are commonly known to provoke depressive reactions in people who are not mental health workers if they are predisposed to depression. In other cases, there did not seem to be obvious precipitation – as is also known to occur in ordinary people. From these accounts, it appears that mental health workers, in Britain at least, tend to become depressed in the same sorts of circumstances as other people.

3. WHAT DID THEY DO ABOUT IT THEMSELVES AND WHAT DID OTHERS, WHETHER LAY OR PROFESSIONAL, DO ABOUT IT?

Again, generalizations are difficult. There appears to be no standard pattern. Like other people who become depressed, our contributors tended both to help themselves and, sooner or later, to receive outside help from a variety of sources, both within and outside the health service. The specifics of their own and outside efforts vary greatly from one individual to another, though most received antidepressants and/or other medications at some stage. The pathways to care were also extremely heterogeneous. Some went through orthodox channels available to all members of the public, some through extra channels which exist for health workers; some sought out their own psychotherapists, others were referred by their GPs, and others bypassed the approved channels and ended up in hospitals after overdoses. Six of the 19 resorted to this approach on at least one occasion — the authors of Chapters 1, 5, 11, 12, 14, and 19.

Many received help from lay sources, including womens' groups, church groups, family, spouses, friends, and neighbours. Some were helped by the example of determination and fortitude in their own patients. Like depressed people in general, depressed mental health workers seem willing to take help where they can find it.

In addition to being helped by others, our authors – like other depressed people – also tended to engaged in active self-help. Seventeen of the 19 reported some form of self-help activity. The activities they engaged in are also typical (Rippere, 1977a). A recent cross-cultural study comparing English- and Spanish-speaking individuals suggested that the majority had clear ideas about appropriate self-help activities for use when feeling depressed (Caro, Miralles and Rippere, 1983). There were 12 major areas of activity upon which members of the two national groups agreed. These were as follows:

1. Attributing the depression to a cause
2. Attempting to rectify the problems considered responsible for evoking the feeling of depression
3. Finding social and moral support
4. Engaging in diverting and distracting recreations
5. Keeping busy and working
6. Focusing one's attention elsewhere than on the depressing problem or depressed feelings
7. Restructuring one's cognitions so as to minimize the significance of the depressing events
8. Engaging in self-care and self-maintenance activities
9. Venting one's emotions
10. Taking prescribed medication and self-medicating
11. Finding compensations and boosting feelings of self-esteem or self-efficacy through useful, purposive activity
12. Taking comfort in one's religion.

Although not every one of our authors who reported some form of self-help activity reported using all the standard approaches, all of these methods for coping with depression were mentioned by at least one, and often more than one, writer. Whether the activities involved doing crossword puzzles, talking to one's girlfriend, participating in a women's group, watching television, reading Shakespeare, learning to play the recorder, or changing careers, they are all aimed at the common goal of alleviating the sufferer's depression, either by removing precipitants or attenuating negative feelings. Both in the fact of using self-help and in the particular techniques they used, our authors show another basic similarity to other depressed people.

Another aspect of what others did about our authors' depression is the reaction of colleagues and employers to learning of the writer's affliction. Like other depressed people, our authors met with mixed receptions. Again, global generalizations are difficult, especially since particular individuals met with different sorts of receptions from different colleagues or employers at different times. These responses may be broadly characterized as conforming to one of three types: active support, seeming indifference, and overt hostility.

The components of active support, as described by our contributors, include provision of active reassurance that the sufferer is still an acceptable person. Two particular instances are the visit, described by the author of 'In the wilderness' (Chapter 5) during his last hospitalization, of his supervisor, who came to assure him that his job was safe and that she could not possibly sack all staff who suffered from depression or she'd have no staff left. In a similar vein, the author of 'Surviving depression' (Chapter 3) describes how, when one of the consultant psychiatrists she worked with while on her postgraduate training course discovered that she was anticipating difficulties in meeting the course fees, he arranged for her to pay them in instalments over an extended period, which eased a major practical problem in her life at the time. The message of providers of active support was 'You're OK, we still want to know you', and, coming at a time when the recipients were in some doubt about their continuing acceptability, it was a very welcome message.

Apparent indifference took the form of colleagues and employers either apparently not noticing that the writer was depressed or, at the very least, making no adverse *or* helpful comments. The author of 'Beginning to live' (Chapter 9) notes that at the time of her depression, her colleagues appeared not to notice that she was not functioning very well. The author of 'Wading through mud' (Chapter 10) notes the absence of direct adverse feedback from colleagues at a time when she was aware of functioning poorly. She was told by her psychiatrist to assume she was functioning adequately at work until told otherwise. On the other hand, she notes that people were 'consistently kind and helpful', so that the indifference was perhaps more apparent than real.

Overt hostility, which other contributors reported encountering, was quite unambiguous. The author of 'Hitting rock bottom' (Chapter 2) describes in detail the efforts of her employers to get rid of her after the onset of her depression. The author of 'In the wilderness' (Chapter 5) mentions a very hostile reception from the Head of Nursing when he returned to work after his first hospitalization, as well as tactless and discouraging comments from colleagues who visited him during it. The author of 'It couldn't happen to me – could it?' (Chapter 4) tells of having an unwanted change of posting foisted upon her 'for her own good' when she returned to work after her leave.

However, such overt hostility was more often anticipated than actually encountered. Four authors (see Chapters 1, 3, 16, and 19) mention dread of psychiatric stigmatization as something which affected them personally and another (see Chapter 15) as something which generally affects members of his profession. Other authors reported feelings of shame, guilt, or embarrassment when contemplating the prospect of becoming a psychiatric patient, whether or not they were mental health workers at the time (see Chapters 4, 9, 10, and 13). This reluctance to assume the role of psychiatric patient and the attendant anticipations of stigma are yet another way in which the depressive experience of mental health workers is similar to that of other people.

4. WHAT OF ALL THIS DID THEY PERSONALLY FIND HELPFUL AND WHAT DID THEY FIND UNHELPFUL?

Generalizations about what our authors found helpful and unhelpful when they were depressed are considerably easier than those concerning the nature and circumstances of their depressive experiences. Perhaps the most important generalization is that an enormous range of experiences and conditions can be either helpful or unhelpful; formal treatment is by no means the only modality of help – or otherwise.

As far as formal treatments are concerned, many of our authors agreed that conventional physical treatments – antidepressants, lithium, hypnotics, and ECT in particular – were reasonably effective in containing their depressive symptoms. However, some tried many drugs and found only a few to be beneficial. Several drew attention to unpleasant side effects of pharmacotherapy. Several reported rejecting tranquillizers – and, in one case, a tonic – as either irrelevant to their needs or unacceptable as crutches in their efforts to cope with, rather than suppress, their emotional distress. The potential of some drugs for producing dependence was also noted as an unhelpful aspect of physical treatment. Of those who accepted medication, several commented on the helpfulness of being given responsibility for adjusting their dosage as required.

Our authors' responses to formal psychological treatment were mixed. The one who underwent cognitive therapy (Beck, Rush, Shaw, and Emery, 1979) reported finding it extremely helpful. By contrast, of those who underwent more conventional dynamic psychotherapy or formal counselling, there were more who reported disappointment than who commented on its benefits. Insensitivity, coldness, lack of empathy, and a critical attitude were noted to characterize unhelpful therapists, thus confirming the view of Truax and Carkhuff (1967) that effective therapists possess the qualities of accurate empathy, non-possessive warmth, and genuineness. Less formal, primarily supportive therapy over an extended period with a respectful, warm, understanding, and encouraging therapist, whether GP, psychiatrist, or other professional, was reported to be extremely helpful by all who mentioned it. This long-term supportive therapy was commonly combined with drug treatment. The few authors who mentioned group psychotherapy were generally positive in their evaluation, but one author who tried several groups found that one helped and two did not. One author commented very favourably on the helpfulness of occupational therapy.

Besides formal therapy, informal interactions with nurses, ambulance drivers, or ward attendants – not to mention fellow patients on the ward – were often reported to be supportive and encouraging. Incidental displays of human interest, warmth, or humour on the part of staff and patients were appreciated whenever they occurred. But the behaviour of staff, whether medical or nursing, could also be extremely unhelpful. Brusqueness, rudeness, lack of respect or consideration on the part of staff, failure of staff to introduce themselves, or failure to specify when the next appointment would take place were all experienced as unhelpful, as was the constant turnover of staff on at least one ward. Facile 'explanations' concocted for the author's condition or asinine and fatuous 'advice' were rejected as worthless. One author commented unfavourably on the 'staff only' sign on a lavatory door near the patients' waiting room in the hospital where she had her out-patient appointments. To her, the sign represented a kind of staff–patient apartheid which was especially distressing to one on the wrong side of the fence.

As well as from professionals involved in their care, our authors also received support from family, friends, spouses, colleagues, and even, on occasion, their own patients. Some insensitive relatives and colleagues, who made stupid remarks while visiting, were perceived as very unhelpful. One such had a Gideon Bible thrown at him by our irate author! Several contributors commented on the futility of being told to 'pull themselves together' or 'snap out of it' People who said such things were regarded as showing their lack of understanding.

Lay groups in the community as well as individuals were also reported to be helpful. Church groups were noted by two authors and women's groups by three as effective sources of support. Whether the focus of the group was learning to play the recorder, discussing the oppression of women in our society, or 'prayer and share', the opportunity for regular contact with friendly and caring people was extremely important to those in need. In a similar vein, one author noted that he found it helpful, when depressed as an undergraduate, to move from digs into a hall of residence, where he had more contact with people. Seeing and talking to other people are amongst the most helpful experiences for depressed people generally and our authors are no exception.

Besides help provided by others, our authors also used self-help, in the forms of short-term strategies to improve mood, keep going, or reduce disability, medium-term ones to work through emotional problems, and long-term ones to alter their depressing circumstances. Of the first kind, distraction methods, constructive activity, reading, the use of reminder lists, and continuing to go to work were noted especially. Medium-term strategies included reading philosophy and seeing heart-rending films. Longer-term strategies included choosing and training for a mental health career. While some authors noted that their techniques for banishing everyday depressed moods were ineffective against their clinical depressions, the majority of those who reported using self-help techniques found some or most of them helpful. In this respect, they are also like depressed people who are not mental health workers.

5. HAVING SURVIVED TO TELL THE TALE, WHAT DID THEY FEEL THEY LEARNT FROM THE EXPERIENCE, BOTH PERSONALLY AND IN THEIR SUBSEQUENT WORK AS THERAPISTS?

This is the question our authors seemed to find hardest to answer. A few did not even attempt it. Those who did tended to leave their comments till last and to pass over the issue in a few sentences, though a few wrote at greater length. Our contributors' apparent difficulty in dealing with this question suggests that the lessons to be learnt from a depression, if any, do not lend themselves to ready formulation. They are evidently not didactic sorts of lessons like the times tables or the conjugation of a French verb, lessons that can be obediently recited. They seem, rather, to involve subtle changes in outlook and under-standing.

The lessons our authors learnt from their depressions appear to be of a number of kinds: lessons about depression in general, other people's, and one's own in particular; lessons in relating to, understanding, and helping depressed patients; lessons about one's own character; and what might be called lessons in living. The majority appear to be straightforward generalizations from the writer's experience of depression and the remainder concern changes in outlook and interpersonal functioning attributed to it.

Lessons about depression included the observations that depression is no respecter of persons, that one cannot take one's professional status for granted, that depression may go hand in hand with tiredness, that it may render both logic and religious faith ineffective, and that a person may still manage to carry on a superficial sort of functioning despite an extreme degree of depression and anxiety. These lessons are evidently not the stuff of which psychiatry textbooks are made, but they do reflect a personal knowledge of what it is like and what it means to be depressed. Psychiatry textbooks might be more informative if they contained more of this kind of subjective knowledge.

As far as lessons about understanding and helping depressed people are concerned, the single most frequent comment was that the author's experience gave him or her more understanding of and empathy with depressed patients. This lesson would not seem to be unique to mental health workers who have suffered a depression. Thus Cecil Todes (1983), a psychiatrist suffering from Parkinson's disease, wrote in the *Lancet* that when he returned to work after obtaining treatment, 'New zeal as a therapist seemed to emerge from the straitjacket of my former training alongside my experience of illness. I was able to treat my patients in a more active and participating manner' (Todes, 1983, p. 977). Suffering as a patient oneself may go far towards breaking down the 'them versus us' distinction between staff and patients which at least one author noted she became aware of having unconsciously subscribed to before she herself became one of 'them'.

The specifics of the lesson again reflected the individual author's experiences.

They included recognizing the importance of relating to patients as whole and potentially viable people, of encouraging them rather than trying to destroy their defences in the name of some abstract therapeutic ideology, of refraining from judging, and of listening, trying to respond to patients' needs, and trying to provide the kind of help they want.

These lessons seemed to derive from different sources: 'good' experiences and 'bad' experiences. Thus one author noted that her helpful psychiatrist's behaviour came to serve as a model, while another noted that her unhelpful psychotherapist's behaviour served as a negative model, exemplifying 'the kind of therapist I do not want to be'. However, from her helpful GP, this same author came to appreciate the importance of continuity of care; the first, likewise, learned the meaning of 'support' from her psychiatrist. A third author, who described being let down by his counsellor when the letter criticized him, noted that he has realized how important it is not to let patients down. A fourth, whose GP fobbed him off with a tonic while his father and girlfriend gave unstinting support, concluded that professional helpers may underestimate a depressed person's distress and that depressed people may get more help from their families and friends. And a fifth, whose depression occurred in the context of an orthopaedic problem, learned that doctors and nurses need to be told that depression and physical disorder are not mutually exclusive and that depression may be the worse affliction. It is our impression that lessons learnt from unfortunate experiences tended to be formulated in a more discursive and explicit manner than lessons learned from good experiences.

Lessons concerning character tended to be formulated either as basic discoveries about the self – such as having a propensity to recurrent depression or the ability to survive – or as a description of changes in attitudes and social behaviour attributed to the experience of depression. The majority who noted such changes mentioned beneficial ones, but one writer could not honestly say that she had gained anything from her breakdown and both she and another author noted the emergence of a much more wary and guarded approach to life. The second regarded depression as 'an extravagantly wasteful means of forming character'. A third commented that his experiences caused him to recognize a limitation in his commitment to change. These writers' experiences contrast sharply with the beneficial changes reported by the majority who reported changes: reductions in anxiety, social distance, self-consciousness, ruthlessness, and pomposity, and increases in self-respect, effectiveness, autonomy, ambition, and responsiveness to the needs of others. One author described his pre-depressive self as 'a right little creep-arse' and his post-depressive self as more humble, accepting, and mellow. Another described her post-depressive self as less straitlaced, better balanced emotionally, and easier to live with. These are not the sorts of characteristics usually attributed to recovered depressives, who have been depicted as lacking in self-esteem, having an unhappy outlook, helplessness, and narcissistic vulnerability (Altman and Wittenborn, 1980).

Finally, lessons in living included a variety of existential conclusions which our authors derived from their experiences. One came to construe his depression as a sign that he was not dealing honestly with his problems. Another concluded that people have the seeds of their own revival within them. A third noted that the struggle with depression leads to consciousness and consciousness leads to change. A fourth noted that her depression threw her back on her own resources and caused her to begin to discover what she wanted for herself as an individual rather than merely inheriting her values from others. And, finally, a fifth author concluded that, however invaluable, help provided by external sources is limited and that beyond those limits survival becomes a matter of individual initiative and choice: 'If you want to survive, you're on your own', Unlike the lessons we have examined previously, which all showed considerable diversity, these all seem to converge on the twin themes of self-awareness and personal responsibility.

Having reviewed our contributors' answers to the guideline questions, we are now in a position to draw a few conclusions. The first is that having a history of depression does not by itself automatically preclude effective professional functioning in subsequent mental health work. The majority of our authors appear to have made a complete recovery and some regarded themselves as functioning more effectively after their depression than before, though they may have been moderately to severely disabled at the time of their illness. Only a small minority either retained some degree of disability or did not survive at all. Of our 19 authors, 14 (73.5%) are still working in a clinical capacity, one is in a less emotionally demanding field of medical work, two have retired early on medical grounds, and two are dead, one by suicide and the other of natural causes in old age. Though the samples are not strictly comparable, our contributors as a group appear to have done better than the sample reported by Small *et al.* (1969), in one of the very few follow-up studies in this area, of 40 doctors hospitalized with psychiatric disorder during a 13 year period, only 57.5% of whom were still in active medical practice at the time of follow-up. Because of differences in the composition of their sample and our own group of self-selected contributors, we do not wish to lay too much emphasis on the difference in the rate of good outcomes. But we would suggest that our authors' experiences – which are probably more representative of the spectrum of depressive disorders in mental health workers, not all of whom are medically qualified or need to be hospitalized – give reason for hope of a good outcome when a mental health worker becomes depressed.

In view of the likelihood of a good outcome and in view of the enormous range in the nature, severity, and duration of mental health workers' depressions, our second conclusion is that uniform institutional policies assuming that, having once been depressed, mental health workers must be unsuitable for further mental health work, are unwarranted. Small *et al.* (1969) commented on their findings as follows: ' . . . it seems to us that the attitudes of medical societies, hospital committees, and licensing authorities [to doctors with a history of psychiatric disorder] should be supportive and encouraging rather than restrictive or punitive' (Small *et al.*, 1969, p. 1340). We can only agree with this point of view and would extend it to depressed mental health workers other than doctors. While we would also agree that the public quite obviously needs to be protected from mental health workers who as a result of illness are unable to fulfil their duties towards patients (Murray, 1974), it also seems to us that depressed mental health workers need to be protected from involuntary martyrdom to other people's prejudices. At least one of our authors (see Chapter 5) got a very raw deal from his employers, while his subsequent track record has established that he was perfectly capable of carrying on effectively in a professional capacity. The author of 'Hitting rock bottom' (Chapter 2) was also dealt with harshly. While their experiences of being rejected by their employers may be the exception rather than the rule, even a 10% incidence of wastage of good and competent people, if unwarranted, is much too high. It should not happen at all, either for humanitarian or for economic reasons.

The economic reasons for opposing attrition of mental health workers because of depression are that, since most are trained at the public expense, they represent an investment of public funds that should not be discarded lightly, and that, with the increasing cutbacks in state expenditure on health and education, their economic value is also constantly increasing. Even if it were not humane to do so, depressed mental health workers should be conserved because of the tremendous waste of scarce resources entailed by failure to do so.

But conservation of depressed mental health workers is also humane. With the proviso that our views extend to all mental health workers, not just doctors, we agree with Crammer (1978). He argues that an individual who has recovered from a breakdown should not be excluded from further clinical practice unless there is 'positive evidence of his potential dangerousness to patients instead of an automatic assumption of his unsuitability' (Crammer, 1978, p. 561). He notes, further:

'In judging him and his work before and after breakdown the standard to be applied is not that of the best, but simply the minimum that is accepted from his healthy peers. Why should a doctor who has had a mental breakdown be expected to do better than one who has not? Thirdly, much nonsense is talked about the 'stress' of clinical practice. It is unwise simply on the basis of psychodynamic hypotheses to decide that anyone needs protection from everyday life, and the proper test is to let him try it and see' (Crammer, 1978, p. 561)

It would obviously bring discredit upon any helping profession – not just medicine – if many of its members were known to be actively crazy and causing untold damage to the vulnerable clients they were supposedly trying to help. But it is not particularly to the credit of any helping profession, either, to be known to reject out of hand members who have been depressed (or even to be suspected of so doing), especially not when a history of depression, as so many of our authors have remarked, may enable them to function more empathically in their subsequent work.

We have already noted Todes's (1983) report of increased involvement in his patients' treatment after he developed Parkinson's disease as corroboration of our authors' views of the professional benefit to be gained from being a wounded healer. Further evidence that their experience is not atypical comes from an American psychiatrist, Martin Lipp (1980), who remarked, 'My wounds become my spectacles, helping me to see what I encounter with empathy and a grateful sense of privilege' (Lipp, 1980, p. 107). Small et al. (1969), likewise, reported of their series of psychiatrically hospitalized physicians:

> 'The practicing physicians confided that they considered that the episode or episodes of mental illness had provided them with useful insights into the unhappiness experienced by their own patients. . . . Many of them began to take a greater interest in caring for patients with mental disorders, as, for example, one surgeon who currently spends half his time in marital counseling, putting into practice many of the things he learned in therapy himself. Many times the physician's growth in emotional maturity, warmth, and flexibility was impressive' (Small et al., 1969, p. 1339).

So our authors are by no means isolated in their belief that their experience of depression contributed to improved social and professional functioning. In view of the importance of personal qualities such as warmth, empathy, and flexibility in therapists of whatever profession, it is not only uneconomic and inhumane to exclude depressed mental health workers from further practice but also potentially very inefficient, since some, probably many, who were rejected a priori on these grounds might have been better at their work afterwards than before.

Being depressed is, however, a pretty miserable way of coming to understand the pain that depressed patients are going through. We are decidedly not recommending it as a training experience to anyone who can avoid it. But miserable and undesirable as an episode or episodes of depression may be for anyone to undergo, it is not necessarily an entirely negative experience. We should hope that our contributors' accounts will make it possible for others who have not shared the experience to appreciate the potentially positive side to being a wounded healer.

References

a'Brook, M.F., Hailstone, J.D., and McLauchlan, I.E.J. (1967). Psychiatric illness in the medical profession. *British Journal of Psychiatry*, **113**, 1013–1023.

Altman, J.H., and Wittenborn, J.R. (1980). Depression-prone personality in women. *Journal of Abnormal Psychology*, **89**, 303–308.

Alvarez, A. (1974). *The Savage God: A Study of Suicide*. Harmondsworth: Penguin.

Beck, A.T., Rush, A.J., Shaw, B.F., and Emery, G. (1979). *Cognitive Therapy of Depression*. Chichester: John Wiley & Sons.

Bennet, G. (1979). *Patients and their Doctors: The Journey Through Medical Care*. London: Baillière Tindall.

Blachly, P.H., Disher, W., and Roduner, G. (1968). Suicide by physicians. *Bulletin of Suicidology*, December, 1–18.

Blachly, P.H., Osterud, H.T., and Josslin, R. (1963). Suicide in professional groups. *New England Journal of Medicine*, **268**, 1278–1282.

British Medical Journal (1964). Suicide among doctors. *British Medical Journal*, **1**, 789–790.

Brown, G.W. (1974). Life events and the onset of depressive and schizophrenic conditions. In *Life Stress and Illness* (E.K.E. Gunderson and R.H. Rahe, eds). Springfield, Ill.: Charles C. Thomas, pp. 164–188.

Brown, G., and Harris, T. (1978). *Social Origins of Depression: A Study of Psychiatric Disorder in Women*. London: Tavistock.

Brown, G., Ní Bhrolcháin, M., and Harris, T. (1975). Social class and psychiatric disturbance among women in an urban population. *Sociology*, **9**, 225–254.

Burns, D.D. (1981). *Feeling Good: The New Mood Therapy*. New York: Signet Books.

Caro, I., Miralles, A., and Rippere, V. (1983). What's the thing to do when you're feeling depressed? – a cross-cultural replication. *Behaviour Research and Therapy*, **21**, 477–483.

Chesler, P. (1973). *Women and Madness*. New York: Avon Books.

Craig, A.G., and Pitts, F.N., Jr (1968). Suicide by physicians. *Diseases of the Nervous System*, **29**, 763–772.

Crammer, J.L. (1978). Psychosis in young doctors. *British Medical Journal*, **1**, 560–561.

De Sole, D.E., Singer, P., and Aronson, S. (1969). Suicide and role strain among physicians. *International Journal of Social Psychiatry*, **15**, 294–301.

A Doctor Patient (1981). A doctor's depression. *The Practitioner*, **225**, 1692–1693.

Endler, N.S. (1982). *Holiday of Darkness: A Psychologist's Personal Journey out of his Depression*. Chichester: John Wiley & Sons.

Forrest, A.D., Fraser, R.H. and Priest, R.G. (1965). Environmental factors in depressive illness. *British Journal of Psychiatry*, **111**, 243–253.

Franklin, R.A. (1977). One hundred doctors at the Retreat. A contribution to the subject of mental disorder in the medical profession. *British Journal of Psychiatry*, **131**, 11–14.

Fredén, L. (1982). *Psychosocial Aspects of Depression: No Way Out?* Chichester: John Wiley & Sons.

Freeman, W. (1967). Psychiatrists who kill themselves. A study in suicide. *American Journal of Psychiatry*, **124**, 846–847.

Friedan, B. (1963). *The Feminine Mystique*. London: Victor Gollancz. (Cited from Pelican edition, Harmondsworth: Penguin Books, 1983.)

Garfield, S.L., and Bergin, A.E. (eds) (1978). *Handbook of Psychotherapy and Behaviour Change: An Empirical Analysis*, 2nd edn. Chichester: John Wiley & Sons.

Hammen, C., and de Mayo, R. (1982). Cognitive correlates of teacher stress and depressive symptoms: implications for attributional models of depression. *Journal of Abnormal Psychology*, **91**, 96–101.

Herzlich, C. (1973). *Health and Illness: A Social Psychological Analysis*. London: Academic Press.

HMSO (1968). *A Glossary of Mental Disorders*, Prepared by the Sub-committee on Classification of Mental Disorders of the Registrar General's Advisory Committee on Medical Nomenclature and Statistics. London: HMSO.

Holmes, T.H., and Rahe, R.H. (1967). The social readjustment rating scale. *Journal of Psychosomatic Research*, **11**, 213–218.

Jones, K. (1960). *Mental Health and Social Policy, 1845–1959*. London: Routledge & Kegan Paul.

Kraupl-Taylor, F. (1979). *Psychopathology: Its Causes and Symptoms*, revised edn, Quartermaine House, Sudbury-on-Thames.

Lacqueur, H.P. (1962). Epilogue. In *One Hundred Years of Psychiatry*, by E. Kraepelin. London: Peter Owen, pp. 157–160.

Lehmann, H.E. (1982). A trouble in the brain-mind. Self-description of a depressive episode. *Canadian Journal of Psychiatry*, **27**, 216–217.

Lipowski, Z.J. (1975). Psychiatry of somatic diseases: epidemiology, pathogenesis, classification. *Comprehensive Psychiatry*, **16**, 105–124.

Lipp, M.R. (1980). *The Bitter Pill: Doctors, Patients and Failed Expectations*. New York: Harper & Row.

McCue, J.D. (1982). The effects of stress on physicians and their medical practice. *New England Journal of Medicine*, **306**, 458–463.

McGhie, A., and Chapman, J. (1961). Disorders of attention and perception in early schizophrenia. *British Journal of Medical Psychology*, **34**, 103–116.

Marshall, J. (1980). Stress amongst nurses. In *White Collar and Professional Stress* (C.L. Cooper and J. Marshall, eds). Chichester: John Wiley & Sons, pp. 19–59.

Maslach, C. (1982). *Burnout: The Cost of Caring*. Englewood Cliffs, N.J.: Prentice-Hall.

Metcalfe, M. (1968). The personality of depressive patients: I. Assessment of change. II. Assessment of premorbid personality. In *Recent Developments in Affective Disorders* (A. Coppen and A. Walk, eds). Ashford, Kent: Headley Brothers, for the Royal Medico-Psychological Association, pp. 97–104.

Mostow, E., and Newberry, P. (1975). Work role and depression in women; a comparison of workers and housewives. *American Journal of Orthopsychiatry*, **45**, 538–548.

Murray, R.M. (1974). Psychiatric illness in doctors. *Lancet*, *i*, 1211–1213.

Murray, R.M. (1977). Psychiatric illness in male doctors and controls. An analysis of Scottish hospitals' in-patient data. *British Journal of Psychiatry*, **131**, 1–10.

Nunnally, J.C., Jr (1961). *Popular Conceptions of Mental Health: Their Development and Change*. New York: Holt, Rinehart & Winston.

Office of Population, Censuses and Surveys (1978). *Occupational Mortality 1970–1972. Decennial Supplement, England and Wales*. London: HMSO.

Paykel, E.S., Myers, J.K., Dienelt, M.N., Klerman, G.L., Lindenthal, J.J., and Pepper, M.P. (1969). Life events and depression. A controlled study. *Archives of General Psychiatry*, **21**, 753–760.

Pitts, F.N., Jr, Schuller, A.B., Rich, C.L., and Pitts, A.F. (1979). Suicide among US women physicians, 1967–1972. *American Journal of Psychiatry*, **136**, 694–696.

Pond, D. (1969). Doctors' mental health. *New Zealand Medical Journal*, **69**, 131–135.

A Practising Psychiatrist (1965). The experience of electro-convulsive therapy. *British Journal of Psychiatry*, **111**, 365–367.

Rachman, S.J. (1978). *Fear and Courage*. San Francisco: W.H. Freeman.

Rahe, R.H. (1968). Life change measurement as a predictor of illness. *Proceedings of the Royal Society of Medicine*, **61**, 1124–1126.

Rich, C.L., and Pitts, F.N., Jr (1979). Suicide by male physicians during a five-year period. *American Journal of Psychiatry*, **136**, 1089–1090.

Rippere, V. (1977a). 'What's the thing to do when you're feeling depressed?' – a pilot study. *Behaviour Research and Therapy*, **15**, 185–191.

Rippere, V. (1977b). Commonsense beliefs about depression and antidepressive behaviour: a study of social consensus. *Behaviour Research and Therapy*, **15**, 465–473.

Rippere, V. (1980a). Predicting consensus about propositions concerning depression and antidepressive behaviour: another cognitive dimension of commonsense knowledge. *Behaviour Research and Therapy,,***18**, 79–86.

Rippere, V. (1980b). Some historical dimensions of commonsense knowledge about depression and antidepressive behaviour. *Behaviour Research and Therapy*, **18**, 375–385.

Rippere, V. (1980c). More historical dimensions of commonsense knowledge: spiritual consolation for the depressed. *Behaviour Research and Therapy*, **18**, 549–563.

Rippere, V. (1981a). The survival of traditional medicine in lay medical views. An empirical approach to the history of medicine. *Medical History*, **25**, 411–414.

Rippere, V. (1981b). Depression, common sense and psychosocial evolution. *British Journal of Medical Psychology*, **54**, 379–387.

Rose, K.D., and Rosow, I. (1973). Physicians who kill themselves. *Archives of General Psychiatry*, **29**, 800–805.

Rowe, D. (1978). *The Experience of Depression*. Chichester: John Wiley & Sons.

Schutz, A. (1972). *The Phenomenology of the Social World*. London: Heinemann Educational Books.

Simon, W., and Lumry, G.K. (1968) Suicide among physician-patients. *Journal of Nervous and mental Disease*, **147**, 105–112.

Small, I.F., Small, J.G., Assue, C.M., and Moore, D.F. (1969). The fate of the mentally ill physician. *American Journal of Psychiatry*, **125**, 1333–1342.

Stanley, L., and Wise, S. (1983). *Breaking Out: Feminist Consciousness and Feminist Research*. London: Routledge & Kegan Paul.

Stengel, E. (1964). *Suicide and Attempted Suicide*. Harmondsworth: Penguin.

Steppacher, R.C., and Mausner, J.S. (1974). Suicide in male and female physicians. *Journal of the American Medical Association*, **228**, 323–328.

Strauss, A.L. (1975). *Chronic Illness and the Quality of Life*. St Louis: C.V. Mosby.

Sutherland, S. (1976). *Breakdown: A Personal Crisis and a Medical Dilemma*. London: Weidenfeld & Nicolson.

Thomson, K.C., and Hendrie, H.C. (1972). Environmental stress in primary depressive illness. *Archives of General Psychiatry*, **26**, 130–132.

Todes, C. (1983). Inside Parkinsonism – a psychiatrist's experience. *Lancet*, *i*, 977–978.

Truax, C.B., and Carkhuff, R.R. (1967). *Toward Effective Counselling and Psychotherapy: Training and Practice*. Chicago: Aldine.

Weissman, M.M., and Paykel, E.S. (1974). *The Depressed Woman: A Study of Social Relationships*. London: University of Chicago Press.

Wyler, A.R., Masuda, M., and Holmes, T.H. (1971). Magnitude of life events and seriousness of illness. *Psychosomatic Medicine*, **33**, 115–122.

Yaryura-Tobias, J.A., and Neziroglu, F.A. (1983). *Obsessive-Compulsive Disorders: Pathogenesis – Diagnosis – Treatment*. New York: Marcel Dekker.
Zilboorg, G. (1941). *A History of Medical Psychology*. New York: W.W. Norton & Co.